DARK LADIES

Dark Ladies

*A Mennipean masque
and user's guide to the tragi-comic
incorporating a new philosophy of the joke*

Steve McCaffery

chax 2016

ISBN 978-0-9862640-4-7

Designed and Published by Chax Press
PO Box 162
Victoria, Texas 77902-0162
USA

Cover ink drawing by Charles Alexander.

Chax Press would like to thank the University of Houston-Victoria School of Arts and
Sciences for its support, and to thank several students, student interns, and press assistants
from the University of Houston-Victoria, particularly Enkeleta Dervishi, Drenica
Dervishi, Melissa Cluff, Laura Hicks, Georgette Walker, Katrina Rose, Jaime Flores, and
Mareesa Johnson, who worked with Chax during the time in which *Dark Ladies* was being
prepared for publication.

TO THE
ONLY BEGETTERS OF THIS ENSUING TRAGI-COMEDY
MR. W. S. & MR. S. McC.
ALL HAPPINESS
AND THAT ETERNITY
PROMISED BY OUR EVER-LOVING POETS,
WISHETH THE WELL-WISHING ADVENTURER
IN SETTING FORTH

C.A.[1]

---

1. C.A. Charles Alexander

AND

To the Dead and Dying on a continuing basis.

"Writ thus odde bet; rid aweg; Shaxpaer Patta fox, thou wilt swingan Stefan cild."

To be poets confers Death on us:
Death, paradisal fiery conspectus
For those who bear themselves always as poets.
Robert Graves

Death is more "jest" than life.
Thomas Lovell Beddoes

… he is a fool which cannot make one Sonnet,
and he is mad which makes two.
John Donne
in a letter to Sir Henry Goodyeare

Dandyism is inconceivable without the sonnet.
Valerian Gaprindashvili

ACT I Scene 1. *Enter Polonius.*

You know for a fact I may *be* Denmark's politician of the decade (having lied my way into World History) but I'm so cognitively constipated these days that a thought from me instantly becomes an endangered species; all my judgments are influenced by my favourite color.[1] The shocking thing is that come election time I'm actually entitled to vote. In fact it's amazing that I've made it so far in politics, believing truth and the logic pill are paramount, living professionally with a neutral vocabulary and having never approached life with that eschatological indifference that proved so popular during the dissolution of the monasteries. Wealth and symbiosis emerge through dialogue not intelligent design, however the last thing a schizophrenic like me needs is a diversified portfolio. (I'm sure it's from my multi elegiac personality and not from the memory of Beethoven eating his final bratwurst, that Elgar got the idea for his Variations.)   I'd compare the politician at his best to the brain surgeon at his worst. But to turn to the temporal matter at hand, once upon a time seems reasonable, in fact I love the idea of being upon time as I'm rarely in it—avoiding as I do most of the calamities consequent to the practicalities of courtly living. That said, I'd love to overcome my *niggarding* attitude to the contemporary and make a significant contribution to the world of letters. I know it's hard to keep a steady balance on the *content*-slope with such morsels of a mouthful as "cacozelia" and "soraismus;" they put me in mind of primitive man at breakfast. Truth is I love smothering language with decayed words. With such parsimonious old oddities I could jump the precipice into another Arab *Spring*, take a stab at ekphrasis and that way satisfy my insatiable desire to add *ornament* to my statecraft in the old Parnassian way. Or perhaps I should invent a mode of tragedy that evades the universal and the personal alike. Either way I'm sure glad I escaped the *cruel* pitfalls of an insignificant baccalaureate to end up the man I am. I remember those *lies* told me by a matriculated nutter from the Massachusetts Institute of Technology, such as "fossil *fuel* was a post-Renaissance by-product," and that "the *eyes* of every U.S. President are slightly strabismic of necessity." (But what are untruths if not mischievous facts.) In any event truth posits a nod back to some *memory* of that other more optimistic speech-act theory, the one in which "starting to *decease*" means "not to *die*" (in that scenario death's left for the other one who never says no to the category *increase*). It's never enough though, that meta-linguistic striving to *increase* the possible ways for us to *die* in language. Ah puce remorse! I failed miserably in my attempt to give knowledge back to thinking and so saddened by my *decease* in believing that the deepest truths are found in a *memory* of bedtime stories. But at this point I should turn my *eyes* to those constitutional dialogs around here that merely *fuel* my urge to evade an answer to the single burning question of what *lies* beneath that community named The Dead. It's a *cruel* reassurance that this castle has windows but no *ornament*. One can look out beyond the parterre to the car-park and set off a car alarm with a cough or a sneeze then hear moisture unmuttering a twitch of *Spring*, coiled in a readiness, *content* to arrive on time and repeat any number of seasonable possibilities in its gene-pool, despite its *niggarding* attempt to block the moment that occluded my own chance to *be* elsewhere. It all leaves me wondering whether mixing memoranda with ambition helps *you* escape from the atmospheric sadness of the Middle Class. Oh oh, I see the grown-ups are coming.

1. Muddy brown.

Exit

Enter Justice Shallow, Slender, Sir Hugh Evans, Master Page, Falstaffe, Bardolffe, Nym, Pistoll, Anne Page, Mistresse Ford, Mistresse Page, Simple.
One is always exiled to the present, *cold* as that sounds to us here at the start of this *old*-style piece of theatre. It takes a down-to-earth philosophy like *yours* truly's to argue convincingly that community's only promise is extinction. Why not take on the name Angesilaus Santandor like Walter Benjamin did and step out into the Pyrenees as one of the ones not counted? *Excuse* me for fffpharting in your fffface like that but *mine* is a truly a posteriori vision

of the Promised Land. I mean what's the *use* in Affffrican amnesty exchange when it involves unconditional *praise* ffffor the exploits of Idi Amin, Robert Mugabe and the Botswanaland Fffive? That's hardly a recipe fffor happy living, in ffffact I'd rather be a dyslexic Patagonian in rehabilitation than a Justice of the Peace around here, yet it sure beats one hundred and ninth place on Lithuanian Idol. In retrospect I should have become a lawyer, they get paid for everything, when they take a break they take it from someone else's wallet, and if they fforget to take a Beano and happen to fffphart down the phphone they send you a bill ffor it). I'd like to know who dropped us here in the fffirst place, life seems narrower in this aeon and if we are on a mission ffffrom God then how come we're all atheists standing among strangers dressed in cute italics? I appreciate we got airmiles fffor the trip here and I know God works in mysterious ways, like Pantisocracy and the I.R.S., but what are we supposed to do, skip around as if we're heroic adolescents in a Japanese Manga, or act out some cliché plot stolen fffrom Pirandello until we disappear into the mute choreography of Beckett's fffinal work? I don't know which Tantric chakra we've landed in but it sure don't feel like Nirvana and I'm convinced those plutocrats fffrom Pluto are enjoying this uncertainty. Perhaps we're somnambulating into other peoples' dreams. Wait, don't these corny Elizabethan plots usually have a play within a play? If so we could stage Waiting for Godot (as we seem to be doing that already). Personally, I had high hopes of being vaporized into a highly disjunctive, agrammatical, post-referential piece of écriture ffffeminine not a bloody ffiction yet-to-be. It may well end up being one of Sir Arthur Wing Pinero's happy plots in which case we might meet Dandy Dick and the second Mrs. Tanqueray, but what if it turns out that we're all refugees from Readers Digest thrust into a Jacobean plot like Cyril Tourner's in which the entire earth is a villain's abattoir? We might fffind ourselves with both *eyes* held open with rusty tooth-picks fffor *days* on end, our necks stretched to the point of strangulation before the King tells the torturer to relax, cuts us down, *lies* us on our fffaces, then cleans the blood off the hooks that *held* the corny narrative in place.[1] The only thing worse than dying is living forever, but *now* it's Spring and All in every *field*, as the good poet saith, the primrose atop the *brow* of Surrealism tells the *brow* itself to automatize among soluble fish and a magnetic *field* full of André Breton look-alikes. I'm sure such Saran-

Wrap Surrealism is possible *now* that sprung rhythm's disappeared into a lassitude of floral collage, all *held* together by an irresistible urge to go out and buy a new pair of socks. Remember those *lies* our mothers predicted we would tell on *days* like these,[2] convinced that we were groundlings in a globe of disaffiliations, turning our *eyes* to alternative ways to *praise* ourselves in the Temple of Thespis? Perhaps we should *use* the knowledge that we have to reconceptualize our origins, maybe *mine* as an ethical act in time permitted by the lame *excuse* that to be historical is to be reversible. Perhaps *yours* as an *old* entechnoid singularity trying to derive some sense out of the fact that one *cold* beggar times arithmetic equals more unwanted etymology.

1. Not to interrupt the flow of this discussion but surely resurrection before dying constitutes the ideal theological aporia.
2. For instance that a condom is an angel in a plastic bag.

Exeunt

It is easier to die than to remember.

Basil Bunting

Scene 2. *Thunder and Lightning. Enter the three Witches.*
Remember how I found *you* both buried under a snow bank during the Blizzard of Oz, the week we stayed at the Nutcracker Suites and we all took up ballet for charity? To write people into history means giving dates their faces[1] yet to *be* interior to the historical is all that memory requires. History is a wind and clouds the events that historiography records. This is not a novel proposition, it is the propelling insight behind the holy Muslim saint Sidi Mahrez's elegy on the disappearance of Carthage. Stone for the permanence and a pen of iron to write it. The space of history always reminds that for the vast majority memory's a graveyard without head-stones. I'm remembering the *time* when I thought I could *see* Munich superimposed on a wartime map of Florence in the *prime* of winter and a marvelous muteness fell upon me. For a moment I was at home in the univocity of bodies where a voice is always a fingerprint of sound. Moving back to our philosophical discussion of the a posteriori method (that those previous people introduced), *you* really should

14

see a proctologist about my migraine, I'm convinced it's related to the way we don't sit during hexing. And what's *posterity* after all? Just a *tomb* for those brave victims torn between pain and animal *husbandry* caught out there in the fields of pastoral patinated with incontinence unable to bivouac in the *womb* of a different genre like those clerihews[2] my *mother* sang me. Hope *renews* however with *another* version of One Flew over the Cuckoo's Nest and we should all pause to reflect how ornithological studies lend a tad of plumage to the way we *view* our favourite bird, the vulture. I take the *view* that some things never change, like *another* one of those eternal alternative returns by which political theology *renews* its campaign on behalf of the village idiot. Interestingly, that's how I conjure up a thought a *mother* might have planted in the *womb* of her andropausal circuitry. Even accidents reveal themselves as new coordinates, your fist comes tightened around the epicenter of the word "*husbandry*" arriving at a *tomb* somewhere in a Mississippi graveyard marked "In Loving Memory of *Posterity.*" *You* know it's a little known fact that the culinary behavior of evolving primates offers an a priori possibility to actually convert a *prime* rib-eye (via the heterokaryon test) into a phenotypical chloroplast and actually *see* a green colored *time* stand still on the barbecue and smile.[3] But something tells me evolution's not the place to *be* as *you* sit down to a sunny breakfast egg cracked over yet another human disaster.

1. Walter Benjamin, *Arcades Project* N11 2, p. 476.
2. A somewhat less than epic form invented by E. Clerihew Bentley (d.1956) e.g. "Said Sir Christopher Wren I'll be dining at ten and if anyone calls say I'm building Saint Paul's."
3. A full scientific explanation of this test is too complicated for a modest footnote.

> The destructive character lives from the feeling not that
> life is worth living, but that suicide is not worth the trouble.
> Walter Benjamin

Enter Hamlet.

The perpetual sadness of God comes from his awareness that he can never die, but it leaves me wondering whether he's ever contemplated suicide. My ontological debut was a dying into life born into the decade with no name and such a non-prophetic childhood despite being suckled at the breasts of ocular suffocation as well as saturated in all the humanistic comforts of a courtly crib 'n rattle and constantly bombarded with all that phrasal politesse, such as "who's a lovely little Princey wincey?"! My lullabies were conditioned by the logic of the still-born song with its singer catabolized. (It didn't help matters that as a baby I was nursed by a nanny internationally renowned for restless knee syndrome and who spent most of the day on a suicide chat-line.) My youth was commonplace enough as "an orphan among prosperous boys."[1] Bullied at playschool and kindergarten, contracting mumps at the age of eight, measles at ten, first signs of puberty at twenty-seven, weeping under willows, witnessing the partial death of social democracy and other same-sex segregated activities, while indulging in a litany of French inventions such as preciosity and fish sauce and each week I celebrated the anniversary of art. Pausing to answer the odd Renaissance conundrum dropped by a witty courtier, I grew to love the beauty of wilted things. Every morning without fail I would wake and think upon the perfection of an unlaid egg, every night reinvent my childhood fears of aristocratic binary accessories and sometimes dream I was taking Sartre back to Paris courtesy the airline of the anti-vowel to join the audience at a Party Political Broadcast by René Magritte. My true Beatrice was Cicero who came to me as a vast not-for-profit prophet disguised as Mahmoud Ahmadinejad, wearing a worn sombrero, telling me poetry always needs an unborn reader. I inherited my gender fear and piety from the Holy Anchoress of Pyongyang, and by various sinuosities still practice those habits of a nun, pious, pristine and regular across a year marked out for prayers. Each hour my eyes settle on the wrinkled surface of a homily (occasionally choking on the odd maxim from Lao-tse). A skull and crucifix are always near my lips, at such time I contemplate the commonplace in abject things. Each thought I have intersects with its corresponding miracle, each point of light ignites an incognito. In momentary audacity, I try to think of new hobbies such as hand-gliding and shooting families for fun, until I remember that the Incas had no wheel. I fantasize yin/yang experts congregating near off-shore wind farms to discuss the outlook on Confucian profit possibilities, and wake each morning to myself and things then, in my fancies, fly with Yeats and Icarus among the wild swans of Coole feeling good to *be* alive. I learned from Thomas Wentworth Higginson the other day (while helping him knit a brand-new edition of the Poems of Emily Dickinson) that the soul, like the Siegfried Line, is built entirely of concrete, protected by barbed wire and remains dormant until tenanted. An empty, subvital place, it is the textual somatic haunting the neighborhood of real-estate in the personality of the one who walks away.[2] When *you* consider time by itself then the position of the future is merely the past viewed from a different angle while the present is always happening elsewhere and one doesn't get far unless one looks a little further than the future, but what a sprawl is a past! Ernest Hemingway appears in it as the Poet Laureate of the local Taco Bell, arthritic tango-dancers leap in mid-air into long and distinguished careers as TV judges, machines turn into shops as a toad pharts into custard then leaves by a bookseller's alternative to deletion until the burning bush in front of the White House finally yields the empirical evidence of empire. And each vacation an ideogram composed from the vestiges of black and white according to a child's logic captured in some proverbial distich. Can it still work in my diagonal worlds, impatient to *leave* without a sound across all those deciduous years that are too soon *gone*? It's an anxiety I share with Harold Bloom and other multi-cellular organisms consumed by the fear of "the one strong among us." Still, there's no need to *deceive* myself into thinking I'd experience this *alone* and it's best that I *live* frugally and *use* my Princely wealth altruistically, *give* my own charity a chance to offset my dear parents' recreational drug *abuse*: that way, when I give it away *free*, it'll *lend* a *legacy* for someone else to *spend*. Happiness is not included in my post-Epicurean lifestyle, but right now I need to *spend* some time relaxing, take a holiday with a fellow amateur social worker in some insalubrious barrio in Guatemala City—and I won't have to dip into my *legacy* for that, in fact thanks to the internet I can take a boat trip to the Yucatan and not even get off the throne. Or else I could *lend* a hand to a one–eyed quantity surveyor, test drive a new sleeping pill, design edible underwear thicker than bibles, exercise *free*-will, *abuse* the social system, *give* metempsychosis a new *use* in organ transplants and *live* on to keep telling it the way it really wasn't. Perhaps the old cliché holds true that life is a dream from which no one wakes and at death one passes into nightmare. In which case I hope I'm reincarnated and return as an alligator so successfully attuned to my habitat that I'll survive in an evolutionary time-warp like Peter Pan or the Lawrence Welk Show. Then again I might go it *alone* as the Boston Strangler did and *deceive* the crime scene investigators into believing that I've *gone* to *leave* my passport for safe keeping at the local crack house. *You* can *be* sure of one thing: I'll keep those international migraine engineers in lots of overtime—and as Moses said: if I go the Red Sea goes with me.

1. Try guessing this one: Louis Zukofsky, Matthew Arnold or R. W. Emerson?
2. This is not the picture his mother paints. "Hamlet was born out of the anger of hasty worlds. We swaddled him in a trench-coat designed for the KGB, gave him CIA regular issue sunglasses for his first birthday. The King and I kept him in a maximum security nursery with armed guards at each corner of his crib and he still got out. At that point we tried to trade him for an underwater flashlight with a magician on a cruise ship. Soon he developed a curious penchant for sitting on top of other children at playtime. Child psychiatrists despaired of him and recommended we put him in a Cecenian orphanage for hopeless cases, but fake ID quickly got him into the better of the more insalubrious kindergartens. He slipped prozac into the evening soup, dropping worms down girls' blousers, lighting cannabis for arson, singing the Internationale as a favourite lullaby to gullible younger inmates. By four and a half he'd quit that dormitory for ragged boys, developed the full-scale enigma strategies of Rasputin and perfected the vanishing acts of Howard Hughes. It was then that he started his famed knife collection with the stilleto of Agesilao Milano (a gift from King Bomba of Sicily). He took Shakespeare on as his agent after one of his random eye-poking expeditions in Stratford and wrote manuals for revolutionizing poltergeists, while renovating post-industrial Cleveland as a weekend hobby. We used to rent him a hooker on his birth-day and, on his having successfully bi-passed libidinal normalization, we suggested sex with a pig preferable as a more regular, affordable alternative. Soon he turned to socially sanctioned homoerotic rituals such as pole vaulting and morris dancing, then puberty came on and, changing his name to the Elisnore Sperminator, developed the need for those unbearable soliloquies, but he always thanked his parents for making them possible … ."

Exit omnes

Enter Bardolffe and his Boy.
It's *sweet* of you to *meet* me here among as many frangible ideas as possible, and if the deal *was* winter to your mind *bereft* of quietude, then I will raise a *glass* to somnolence and place it slightly to the *left* of thinking, close to *where*

18

another dropped a message that's long *gone*. And if you trace *there* a pressure *on* that shawl of sample quilt you made *excell* all possibilities it would all be the *same* to me. I mean a house in town's okay but let's *dwell* in a more exciting *frame* of mind. It's interesting that Bernard Cache tells us image is *frame* and vector plus inflection, a thought methinks attractive to tree-hugging hippies.[1] But how could we *dwell* in a house built to be a picture with a moving twitch in it? Marinetti and Heidegger might feel the *same* as me and I'm sure that human baboon André Breton would still prefer to *excell on* those volcanoes of unconsciously generated automatic sentences than build inflected housing. For goodness sake, don't get too uptight about frames and inflections, *there* may be a good reason to chill out for a bit and save some of our energy for rethinking the position of that transitory Pinecone Air-freshener in the village pschithouse before it's *gone*, whisked away to the local slaughter-house for obsolete commodities.[2] *Where* can sympathy be *left* in such a world of built-in obsolescence? Relax, don't get your talents in a twist, have a *glass* or two of my bio-technic philanthropy, it's magical in its ability to render the most erotically *bereft* scenario a Lupercalian extravaganza. But is that too Classical for you as a boy without body hair? *Was* I thinking too "nanotechnically" when I suggested it? Let's leave it at this: when two vectors *meet* in the *sweet* morass of an otiose anthropomorphism Le Corbusier's policeman (known as "London Bobby") won't be there to help you reconstruct your tower.

1. See Bernard Cache, *Earth Moves: the Furnishing of Territories*. MIT Press, 1995.
2. *L'abbatoir* you used to call it when your French was better.

Enter Leonato Governor of Messina, Imogen his wife, Hero his daughter, and Beatrice his niece, with a messenger.
Pardon us for interrupting but as *heir* presumptives to that conversation may we suggest aiming for a parsimonious deceleration into coryambic meaninglessness in your next discussion as I do in my annual Governor's address—it's delivered in the style of George W. Bush and it finally rescued him from being the only pig on a pork pie express. Quid tum? Shall we write *fair* trade sonnets in support of illegal immigrants or is that a little too politically correct to gain us *posterity*? Best click on the menu then *depart* for anywhere *you* want to go. In the *art* world of the

Fifties it was called a "happening" by which *one* blended aesthetics into life and vice into versa. Sounds to me like a neat unlogistic covering for strictly material interests. If *you*'ve got a problem with that then I've got negations—lots of them in fact. So instead of simply "happening" why not be inventive, take a *loan* out on the word *"usury"* and try selling it to Ezra Pound. And now an integral to ponder on: upper limit cacophony, lower limit where we live. Geez, it's so dead in this *self-killed place*, it's got all the allure of a puddle in a pediatrician's waiting room and it's hardly the morada vital my swami Vivekananda promised. It's impossible to flaneurize in this Carthusian monstrosity, in fact I'd sooner share a cell in an East-European ghetto with Hannibal Lecter. Yeats claimed maps provide metaphors for poetry[1] but stuck on this chain of being-and-nothingness makes me want to burn them all. What an irony to be out of drink in such a *distilled* moment of quintessential history and not a public building worthy to *deface*. If only we could collide with another planet and get it over with. Meanwhile let's continue to *deface* the latest multinational allegory. The wine's still in the grape waiting to be *distilled* into the next barrel of Chateau Murder Incorporated, so let's get out of this *place*—it's as stuffy as a sonnet in a style of *self-killed* petty verbalism and makes me wish I'd been constructed in a laboratory of test rats. Remember, a becoming always starts in a middle where the tires of the paramilitary Junta's Hummer roll over butterflies who miraculously survive to bolster the resistance in a meso-American coup. If at this point someone cried "that's conceptual *usury*" I think I'd shout out "*loan* thyself to a nunnery and give the Pope a lap dance."[2] *You* only get *one* chance to learn the *art* of the circle in this Castle of Perseverance, but who's to say what still might happen? Perhaps each of us is destined to have our very own September eleven. *You* may be right to claim with Derrida there's nothing outside the text, it's just that the walls of this room are now starting to *depart* from the ceiling and threatening to end in a rather invidious slide towards *posterity* as the domestic detritus that buried both messenger and message. Most least is less, a face none eyes, no smile, a listening. Does that seem a *fair* way to go as *heir* apparent to someone else's memorabilia?

1. See Yeats's *A Vision*.
2. A new personal low.

Exeunt

> Sure all the world runs mad with elegy.
> From the 1695 anonymous
> *The Mourning Poets*

Scene 3. *Enter King Lear, Cornwall, Albany, Gonerill, Regan, Cordelia, and attendants.*

Rilke, quiet conjuror,[1] bard of the thorn prick and Poet Laureate of Leukemia! I wish I had a *son* like him—the grandest landlord in the mortuary of Reason and such a genius with sarcophagi and sadness, mastering the elegy for an epoch of genocide. You can smell the body odor of all our Neolithic avatars in each of them. I read three on the Oprah Winfrey show at *noon* today to a sitting ovation in the *way* Rilke intended wrapped inside a cool cerulean blue (those kinds of blue that *are* usually reserved for café walls and holding cells). They say the new eternity is the event by which the network of chance becomes the axis of necessity, but what a year that *day* turned out to be, a veritable star spangled bummer. I thought I'd end up either the denizen of Hell or the arsonist of Heaven! It was the kind of Christmas you'd expect to spend with a family who thought Santa Claus was a town in Southern California. On Boxing Day I was late for court as I couldn't find a kosher *car*-park in the entire Kingdom; the kids (erstwhile Byronic teenagers bumming around experimenting on drugs and rape date pills) did a volte face and returned from their *pilgrimage* to Finsbury Park mosque as radicalized jihadists, and grandfather, recently defrosted from the Dark Ages and wearing a fossilized back-pack, *still* insisted he was the Peter Pan of Dialectical Materialism. I couldn't believe it was happening to me and quickly joined the ranks of the Depressed Dads. I was a self-declared deprivation zone. The last thing I need at my *age* is an ontology of the exception and then, amazingly, beside the poem I was reading, stood a *hill* in all its *majesty*. It felt as if a moonlight holocaust had transplanted me: Duino appeared from a distant elevation, a uterine halo above the summit of the Four Last Things! (Quince came here to crouch once with a satchel full of Aeschylus.) What a *sight* to the injured face that only has one *eye*, deprived of the wonder of all this binocularity of *light*. Simplicity never occupies the tenebrous, altering its *light* to grasp the *eye* in its *sight* of *majesty*, the corpse of a galaxy seen on a final event horizon with a Soviet summer to the east. However when faced with the Sublime you reinvent the ridiculous. Next day it was sex with Cordelia at first sitting and felt like I was getting a back-rub from an orgasm, other than that the same old biotopologies and beyond the *hill* an endless vista of preventable foreclosures. Perhaps this is the *age* awaiting its own anamnesic Proust but it's *still* better than a statutory *pilgrimage* to Disneyland in the family *car* on a *day* one wanted to devote to proof-reading the obituary columns.[2] If any of you *are* aware of a different *way* to avoid this cul-de-sac, please let me know. I mean, it may well be high *noon* for the rest of the millennium but is midday the best time to call it quits to that meridian *son* of a bitch?

1. Rilke's name for Orpheus.
2. There's always a story in a nameless name.

Enter Prospero (disguised as Harold Bloom).
I prefer allergies to elegies, that purple swelling on the edge of critical insight. Incidentally, *none* of the above seems relevant to poetry except the *one* sentence mentioning sarcophagi. How like a fossil that word seemeth to *sing* putting me in mind of a different text my *mother* extolled when *ordering* uncle's cremation sermon. What a speech that was, hitting the congregation as a veritable sermon-on-the-mount issuing from the very lips of Mae West. It ushered closing time in concept country where Death leads to *another* development in Necropoetics as all poems *bear* themselves along in a Heraclitan flux of anxiety (thanks to my revisionary ratios). But the thought of poetry and leukemia *confounds* my *ear*. It *sounds* as if it's best to leave that particular connection to those with ideological investments in critiquing the cultural imaginary such as Slavoj Zizek and Jacques Rancière. Like poor old etymologies, there's hardly any concepts left to *annoy* those who *gladly* didn't stand in line to experience

joy so *sadly* in the absolute condition of present things.[1] Yet *sadly* it's a *joy* to be alive playing tennis with John Ashbery. I never admitted it in my growth-onset anxiety of influence but it's not all that difficult to write a good poem like he does and even easier to write a great sestina, but to write a bad poem takes a lot of practice. I know, a good poem should always fuse the butterfly with the philosopher, but my penchant is for those with an oriental flavor like that great decadent one by Ella Fitzgerald.[2] [Slipping Cordelia an unused poem.] Strong poems raise questions such as how many letters are there in the word "literature," or what would happen to free speech if the shelves of the Library of Congress suddenly went mad in a glossolalia of silence (as James Longenbach might put it?) It's hard to conceive the ineffable in the all-that-is-human when it's not even human. Is there a space beyond species in which I can *gladly* add a person to my verb and not *annoy* Helen Vendler and her friends who only like the *sounds* of Keats with an *ear* misplaced beneath a tip-toe on a hill? An answer is the saddest place to end up in, but what *confounds* my brain at this point is why that brown *bear* from Jellystone Park is still in the Faculty Club claiming it's Louis Althusser and why *another* goat is *ordering* a glass of milk from that *Mother* Superior selling rosary beads to a group of Japanese tourists? With such unanswerable questions it might be possible for me to *sing* a final chorus from The Mikado and rouse New Haven to *one* final cough before I pass, like Charles Eliot Norton, along the fractal shoreline into the solitary *none*.

1. Melville.
2. The Rubber Yacht of Heimey Cohen.

Exit pursued by a Beare

Enter Sir John the Bastard, and Conrad his companion.
What a goddam shame that Sheakspeare always *commits* the intentional fallacy. I'm convinced interpretation's not his Beatrice, that gal always *sits* alone on a barstool, knowing that sooner or later her agent from Hollywood will appear announcing that *it* is Spring and Act Three again in another one of the Bard of Avon's comedies and by the *end* of act five she'll be dead again

or alive once more (*it* doesn't matter where or how you *spend* your lives in his kind of plots). Knowing that now the dance of the intellect is all the rage brings to *mind* that the only legitimate poet is the ballerina deciphering space in the anterior moments to her leap. We need to *keep* a seat vacant somewhere for all the forgotten choreographies philosophy left *behind*. I never *weep* to my *wife* over botched solutions to problems, in fact I always take "No" for a question. Best give your neighbor a big hug, let the fire of sociability *die* down and *life* eventually expire. I'm sure glad we're all characters made out of cardboard[1] posing the practical question of how to die without ink smudges, but this *eye* for an *eye* approach in real *life* makes me want to stay in fiction as the Man in the Iron Mask or the Prisoner of Zenda and eventually *die* at the hands of the *wife* of Bath having my life drained out according to the rules of the Canterbury Guild of Sewage and Drain Repairers.[2] Chaucer would *weep* for joy at that scenario, knowing psychosis is an inevitable consequence of leaving pilgrimage *behind*. I suggest you *keep* your *mind* focused on appropriate opinions on evolution from whale blubber up to crystal chandeliers—and don't forget to *spend* a little time hobbling on the crutch of cheapness, among those unpaid poverty bills, pondering the difference between herrings and heroes. Philip Johnson would have liked *it* as a final transcendence into the architectural collapse of all evolutionary patterns before reaching a summit from which to *end it* getting smothered by an enormous marble cloud.[3] Meanwhile, far from cult-heroism, a philosopher *sits* still and ponders the fact that a laugh is always the shortest distance between two catastrophes then *commits* cognition to the pun as language still waits for what happened.

1. Polyvinyl in the case of Hamlet.
2. The history of this image, from Irene to Theodosia is collected in Boronius and Pagi.
3. "Marmora pelagi" Catullus noted.

Exeunt

There is so much trouble in coming into the world, and so much going
out of it, that it's hardly worth while to be here at all.

Bolingbroke

Scene 4 *Enter Falstaffe, Pistoll, Robin, Quickly, Bardolffe, Ford.*
"Either it goes or I go." Hey, that's not a nice thought for *you* to entertain and
besides it's not even original. The context and occasion, maybe—but it falls a
tad short of that brush with thanatopraxis Oscar Wilde managed to pull off so
successfully with that bon mot at his witty departure from being. As for *me*, I
worry more about my pension plan and the fiscal crisis in the Euro Zone not
to mention all those botched attempts to *prove* why Cavalcanti depicts death
as female in his 28th Canzone. It's *kind* of like proofreading the Da Vinci Code
on a trampoline. Speaking of trampolines I'd *love* to kiss that mouth of yours
as soon as the breath mint takes effect, we really need to stop using the same
toothbrush. Speaking of corporate flossing between brushings, the only thing
those card-carrying, *mind*-bending capitalists *desire* is to *ruinate* all entelechial
notions of justice under the pretence of leveling the global playing field—it's
enough to put a fellow off soccer for life. It's obvious that they all *conspire* to
corner the international market in Capitalist accumulation, warming their warts
and hairy nostrils in their little log-cabins of greed and *hate*, but it's *evident* too
that *many* of us with dicky tickers have resorted to triple by-passes in order to
enjoy the fringe benefits of neo-liberalism. The rich as we know are a species of
politics unlike the poverty of anti-matter that used to be called the Proletariat.
No one cares a troy ounce these days about the spread of AIDS in Africa, or
the *unprovident* genocides taking place in someone else's back-yard. If there's
any hope left it's in the fact that there's *any* number of ways we can fabricate
happiness, (my favourite is biting the heads off pet hamsters). Providence is
sometimes *unprovident* but for the most part the *many* options on the matter
leave us an axonometric of contentment. It's been *evident* since the 1930s that
hate normally arrives by way of a dictator's dream or a Papal prohibition.
However, if we *conspire* to alter truths (like that flat earth claim) we'll end up
on a skewer disemboweled by a cheap potato peeler and that'll *ruinate* our
plans for Necrophile Awareness Week. When Descartes and Parmenides were

around *desire* equaled a solitary *mind* thinking; they both knew a thing or two about cost reductions. But *love* or liposuction will always be there to kiss us and our *kind* phat families and sweeter, phatter pets. So don't *prove* to *me* that it's all "I" "I" "I" with the egotists, but rather that Rimbaud knew how *you* is the other of the final matter.

Enter old Capulet in his gowne, and his wife.

Let living listen while the dying sing.

Sidney Keyes

"and a coward can't squirm when he's supper for a worm"
"and a woman can't love when her soul has passed above"
"and a widow can't yearn when her ashes plug an urn"
"and a sailor can't swim when there's guppies eating him"
"and your lover's out of breath when you've tickled her to death"
"and a child can't count sheep when death's put him to sleep"
"and a man can't shave when his chin is in a grave"

Dirge like it came over me, all those other ways to *die* outside quotation. *Thereby* fell a tear upon the airfield and it was rain because it wasn't rain. Personally, I *cherish* the bounty from that kind of poetic logic *more* when I turn around and say *perish* the thought of common-sense. The cry and laughter still remain for me the two grace notes of transrational defiance. You can *store* that one *away* as my gnomic utterance of the month but I bet you'll never hope to *cease* hiccupping. Thanks. Remove your personality and you're quite a nice man. Let's hope your tooth *decay* manages to resuscitate all those oral traditions that disappeared with the invention of the printing press. Give molars a chance to meet our wisdom teeth and *increase* conversation via ethnopoetics. How's your feet? Better, they don't seem to smell as much, but I sure found those odor eaters hard to chew and swallow; I also hope death comes as a cold shower to finally wake me up, my life's so sedentary these days that my buttocks are finally turning into fossil fuel. Don't blame your hormone scarcity or lack of exercise for being soporific all the time, blame it on the bloody culture industry, there's no surer way than it to *convert* a revolutionary paragon into an imbecilic TV mini-series. Popularity *bestows* a shallowness on profundity, the latter *departs* like Baudrillard to a bathroom of the Ecole Normale Supérieure with eyes the color of agate lanterns staring into the hyperreal of the nouveau néant. It is a mirifical land cleared of illogicality, complacence *grows* with its Velcro grip to become the dominant aesthetic premium, and normality a mirror to a mediated multiverse. But I'm beginning to sound like the sort of letter one writes but doesn't mail; I'm afraid my lucubration *grows* to sound like a jacket blurb for The Collected Dreams of Rip Van Winkle, it *departs* from the common-sense paradigm that made Thomas Reid such a successful philosopher. You see, it all depends upon deploying an optimism that *bestows* on life a certain carmen joculare. For instance, would a dozen or so optimistic *converts* to orthodox Druidism help *increase* the ratio of terminal sainthoods to christenings? It's a stab at least in recovering the endless multiplicity we were. Did you know that the patron saint of bomb technicians is Saint Barbara? Figure that one out as it threatens to *decay* into a footnote on the Nicean Creed, but don't ever *cease* to make your own saints viable, we'll need them to protect us from those swarms of inter-galactic gold-diggers and serious outbreaks of interdepartmental memos. And don't throw *away* that instant beatification powder, keep it available in every dime *store* you own and don't let sainthood *perish* into Spanish street names. There's too much down-time in Christianity, it feels like Saints have birthdays once a week, in fact the less I think about it the *more* I *cherish* those early Christian masochists who knew that "I think *thereby* I am" is actually a way to *die* inside a torturous syllogistic prosthesis. I didn't know that about Saint Barbara, but I did know that the patron saint of art dealers is John the Apostle, that Saint Zita is still the patron saint of lost keys, and that prison guards actually have two saints to guard them: Hippolytus and Adrian of Nicomedia *hence* the low escape rate. But they sure need that hagio *defence* in those carcieri. Piranesi had the right idea, forget about the welfare of the inmates and allow the material ambience to *grow* into a spatial contradiction. I mean if you unshackle your manacles, *forsake* the safety of the ground and *go* try and climb one of his stairs to *make* the third-floor men's room you'll fall right off the edge onto some rotary machine with revolving spikes. That'll cause the whiskers of your *beard* to curl into *sheaves* of ontological agony! In fact, Piranesi still remains the patron saint of Guantanamo Bay. I've never been one of the *herd*, like my neighbor who *leaves* his market economies under the *white* lights of another sub-*prime* catastrophe. *Night* seems the best *time* to exercise my opposition to all those Wall Street fiscal fairy stories and tell the world that twelve o'clock is the *time* of *night* when all *prime* rates manifest as forgotten adjectives, *white* corpuscles cobbling through the *leaves* of paper currency into a *herd* of gerunds with suits on and bearing briefcases; Visigoths, *sheaves* of grease in Walt Whitman's *beard* ready to *make* you *go* willingly back to Social Credit and *forsake* the very concepts of hedge funds and insider dealing. It's time to learn how to *grow* astute in situ and wise up to your opponent's uncanny form of *defence* which isn't counter-strategy at all, or even supra-tactics, but simply knowing how to make each day feel like a hand-tooled guide to the Aztec civilization. From *hence* it will be anthems to anagrams for me in a secluded corner of the then and there.

Enter Macbeth and Banquo.

So now you *know* why we came prepackaged with hypocrisies and Hippocratic oaths (if they're related), *cold* packed arrière-pensées (as they say in Glasgow), vacuum sealed by Machiavelli and equipped each *day* with a brand-new regiment under our kilts. That's what I like about zuccini implants, best cosmetic surgeons in Bangladesh *uphold* the value of their captivating fungibility. Pity about the tooth *decay* from those treacle-filled haggises, just grin and *bear* it I suppose. I'm surprised at the startling rate of *decease* in all those wood pigeons we used to light the fire with. I'd trade my basker-hilted claymore back to the Laird of Killiekrankie to have them returned for the impending Scottish annunciations. Ouch, my water's just broke, must be giving birth to another Highland slaughter. Ah the joys of clan warfare, those *were* the days when a *lease* on a lipstick got you to the most transparent Petropolis in the United Emirates. Best *give* in *prepare* to *live* among the bed and breakfast agit-prop with a Monteverdi profile plus false teeth, dark spectacles and a crenellation inventory. Like my cousin Mao's Cultural Revolution, we *are* what is becoming. Pardon me for interrupting your radical musings but *are* you sure this is the right track back to where we ought to *live* and is it a destination we should *prepare* to reach? I hear the bio-agents there have gone derelict in their child-support and don't *give* a damn how many innocent villages get swept away.

It'll hardly inject our sporrans with a new *lease* on Loch Ness Romanticism and even if we *were* informed of the lab reports on those terrorists with crop dusters, would knowledge of that fact forestall the *decease* of highland heroes? I tell you, death overshadows diplomacy and that's an adage to *bear* in mind as we *decay* into the anonymity of endless gorse, still hoping to *uphold* the truth that even the pater familias is subject to hair loss just like us. I wonder what the rest of the *day* has in store for us, men on the moon perhaps or a *cold* shower with God and his apostles, or possibly a different epoch than the project scream we *know* to be *so* burdensome to bagpipes?

Exeunt

Enter Bernardo, Francisco, two sentinels.

Whadder you mean September ten? You always get the *date* wrong. Rather than buying yourself a watch, you prefer to *prognosticate* from the scales on our dead goldfish, Kipper. If we could determine the optimum moment for a brand-new awen[1] we could *convert* tactics into teleology and that way *thrive* in the *art* of the fin de siecle. Alternatively we might *derive* some comfort from the possibility that one of us may *find* a way to turn this badly written comedy into one giant human farce. It's all *well* and good to ask your neighbor to *wind* up her clock and wake you up at eight with a loud chorus of "Arrivederci Roma" but I *tell* you this is hardly the time in life to become a subject-in-process, such a *quality* of being in motion always makes me think of phlegm and Hitler's name for human beings.[2] I'm glad his *luck* finally ran out. Think what those Nazi rockets would have done to *astronomy* and our celestial mean aggregates had he got more off the ground, it would have almost been as bad as swallowing toothpaste. But now that we've donated Kipper to the local Gay and Lesbian taxidermy club we can elegize upon it with a living chicken we can *pluck*. The guitar you *pluck* all night makes me think of *astronomy* in Granada and it's just my *luck* to be lacking that *quality* of product management to turn your starlit slum into my galactic dream home. If you *tell* that to the local mayor of Casterbridge you'll *wind* up in jail or a deep *well* of consequence perchance described in detail by Maxim Gorky where you'll *find* yourself forced to *derive* new *art* forms from several amino acid complexes that *thrive* on satiated optimism; you'll have to *convert* idea into specimen, *prognosticate* the future from historical mistakes and *date* your birth from the moment all your nightmares went suburban. Sounds like Paradise to me.

1. An ancient Cymric word for bardic inspiration.
2. "Planetary bacilli."

Enter Bastard.

Retirement under this *new* deal isn't what it used to be. *You* remember the old days? Banging a tortoise around a croquet lawn with a glass of bootleg Martian gin and a handshake beside Lake Proposition before the *night* brought out the crocodile safari, that was the real guacamole for the future. Now it's all about rummaging in other people's woods, sniffing out court truffles for export. What with my addiction to wearing gorilla costumes and my pathetic sense of timing I'd be better off selling life insurance to corpses. And with the *decay* of instrumental reason (courtesy the White House and Pentagon Surrealist Society) it's probably time for me to join the migrating path of the hordes of proletariat trying to re-enact the conversion of Saint Paul on the road to Walmart. In addition I remain unconvinced that two sentinels are sufficiently qualified to be my joint physiotherapists. I mean the *sight* of those dowagers' humps makes me inclined to *stay* away from that clinic of yours; it brings to *memory* the steady *decrease* in previous open-mouth visits to the dentist. Despite being the lovechild of Henry VIII, shuffling around a veritable Toulouse Lautrec in my Hittite jockstrap, and always the flâneur of ambiguities, my own theory of subjective individualism convinces me the body is a path named sarx and the wind that blows along it pneuma, breath freshening to panic as the *sky* turns marble to my thoughts.[1] So any response? Considering everyone's kissed the Blarney Stone there's not much conversation, in fact, I might as well be talking to a jar full of gefiltefish or four dead Bloodhounds. The *increase* in my irascibility needs no further *comment*, suffice to say it *shows* up the *moment* I put my trust in the promised chastity of slumber parties—as the saying *grows*. They say a mollusk *grows* at eight times the speed of a Joshua tree and twice as fast as one of Genghis Khan's erections—another useless fact to stick in my tax-exempt analects the *moment* truth goes out of fashion. However, the fact that acoustic form *shows* shape to be illusionary provides

30

an acrid *comment* on our national anthem. Danger lurks everywhere and we need to sharpen all our survival tactics via sensible questioning. For instance, with West Nile virus on the *increase* should we avoid looking at the flagpole in the *sky* with bare arms and hand on heart and *decrease* our visits to the public swimming pool? Is there a known link to camels or pyramids? Do mosquitoes breed in mosques? Is it an etymological or entomological problem and does it lead to *memory* loss? Best *stay* indoors in the *sight* of the television as it glows back at us, and the *sky* threatens to *decay* into redundancy. That novel I read from, the *night* before last, "My Daddy was an Undertaker," how did it end? *You* only let me get as far as that description of Emile Zola watching Madame Bovary tripping on ice during a hockey intermission and claiming it a brand *new* break-through in contemporary choreography at which point Zola fell asleep. On me.

1. See Hazlitt's *Liber Amoris*.

Exeunt

Enter Evans and Simple.
Didn't Jesus live here once on the fourth floor, or am I confusing him with Che Guevara? Either way it takes eight parts *skill* and two parts luck to fall asleep in a true Spinozan high-rise. Metaphysicians do it all the time, but they're *still* waiting for Zeno at his archery range to shoot down another paradox. Some *men* even doubt the wisdom of the *fair pen* writing the world back into shape, trying to *repair* what television damages in the name of reality. The mental inferno truly is here and only the Poet can finally confront Hell and all its medieval accoutrements. A chilled bee can never dance its message around the *counterfeit flowers* of that shit-honeyed scenario. With brave iniquity *unset* the *hours*, take the hands off the clock and wind time up in spirals, *rhyme* yesterday with tooth *decay* as you run out of *time* for winking the word into another intervention-interface, the *way* a voice asks a labyrinth what's the shortest distance between two points and receives a predictable answer: "what an interesting stammer you have." We should never question the *way time* takes care of its own events, like Rome's decision to decline and then *decay,* or

the way *rhyme* eventually left the scene to vers libre. Think of the *hours* spent writing "anterior but motionless before the *unset* system of cod raptures in a switched Sargasso among *flowers* turned lacustrine, with the heron dipped in the half-fog and a *counterfeit* ferry brought it in for *repair*" or some other non-narrative clap-trap. A good poem always jumps out and mugs its reader. Try telling that to Shakspeyr with his *pen* stuck up the backsides of all the *fair men* of Stratford but it's *still* better than the *skill* you need to paragraph a stanza.

Exeunt

Enter Juliet (disguised as Bessie Smith).

Can a *rhyme* suddenly become a dialectical reflection? *Time* and again I think about that old *song* sung in cabarets and the *rage* I felt when I realized that catachresis is not distortion but misapplication. Every moment I try to wrap my *tongue* around bee bop I feel like an octopus trying to put up a beach chair. The *age* of the swing band's gone, replaced by Afro-American jazz-addict subculture, and who knows what crisis my career *faces* now that tickling the ivories to a dose of skat's gone out of fashion, like my buddies over at the Cabaret Voltaire and my lead clarinetist now playing on an infinite loop of musak. I'm now on a par with classic diabetic legends like BB King and Aretha Franklin because I think of real life as an adoption then double it and try not to worry about what *lies* around the bend. Moreover, the fact that the virus is the micropolitical realization of a Platonic idea hardly *graces* my lyric possibilities. What do I do, where do I go as someone's *eyes* fall on a finger pointing out some shifting body *parts* on a map of the Gaza Strip? I mean world atrocities are terrible but how can you focus on that sentiment when King Kong's sitting in your living room or some equally private recess of the *tomb* ycleped domesticity? Ozymandias taught me all I know about *deserts* but it was Rimbaud who taught me most about the after-life to *come*. He considered eternity to be the sea gone down with the sun. Now, it's all *come* down to this that I've sold my soul to I-tunes and all I've earned are *deserts* of other singers' fan mail. Ah the fate of letters! The *tomb* of linguistic destiny is never fully sealed, nor completely present, *parts* remain errant to the futile dominance of our *eyes,*[1] a remnant of excess free from all the airs and *graces* of the local support group. Every night-club singer knows that Bakhtin's roots were in Plato whose Socratic dialogues supremely dramatize the word, showing it to be the impresario of dialogic festivities, but why seek words when there are no things?[2] and what *lies* ahead for me? *Faces age* more than feet and that's why I have to shave my *tongue* whenever it leaves my fishnet panty hose and gets caught between the dictionary and pure *rage*. Scream a *song* of show *time* a pocket full of *rhyme*? Let brimstone Thespianity attend these mid-life crises to the very end.

1. A phrase stolen from the ever pompous and bombastic cretin, F. T. Marinetti.
2. Victor Hugo in "Dieu."

Enter a Serving man.

Come on Bessie, don't forget the key to happiness is B flat, besides you're much too practical to be a pessimist, standing there looking like Lot's wife in a negligee of pure salt. You see that expression on the faces of distressed ostriches, I haven't experienced you like this since you made whoopee with Jelly Roll Morton. In fact your personality's quite architectural these days, as intimate and particular as a medieval castle and (like it) in constant need of repairs. "Old *thee* and thou," a resurrected, schizophrenic Rosencrantz and Guildenstern if ever I saw them and both waiting to *see* if there's really death after "that faint Shadow called Natural Life."[1] If I was a poet of the old school I'd wax eloquently now with something like the following [clears throat before commencing] "My shadow *grows* into a *shade* when sunshine *owes* the clouds that *fade* to culmination in the west." Unfortunately that kind of weather forecast returns us via the National Poetry Foundation and the Iowa Writing Program back to econometrics when what we need are more multinational investment strategies to disappear into *untrimm'd* budgets avoiding *declines* in our gross national profits. So why don't we sit down and draw up a sketch of the Bolshevik Revolution in both profile and perspective showing Capitalism with all its new abstractions *dimmed* of all abilities to radiate across the Third World. See how light *shines* within the bulbs we planted? Let's pick a *date* in *May* to vegetate alongside them into the Summer of a Thousand Platos. Make sure we choose a *temperate* clime such as Luxembourg in August, or the Bouche du Rhone so we can wear our shorts on a *day* that's warm and friendly to two old mandrakes. Do you remember the *day* when I was a pram and you rolled me down those steps, or was that in a film or on a *temperate* afternoon in *May*? My recollection's bad right now but, given my size, it's the mood of the memory not the *date* that's important. The market puns a bit, nibbling away at some hope that *shines* through never *dimmed* by the fact of all those multiple *declines* on even a bullish market. Did you know that Hitler kept his moustache *untrimmed* throughout the entire Stalingrad campaign as he goose stepped his way toward fate? He thought it would bring his troops good luck as they watched a thin line of strictly theoretical Bolshevism help him and them *fade* into oblivion. Speaking of oblivion, the latest Gallup Poll predicts I'll make a corpulent addition to those "graves of none"[2] but the fact is I'm not very fat at all, I'm simply a neo-realist who knows life *owes* him nothing. [The *shade* lifts just as its shadow *grows* in this very saying and a dim memory of song returns.] Suddenly you *see*, it's not half the poem it used to be there's a shadow hanging over "*thee*" an awkward pronoun at the best of times as we both can judge for ourselves.

1. A phrase of William Blake's.
2. Samuel Beckett.

Exeunt omnes

Flourishe. Enter King, Lenox, Malcolm, Donalbaine, and Attendants.
Why is that "e" on the end of "flourish," it sure makes us sound antiquarian don't you think? I was happy being a cephalopod before evolution gave me language and locked me in a house that Gordon Matta-Clark photographed on the rift of a crisis in human settlement. Shall these bones die? Frankly, I'm beginning to doubt it, in fact I'll no doubt stay *young* and contemporary forever, (thanks to that Christian Science collagen cream I stole from Mary Baker Eddy) and decree it *wrong* to grow old. It's laudable to resurrect the beauty of tradition, yet I'm bound to one such legacy—a permanent premise of doubt. Most *men* don't *allow* skepticism to influence their recreational decisions, preferring to stay hermetically sealed, doting on those crypto-anarcho-syndicalist saints like Chrysostum who put *pen* to paper and bent his *brow* in endless constipated meditation to reach incontrovertible theological

proof that Heaven's a theme-park in Kandahar populated by archangels in full battle dress. Curse the *crime* of oblivion! Does anyone remember Kitty Dashwood, the toast of the Oxford Jacobites and how James Hammond wrote himself to death for her? No doubt one of the less cherished *sweets* in the rich confectionary of the English elegy but a noble act for its *time.* "Streets draw in *fleets*" thinks Hart Crane as he fantasizes three sailors singing disgusting sea shanties as they come home drunk to spawn in a bath of uncorked *blood.* Does that image startle you, do you drop your *jaws* at the thought of such a thing, or do you *brood* perversely on that odd wish of Billy the Kid that every rattlesnake had *paws* with claws? Did you know a temporal inflection obtains with the choice of "pause" instead of *paws* in the last question? Actually, that's a favorite homonym of mine and one I often *brood* on as I'm watching another rerun of "*Jaws* the Sequel," an awful film that's guaranteed to make my *blood* thicken, what with all those *fleets* of small boats with their harpoons manufactured in Taiwan looking for the right *time* to pounce on a poor aquatic creature that seems the perfect synthesis of Attila the Hun and a Kissing Gourami. After all, it's just a cheap rip-off of Melville minus the *sweets* of pulchritude that come from the Melv's mellifluously marvelous mutating sibilants. Boy, that son of Manhattan could have written a great *crime* novel if he'd substituted a gangster for that whale and set it all in Vegas with a high-*brow*, supercilious detective played by Edward Said or William Shatner. Try and *pen* that one if you can and if you can't *allow* me to finish with this final adage from a wise king sliding towards the wrinkled end of life: Let *men* and women always put age before beauty because around these parts it's still always *wrong* to stay *young.*

Exeunt

Scene 5. *Enter Antipholus, Erotes, a Merchant. And Dromio.*
If the *treasure* really is all mine then the *pleasure* must be entirely yours. I know your altruism all too well, *nothing* of your own takes precedence. Others live on in their *defeated* theories of the neo-democratic self and its pre-tax contributions to retirement plans, *doting* over the monad they *created* out of two snotty anachronisms "*amazeth*," with its *controlling* allusion back to Renaissance faux labyrinths, and "*gazeth*," with its *rolling* inclination to stay

out of *fashion*. It's an honor actually to be *acquainted* with the likes of you, or rather the lacks of you, with your absent *passion* around Sunday brunches with that Stabat Mater you never *painted*. While we're on the subject, I think it's time we *painted* our pet sparrow a canary yellow, that way our mutual *passion* for the color inherent in song will be somewhat satisfied. I recall when I first *acquainted* you with aquatints, they were all the *fashion* at the time the Spanish Civil War broke out. *Rolling* out of bed to see them on the wall and believing them to be rejected readymades, you would *gaze* upon them for several seconds absorbing the temporary aesthetics of their paradox and the *controlling* provocation hidden in their displaced commodity logic. Art has never been a problem of depth but a seduction to absence. Should we rethink art then within the broad spectrum of surplus labour as Charlie Chaplin thought we should? Personally I prefer praxis to paint, I mean instead of painting a trash can why not become one? Ours is a life of deception in severely deformed masks, yet it still *amazes* me why God *created* an audience for the fine arts with gullible old pharts conned on weekends into "*doting*" over a masterpiece explained to them in tedious detail by some fatuous art critic. Saccharine obsequiousness of that kind can be *defeated* however by a calculated propensity to take the human condition as *nothing* more than a bad Baudelairean correspondence between "a paragraph of *pleasure*" and "a chimney-pot to *treasure*."

Exeunt

Enter Sampson and Gregory with swords and bucklers, of the House of Capulet. That motivational speaker from the Mormon Tabernacle Choir was pathetic and about as exciting as a vegetarian barbecue. It's not surprising that those complimentary adhesive inspiration notes he handed out in wild abandon soon fell off my fridge door and car bumper. I'm glad you didn't let him *sell* you one of his religious truths, they're simply not worth it and they don't wear *well* in the feisty beer-halls of negative theology. Let things continue one fact at a time knowing Time itself merely wants a night in bed with Space. [Thinks: "The scenery of Switzerland is what rhetoric would be if it were sincere."[1]] Meanwhile in poetry "a lark in clear *air*" serves just as well as "yon *bright* night of twinkling stars." It's a *fair* bet that either one of those platitudinous poeticisms would make you a legend overnight. The critical question remains however: should a poem be a festival or a collapse of the intellect?[2] Either way poems truly are the turds of Pegasus. Gautier thought the sonnet a poetic fugue, a kind of titilation in the tourniquet of words, but pity the poor flâneur who doesn't know the difference between his handkerchief and a raindrop on his ABC. It is said that Mercury invented the alphabet after watching the flight of cranes: "birds which make letters as they fly," but Menw ab Teirwaedd still watches the rowan rods grow from the mouth of Eigigan Fawr with every kind of knowledge writ on them. The ancient Irish Triads warn "it is death to mock a poet, death to love a poet, death to be a poet," although Julia Kristeva believes we reinvent love by writing. However Maurice Blanchot warned me the other day that to *write* is to kill, a trigger-happy assertion don't you think to a verb on the move, body fleshed around language, syntax, a dictionary laid bare? Still the role of killer-writer is infinitely preferable to that of a victim-reader. Reading always *hems* you into a claustrophobic interpretation that's *rare* in the actuality of writing. In "écriture" you're constantly confronted with a desert to cross and precious *gems* to discover. The majority of creative writing workshops allow you in discussion periods to *compare* the last words of Nimrod[3] to the fact that Deuteronomy is the closest thing we get to gay ghazhals, that way words (as poetry) instantiate the manner by which truths happen. As for me, I prefer my poetry to effuse the obscenity of Kalliope phucked by a white rhino on steroids and Viagra. Incidentally, given there's an anamnesis in all annunciation, you might want to *rehearse* your second coming within the sound of the Maharani of Baroda's brand new kitchenette. Distance expands the *use* of aura calling life to *verse* through the aid of the *muse* who leaves alone "what is about to happen." I think the *muse*, like Federal fiscal policy, is a natural gift to humanity. She guarantees that the reader is the poem's collateral interruption and that poets will always be Continental Philosophers at heart, their *verse* registering as a patellar reflex of a *use*-value uninitiated by "luck." She will *rehearse* above what beings below will know as private reading. We might *compare* poetry this way to the living man who's given a cup of coffee before being castrated by a few choice literary *gems* from Swinburne or Robert Frost. That's why I decided to put my gonads in a guppy bag as the Skoptsy advocate and drop them off at the local food bank.[4] The consequence of such *rare* acts of charity perpetually astonish, as do the *hems* embroidered with Latin letters on the gowns of those who never *write*. Imagine the *fair bright air* caught in the brilliance of a blindness, or the accomplished security guard too *well* to be ill and too institutionalized to *sell* off the vital rubbish of things.

1. Arthur Symons.
2. Valéry's and Breton's views respectively.
3. "No more towers like this one."
4. The Russian skoptsy (castrated ones) were an offshoot of a late 18th century sect known as the "People of God" and known for their advocacy of testiculate removal and masectomy as a preventative of lust. Persecuted by the Tzarists and Soviets alike, they survived into the 1920s.

Enter Laertes and Ophelia.
You're hot news baby! Hot news? I'm a national treasure suffering from a severe overdose of the Hall of Fame and I still haven't been upgraded to a proper star-ship. There's no charity in chastity and that's why I'd welcome a multi-national corporation between my legs, but right now I need you to ascertain a distinct technology and market for my contemporaneity.[1] It's just my luck isn't it, winning a complementary car wash for a year four centuries before the invention of the automobile, that kind of luck sends a scintillation through all my microchips. I know a sentient silicon like me turns every head around here, but I hate being the primary target of the male gaze, it's the cultural angst of the times and explains why the guys I'm dating these days are like Ray Charles and all wear dark shades when they push around with their white sticks. I'm pissed off too at having to play the part of some psychotic chick with a flower obsession wearing a corny plastic chaplet happily muttering "here's pansies for power point and hollyhocks for honesty." In fact I hate correctness, if it squeals I squash it, watch it multiply as an unfortunate fungal infection in an extreme male brain with an ethnocentric birthmark to its lethality. There I go *again* taking umbrage at the zeitgeist; measured against the horizon of the Paleozoic I'd say we've got it good. Take the local kindergarten for example, it's relatively free from assassinations and as well as language acquisition, meteoroscopy and advanced string theory, they teach poetry (especially the fate of the lyric

after Auschwitz), biodiversity, astronomy via the sheer arborescence of wave mechanics and learn to calculate gambling odds according to the feast days of all the *slain* martyrs mentioned in the Christian Calendar.[2] Jay Leno was correct in advising my good self (as number one Shakespearian Delegated Damsel) to act more like Mary Magdalene on valium, so I'm putting aside my *ill* rancor and trying to be less *chary* with my sans souci. I might take up origami like the Dali Lama did, no doubt it *will* render my spirit more maudlin, more *wary* of unoriginality in both *art* and life. In real poems breath takes a holiday down the dark boulevards of thanatopraxis, but for *me* death, as a mode of departure, is like the force of transition from bibliography to an ultimate interpretation of the unreadable. Pawn's knight to Queen's bishop two and suddenly voilà the Greek word for "transmigration" reappears. If the Buddhists have it right, the *heart* would be a butterfly and our coffins birth certificates into other lives, but I'm sure my transmigration's guaranteed to take the form of a hoola hoop. *You* should *expatiate* on that phenomenon and *behold* the human condition in all its fundamental contingency. Make a *date* with the aleatoric and some day, when grown *old,* recapitulate those youthful, unfulfilled promises I made. Even an *old* sonnet like this one can be subject to some new kind of mantic setting.[3] Choose the correct *date* for its mise en scène and *behold* how the Flower Maidens dance round some naked Parsifal, in fact that worn-out poetic form can even be arranged into fourteen acrobats in jackboots. *Expatiate* too on everything *you* treasure in Baroque theories of death. Keep your *heart* eponymous beneath all your prejudices against *me* and my *art* of the paradox. Whether Thyrsis and Corydon, or Mutt and Jeff, we'll stay ever *wary* of our twin chagrin. Remember, everything that is not believed remains decorative.[4] Still, I doubt our ideas *will* turn us into idols, and either way we both remain *chary* around the open text, a Vladimir and Estragon feeling safe in the habit of a formal constraint. Two chuckleheads too *ill* to slay or be *slain*. Claustral and methodic once and time *again*.

1. You might consider a cluster bang from that horde of Vikings over there, it's not only their helmets that are horny.
2. One actually dressed up as Ben Franklin with messy white hair and wearing a pair of granny glasses, flying a kite in the rain and claiming to have discovered elasticity.
3. Wasn't it Howard Hughes who asserted "No sonnet is an island even though a sonnet's

page is its castle?"
4. Jean Cocteau in his pretentious book *Opium*.

Enter Polonius.

Hi there! Did you know when *wit* was young professors called it quantum archaeology and *writ* treatise upon treatise to prove it? But you know how I am with my free-love and anti-vegetarianism, with face rubicund and Bacchic, always exhilarated by those operatic umlauts *expressed* in extra doses of the Götterdämmerung. Moreover my sex life's been enormously enhanced by that newly improved ejaculation powder to which you simply add water and stir, it's as easy to prepare as an Irish oatmeal breakfast. Jacques Lacan informs that there is no sexual relation but thanks to that cocaine-looking substance I feel as lusty as the Holy Ghost, however most of the time there's no *recompense* for pan-global testicular collisions with the harpsichord placed next to the supplementary health care plan. How's that for the perfect Surreal image and how ecliptic the *breast* in its apparent cleavability, knowing *eloquence might decay* into a weekend of dynamiting salmon in Alaska, like Sarah Palin does, in honor of the *rite* of Spring. Let's just *say* to the *heart rage* on, play your *part* more upbeat than downcast at this post-transitional *stage* of cultural gout. Dreams fade when you're comatose like I am, as if a minor attack of *stage* fright makes all the world unsympathetic to my attempts to fully Wagnerize my lifestyle. *Part* of the problem comes from my infant *rage* at my triple-breasted wet-nurse, it broke my *heart* when she joined a carnival show in Toronto bidding me farewell with the sign of the cross. Celan believes a poem is always a letter to the Father, but the crucifixion will always be remembered as the poem not the war of pure mathematics—and that text goes to everyone, not as religious dogma, but as a naked monstrance, a proud nudity of integers. What I'm trying to *say* is that when you're in Le Maison des Amies des Morts a *rite* of passage is an algebraic not an ethnological event. We take place as it takes place, oblique yet operational. But how does the skylight rearrange the distribution of its motes as navies, egalitarian crowds before that ineluctable *decay* into percentages, a wave returning to an open sea? You *might* say I'm intellectually well hung and thrill to my own *eloquence* as it curves from groin to *breast* along a trajectory of corpulent Schwartzneggerian anatomy, but it's still sad *recompense* for that inoculum *expressed* in sepia we call a photograph, *writ* with light in a blink to non-entity exchanging the *wit* of a decadent for a nom de guerre along its way.

Exit

Enter Mistresse Quickly, Simple, John Rugby, Doctor, Caius, Fenton.
I was snorting a line or two off stage with Dr Oz the other day and he assured me that it's a medical fact that a person's chance of a *heart* attack is increased eleven-fold by reading this ex-sonnet quickly with her or his mouth full. The *art* of the pastoral in its set scenarios of shepherds piping to *you* in the *sun* doesn't mention that (in fact all my pastorals come semi-skimmed). Meanwhile, back in the city, it occurs to *me* that all we need are more simplified employee pensions. The Beatniks want to suitcase society in its entirety and replace it with a fly-by-night counterculture but when all's said and *done* there's never nobility in mobility, that's why I prefer a sedentary life asleep in an arm chair waiting for a golf cart to eternity. Tacit, like Proust, *eyes* lowered to an orthodox angle, with thought *still* immured from the perilous *lies* of the alpha male, and dreaming of joining the ranks of the great magicians such as Merlin, Cornelius Agrippa and David Copperfield. We lost a magic *skill* with Mallarmé: that absolute *art* of the blank *held* potent if addressed to the *heart* of negativity and silence constellated in *stolen* space. Speaking of *stolen* whatever happened to the works of Sir Phillip Sidney, laughing to himself in the *heart* of winter as he *held* the literary world hostage to his Penshurst poetics, constantly reminding Sir Walter Raleigh that poets are the same as their pens and write themselves to death. Poetry of course remains alive and well, but whatever happened to the *art* of swaddling? Those were the days before saran wrap made life's little problems transparent. It took great *skill* to wrap up a dozen infants per half-hour and make each one look like identical Tutankhamuns in miniature. Meanwhile, back in the land of con, the *lies* and put-ons of every kind of avant-garde *still* dominate the galleries of Manhattan as a pain in the ass and a puzzle to the *eyes*. But what's *done* is kaput as your crippled nephew keeps reminding and the oneness of what's *me* is getting onerous. Look at that smudge called a masterpiece, an eternity of the fatal in a narrow slit scratched onto the *sun* then stretched out into cliché. You cannot speak the saying and though the face

speaks its need it never says I am needy, it remains the meniscus of a *you*, a sad misprision in the *art* of the ethical relation. Still, it breaks my *heart* to think that when I unswaddled that piece of cheese for lunch I completely destroyed a brand-new Christo.

Enter Ghost (disguised as the late Marcel Duchamp).
Now that this old toilet seat's been *removed* from my garret, festooned with cannabis flavoured toilet paper (inhaled to the point of ebriety) and put in the Salon d'Indépendants it really does look like one of my readymades, but to the proletariat, that true subject of History, it'll always be seen as a part of last night's garbage. As a once-*beloved* poltergeist I ought to sigh at that observation and point out the preternatural terrors I *toiled* all night to produce. Being a mainly conceptual artist-specter, thrown into language against my will, I was *quite foiled* at first by the unnatural onslaught of anacoluthon. I was eventually rescued from a labyrinth of Baroque pattern poetry by the natural style, gradually finding a way out of literature to *fight* and *die* in a highly volatile art market towards a condition more brutally crucial than eudemonics. Death after check-mate felt like entering Noah's rainbow ass backwards, a step into the still radiance of the astral silence.[1] Death always meets you before you die so I made sure I was dead before they interred me as a black pawn—and I also made sure to pack an I-pod and a screwdriver. Imagine being *buried* alive like Virgina Macdonald or Madame Bobin, or accidentally misplaced while comatose among the stemma of limbs and craniums in the local bargain charnel-house.[2] (One needs to keep a skeptical *eye* on the lethal *spread* of the cremation industry.) *Most* of the time the fire brought on by optimism melts down the permafrost of depression but the *bars* of this prison house aren't bending. Nowadays even Hollywood wants to *boast* of being a boot camp for its *stars*. The fact is literacy's bad news for the lovers of FX and fast action. Hence the *stars* I admire are the ones in the silent movies who remain Trappist and sepia. Meanwhile, a team of health inspectors *boast* of discovering that all the *bars* in Beverly Hills serve cocktails contaminated with green neurosperm around the rims. *Most* of the customers like it that way, *spread* out around the Californian canyons, governed by the single ethical rubric that you leave your neighbors in peace. [Long silence during which his right *eye* squints through

a Cubist telescope toward a *buried* integer; the number hides in the verb to *die* and hidden in that verb is a key to how to *fight* the fact that, since Heidegger, death has become a philosophical necessity.] Refusing to be *foiled* by my lack of bodily presence I'm *quite* happy to play around as a spirit and park in the rooms next door to séance fiction where I *toiled* away with venture capitals before telling my *beloved* family that I cashed in their long-term disability insurance, *removed* their belongings, and spent all their life savings buying up my own art. It's no use trying to forge the conscience of your race, better to race with good conscience to the latest forgery. Voilà, another fake monstrosity completed, I'll sign this one "Picasso" and try selling it to the local human condition as a valuable addition to its fridge magnet collection. Look how it sags in the wind.

1. Rimbaud's "Fairy" in *Illuminations*.
2. This is not a footnote to be read by taphephobics. Both Bobin's and Macdonald's fates have entered the ranks of the top ten Creepy Campfire stories for the under-thirteens. Mae West, however, preferred premature burials for her lovers to premature ejaculations (chacun à son gout).

Enter Gonerill and Steward.
"Hi, what's happening?" "Mea res agitur." Sounds interesting, so let *me* start off on the dark side of the fact that we're still here as the name of those who have no name. How does that make *you* feel? In one *respect* the same as if I hadn't been asked that question at all, in fact, you're beginning to sound like a discount tampon commercial. I like where we are, here, in our own interior space of being-there and *loving* the way our bio-ethical oscillations consistently provoke an unexceptional *aspect* of the logic of the detail, as we discover a whole in every part. Philharmonically speaking, we could say our names necessitate our *moving* out of predication into a more foundational term, like Plato's khora, and *it* could possibly defend us against the old boar without bristles.[1] *Yours*, of course, is a different desire, *it* seeks a poetics without party, *mine* a conventional politics of tactical incompetence which makes one feel good to be a court misfit free from the necessity of being a success. [Ed. The false *wit* in this kind of *embassage* remains conjoint yet unnamable, *knit* in a fabric of non-description where a remnant of *vassalage* returns in all the splendor of a non-Greek origin.] My kind

of *vassalage* is much more paltry, *knit* onto the bottoms of irreducible gaps in my ontic layers, provoking a need to shift my semiotalia into numerous punctums of ereignis. *Embassage* involves the opposite of *wit*, a veritable *mine* of politesse, concealed agendas and shuttle diplomacy of the kind immortalized by Joseph Goebbels and Henry Kissinger. But is *it* any different from happy hour in the neighborhood brothel where each john gets a complementary curry-flavoured condom for every three they buy? *Yours* is a contemporary ethics, kicking ass with otherness and duty, *it* refers to that unspeakable gift of ego-practicality Mahayana Buddhists call the un-spoke not speaking. I've recently thought of *moving* from here to a greenbelt of anti-matter in the Village of the Damned where I can assume the *aspect* of one of those psychopathic killers they stuff and exhibit to a *loving* audience in the Prague Chamber of Horrors. After that I think I've little *respect* left for a God who turns out to be a squirrel pulled from a magician's hat and shells its nuts on both *you* and *me*.

1. An ancient soubriquet for death. Diligent and masochistic readers can learn more about this exciting anti-Platonic arche-concept situated at the core of Plato's thinking by pondering Jacques Derrida's lengthy and prolix essay "Khora" in *On the Name*, trans. David Wood, John P. Leavey, Jr., and Ian McLeod (Stanford University Press, 1995): 87-127 as I did. [One assumes that women translators wisely avoided it].

Exeunt

Scene 6. *Thunder. Enter the three Witches.*

Don't get me started. Just two months after that home gym equipment was retrofitted this happens—and only three days to go before Walpurgisnacht! So much for home-grown spookiness. It's as bad as when we entered that Festival for Competitive Anorexics each as "The Blonde with the wilting Hibiscus" and with all this atonality throughout the coven, not to mention the problem of buying the proper shampoo for all those Hydra's heads, I'll *find* it hard to turn my *mind* to a *new* way of arranging another scary Saturday-night sleepover for teenagers. We used to be so skilled at being horrible (far better than the Cock Lane ghost and Dame Alice Kyteler rolled into one)[1] but now all our botched excursions into mumbo-jumbo and jiggery-pokery have left us somewhat less than frightening, (we're now eighty-six scare points behind the

Canterville Ghost and as distinctive as a poinsettia at Christmas). We should never have bought our recipes from that Warlock from Porlock. Still it's lovely weather for witchcraft and the *night* beckons us to *view* the latest in potential victims. So let's grant the world the *sight* of a trio of Halloween rejects flying passed on broomsticks in a tight Stealth-bomber formation—while carefully steering clear of Cotton Mather and his posse of witch sniffers. Not all effective necromancy's fled, I can *see* a new deviant tunnel into mischief and it's *wide* enough for us all to squeeze through. I'll just take a dozen painkillers, put on that Black Sabbath album Ozzy Osborne gave me, open up the grimoire, conjure up my imps and sucklings with an "abracadaver" and mix some frogs' throats in a little spider spittle, dried hedgehog dung with badger vomit, read the Lord's Prayer backwards with a lisp and that way disseminate some diabolical law-becoming-action as *you* both *abide* in that bloody lyrical quietude I previously *expired* in. Speaking of blood, Solomon warns that qui nimis emungit elicit sanguinem,[2] but a well delivered punch has the same effect. It would be great to take a hike into canine body language and reinvent the Werewolf, this time, however, we should restrict our malevolence to the standard scenarios, like blighting a pig with measles, putting thumbtacks in Banquo's condoms, or turning Macbeth's milk sour as we burn a few extra bothies and brunstane cooties. Like good old party comrades we can *head* back to our Illyrian fantasies wearing the polka-dot pyjamas of Dame Imagination before those words from our sponsors reappear, *tired* no doubt with the wonders of modern plumbing, as we roll into *bed* and diffract. I hate those nights in *bed*, it's far worse than sleeping with a pair of howler monkeys, no wonder our mutual non-aggression pacts turn sour. The other problem is our *tired* attitudes to failure but then there's also the matter of my insatiable desire for bedtime prolegomena and your obsessive wish for some TV celebrity Satan to conflagrate into manifestation. Television always raises my blood pressure and Theodor Adorno believes it's the precondition for the poverty of genuinely lived experience, it's just there, like some sports utility vehicle parked in front of that *head* one calls a face, and one watches it as it watches back. Others believe it a suitable alternative to sex, but with a little necromantic mischief we could eradicate televisuality entirely. That's hardly the kuan ha[3] I've come to expect. I mean your credit card to profundity *expired* long before we enrolled in the passive majority where I have to *abide* with all those surrogates of *you* as a new improved version of cultural theory while everyone else enjoys the *wide* expanse of image-democracy and *see* themselves in what they're saying. Imagine the *sight* on late-night television of Hannah Arendt kneeling naked in full *view* of the entirety of Western Civilization doing the Charleston in its underpants. Right now though, having the mask of *night* upon my face[4] helps bring a *new* thought to *mind* on the pros and cons of Corinthian glossolalia in an attempt to help bolster state-of-the-art witchcraft. Unlike a guided tour through the entrails of a three-part theory of the psychoanalytic, I think it may help us *find* out the why not where we stand.

1. The Cock Lane ghost was a hoax perpetrated in 1762 London by Elizabeth Parsons and her father Richard Parsons. The latter was pilloried and the former subjected to watching eighteen re-runs of Kitchen Nightmares. Dame Alice Kytler was prosecuted for Sorcery in 1324 by Richard de Ledrede, Bishop of Ossory. The Camden Society published the contemporary narrative (mainly in Latin) in 1843: a stultifyingly boring read.
2. "Too violent a blowing draws blood from the nose."
3. In Mandarin "official speech."
4. The Earl of Oxford, *Romeo and Juliet* 2.2.85.

Enter Rosencrantz (in drag) *and Guildenstern* (dressed as Clint Eastwood).
I know we were heading for Dodge City 'coz that's where all the cowboys hang out but apparently my luggage is going to some backwater of the Louisiana Purchase and Rebecca's still the bad guy. Forget not my friend that the journey, as the horse informs, is across two states of mind. It appears, however, that the direct route diverts us from the detour, so God bless the angel of the swerve! Unfortunately we seem to be stuck here like two possums in a wind tunnel, a problem no doubt inherited by most missionary siblings. Billy the Kid insists that construction's the best way to travel—so if we don't find a city we'll build one (Moctezuma and the Mayans down south did it all the time). Sounds an awful lot to get through in one scene. I didn't know (till John Wayne let drop the fact) that if my bow legs weren't joined at the top I wouldn't be able to ride that wooden rocking-horse. Seems a compelling argument for intelligent design, unfortunately there are *stronger* reasons for moving on than our stubborn cowboy itinerary. We no *longer even* need the stability of

phenomena to collide in the *night* of a master narrative about the afterlife. The majority of folks believe *heaven* is a community center for the old yet *bright* departures from our species where everyone smokes Camel filters and secretes pheromones, but *you complain* that it's probably a museum without a curator and blame *me* for the *reign* of the transcendental duplicity in all its virtual realities. On the other hand, Hell could well be a petting farm run by retired social workers or even Catholic priests and not as warm as we imagined. In a perfect world we would be allowed at least one visit to both on a week-end so we can make an informed decision as to which one will be our eternal domicile. If nothing else Heaven's at least a vertical solution to horizontality: an aerial view of Mount Kilimanjaro protends the ratio of panic to balcony and there we stand with peckers pointing to the Pearly Gates. What life can replace this mutable community called us? Having posed that question I must admit I feel *oppressed* by our current hilarity, we make a perfect synchronized idiot team and if crazy ever becomes an Olympic event we'd have the first two lanes of our relay in place. I mean that open road dotted with cacti sure turned quickly into a cul-de-sac. Here we are with barnacles on our foreskins, lassoed by some formal constraint, forced to spend the day and *night* trapped in the echo of 154 stylized love-poems like two live wasps in an ice cube and we don't even know the sex of the recipient. I don't know how those pseudo guilt-ridden sonneteers slept at night let alone got up in the morning to write all that krapp. It's infinitely preferable to *rest* one's eyes on the shards of a forgotten treatise on the gout or a catalogue raisonée of civil war memorabilia. Remember when the novel was just a tissue of loose episodes and cardboard characters? Those were the times, so much better than today's soul-searching figures like us. Gadzooks I say to the *plight* of Frisbee knowledge! But *plight* often separates the human species by a complex talk-back mechanism and, like the *rest* of the victims, ours is a *night* of mutilated panoramas, aesthetic yet embattled—but not *oppressed*—by the strange *reign* of counter-memory. In these parts *me* is merely a stage of history so I never *complain* about departure time, on the other hand historicity is the gift that no one wants. *You* know all too well how the provisionality of the future brings its *bright* little icons from a *heaven* of tessera and, who knows, my *night* might turn out *even longer* than Kenneth Goldsmith's Day.[1] A Copernican insight no doubt within the *stronger* challenge of a quotidian fourth-dimension.

1. *Day* is a verbatim transcription of a single issue of The New York Times. It appeared through The Figures in 2003.

Enter Leontes and an olde man, brother to Leonata.
Every visit to the Vatican makes me thank God that I'm an atheist. *Kings* commit atrocities all their life then conveniently arrange a death-bed confession that *brings* them safely through Heaven's *gate. Arising* from the fact that such stupid aspirations are a fitting testimony to the world's folle de logis I can now *state* categorically that sanity is deteriorating on a global scale. Politics has always been the secularization of theology, drawing its strength from other people's maladies, a stock-exchange on the left foot of its adversary, but the current debacle is ridiculous! It makes my religious skepticism adopt the persona of Attila the Hun. That's why I'm placing all my chips on celebrity atheists like Giordano Bruno and Thomas Hobbes, I'm now the rhapsodist *despising* the eternal, the quintessential strategist of life and death.[1] Cultural compensation doesn't matter in the *least* at this level, nor does the full *scope* of salvation while I'm *possessed* of a *hope* in a power that never disappoints. *Fate's* where the dead buy drinks for the undying, that's why I've turned my back on the *cries* for wisdom as such and why I'm turning my life into a whole new zip code. Phrased ontologically, I've passed into a *state* of self-redistribution, which explains why my chin's now set between my *eyes*. (When you called it "eugenics" I rolled my *eyes* in a *state* of disbelief.) With my asthma on thermal alert I'm turning *cries* into coughs. I'm not unlike the *fate* of the sentence in the early history of italics, that said I can't wait for the death of the ecumenically correct in an uncontrollable outburst of the latest poetics of vulgarity. Let's *hope* we can handle all the sexually transmitted flesh dimensions in the next asteroid attack. If only we *possessed* a penchant for Helio-arkite superstitions we might be able to widen the *scope* of our tactics and bring down Moses and the rest of them, at *least* we'd have a recipe for living on and *despising* those pro-life Jehovah's witnesses that have a leg in at the palace. The memory of a sphere should recapitulate the amnesia of a cube and together yield the philosophy of the line, limit and desire. But it never does and now the *state* of alert's been suspended from the promises *arising* from this new found liberty,

we can leave through the garden *gate* judged "innocent until proven born." This monochrome momentum *brings* legerity to flatness in lacerating lucidity don't you think, so best leave the casus belli for the doctors of revolution to sort out instead of the *king's* jesters.

1. A phrase of Foucault's.

Exit

Scene 7. *Enter Brutus in his Orchard.*

The continuous work of our life is to build death, as Montaigne eloquently puts it or, if you prefer the Latin, prima quae vitam dedit, hora corpsit, or perhaps more tersely: Nascentes morimur. Whichever way you phrase it death's bad news to ontology and in the *end* there's just your skeletal *friend* emerging from some footnote to upgrade the total to the ultimate nightmare.[1] However, prior to death and being poor of world, I'll need some counter-demand *before* fiscal anxiety sets in and I start to *moan* again about the falling rate of the denarius. I can't get *over* the fact that non-scientific truth is the indeterminate knot emerging from the interaction of epistemological structure with rhetorical assemblages and that's how poems know themselves, it's a *foregone* conclusion that penury and poetry aren't the best of book-ends. Imagine the *sight* of Philip Marlowe in The Big Sleep asking Charles Bukowski for a tranquilizer. *Woe* is me says the assassin who tries to murder his victim with a cat toy during the *Night* of the Long Knives. Termination is a this not a that and the *flow* of thinking never stops it being so. Cute though, how one *waste* idea—*sought* for profit from a *past*—remains too intractable to be hi-jacked by a different *thought.* I "*thought*" therefore I "was" in the way a *past* tense always rhymes an old philosophic sentiment. Giorno dopo giorno across sea and land toward the historical soil of a cloud before the Law covers it. Yet landscape is not a grammar[2] but it does have clouds to read it. Thus I *sought* to reconfigure the entirety of analytic philosophy according to that kind of poetic knowledge and look where it got me. It's a *waste* of time to try and counter the incessant *flow* of disappearing data yet that one final "Roman" question (the one Caligula constantly asked himself) remains: after a *night* at the baths where does one go to get clean? My *woe*-begotten pederastic passions require advanced methods of repentance but the *sight* of a postulant Republican senator kneeling in public before the vacant ass of Albert Einstein haunts my every thought. Unfortunately death moves faster than relativity so it's a *foregone* conclusion that it's *over* and out with the *moan before* the final *friend* expires, a perfect note on which to *end* this pornographic out-take.

1. I wouldn't be too sure about that. Take a look at the many deaths of the prior of Saint Wandrille, burned alive three times after being twice de-mummified.
2. Gertrude Stein.

Enter Afriana and Luciana.
Ah, mon potasson[1] voulez vous some Cartesian reductions avec extra pulp and a guaranteed self-certainty avec pas de down-payment? At least Stanley Cavell had the guts to stand up in a similar interrogation and decry the arrogance of Philosophy. Unphilosophical characters like *me* always approach life entirely through Cantor's Continuum Hypothesis, but *you alone* can *give* it a different twist now that life's *gone* from bogus to bingo.[2] It's a great lesson: to *live* life as a *lie*, successful politicians do it all the time but in my case love behaves as does the sandal tree, which sheds sweetness on the axe that wounds it, for love is always the story of the two placed in movement, still as one – one other into another one. Admittedly, our own love is strictly technologically determined, but it still feels real. It would *appear* to the discerning *eye* that a *tear* is least like the face it comes from, being best considered as a counter-design to those problems *buried* among the broken *parts* of Rimbaud's violinist. (He of flatulent memory, I never knew his name nor the footnote he grew up in.) At *dead* center of this point-grid function is the name for several associated *hearts* symbolically beating in contradictory deep space.[3] Some *hearts* stop beating earlier than you'd like at which point bio-ethics suggests the Karen Anne Quinlan method of lullabies sung to the living *dead*, whistled to a cluster of body *parts buried* to animation but still existing in a vegetable self. The *tear* here is in the fabric of interrogation.[4] Where does it end? Why should it go on? Is this kind of life the afterbirth of death? In any case keep one *eye* focused on the nearest available independent quotation and *appear* to be happy in the *lie* of your cloth-eared goodness. *Live* on through the bio-politics and the base-life brigade to profit from others' financial miscalculations and, when all hope's

gone from the positive practice of margins, *give* a second chance to Lenin who *alone* thought the thought beyond a *you* and a *me*.[5]

1. A neologism coined by the bohemian poet Léon-Paul Fargue, roughly translatable as "buddy" and for that reason never addressed by him to James Joyce.

2. A key premise of Set Theory expounded by Georg Cantor in 1874 stating "There is no set whose cardinality is strictly between that of the integers and that of the real numbers."

3. Viz. Johannes Kepler, Georgia O'Keefe, Bugs Bunny, George Washington, Herman Göering, and Shirley Temple.

4. One of the pioneers in the right-to-die movement. Quinlan (1954-85) was kept alive in a vegetative state for almost a decade.

5. As the Pope says "everyone's a socialist at heart."

Exeunt

End of Act I

Act II. Scene 1

I am so certain of the soul's being immortal that I seem
to feel it within me; as it were by intuition.

Alexander Pope

Enter Hamlet reading of a booke.

"Sandroost in ruttocks bland wist thrumplike thrumbs a butcher's hog vast spread as rawlock wads on grummet copse till foamed throbe throngs in widge of himblit intimate, as hinge-mate sillibub 'pon poutined minutes." Mmm, it seems to be an ancient Lancashire recipe for Yorkshire pudding cunningly encrypted in a gorilla-gram. "Words, words, words" (if I may quote myself); I *love* the way they die, just like pets and people, it goes to *prove* the Dictionary's wrong to fix meanings once and for all. The word *"equipage"* is a good example of a word *brought* back into currency by the Pre-Raphaelites and then peremptorily discarded by the Italian Futurists. The word *"age"* is actually a complex extension of chronometric bio-feedback *thought* through by way of the valves and values of several disciplines starker than lexicography. Some *men* will always give new life to lingo but *rhyme* per se capitulates to more open semantic relations such as semaphore. The *pen* for a long *time* was the instrument of choice for amatory correspondence. A French letter to your *lover* in Sweden arrives suspiciously on time, but a thorough *survey* of pan-mutability needs to *cover* the less predictable coincidences, such as, why the Titanic sank the *day* Fenway Park opened. Each moment of this composition two distinct texts contaminate each other and the viral reader happens to congratulate them both. As usual, the writer's *day* begins symmetrically between a cup of coffee and a filmy reticulum, until a *cover* cracks on the ciliated chamber to reveal the contents of a covert *survey*: a *lover*, in the shape of tiny tetrahedra, that previously spent *time* in the dust particles of a Cincinnati suburb, now attaches to your *pen* and floods each *rhyme* with colloid loci: Anchorage, Salt Lake City, Bangladesh, the British Museum, all finally emerge as a festival of indecipherable "guess words." I remember drinking absinthe and orange juice with Gregory of Spoleto (a proud martyr to conjugal fidelity) who informed me that long ago the *Men* of Harlech *thought* that old *age brought* on prematurely could be cured by a mystical marriage of material form to immaterial accident, a union of the truest *equipage* to *prove* a constant ratio between a *love* of trigonometry and a camel's ass soul.

> This light is thick with birds, and evening warns us
> beautifully of death.
>
> Muriel Ruykeser

> Now the Holy Ghost drips birdshit on the nose of God.
>
> Jack Spicer

Enter Demetrius and Hermione.
Only an eagle could trust itself to paint the Profanation of the Host,[1] but the latest lab tests indicate that the pshitte on your head came from the dove of Mythopoesis and not the Holy Paraclete. Despite this new improved detergent those hermeneutic *stains* are apparently stuck in their molecular assemblages. It beats me why philosophy *disdains* impurity. Long live the contaminants! Speaking of which your tongue resembles a worm on which that same bird has lost its footprints, but your feet look fine from here, a little on the historical side of materialism, but nonetheless a happy pair, like us. Right *now mine* walk in a constant fear of meeting with inanimate surface-tension phenomena, such as Hulk Hogan in miniature, attached by the internet to the labouring poor. The high-*brow* intelligentsia go in fear of Hulk's style of rhetoric, and shun the *shine* from his scintillating one word questions. He truly marks the difference between phlogiston and fogbanks. It's a *disgrace* the way he turns to *hide* his pudgy *face* from his fans when a simplified chemical ambiguity is all it takes for the *ride* from professional wrestling to designer *alchemy. Green* to the *eye* that's looking for envy, his smell is of a lilac mist descending on the ones that can't be *seen.* William Blake informs there is a place outside the wrestling ring

at the bottom of the grave where contraries meet, which reminds me why your outside is my inside at this stage in our relationship. Instead of a mirror image (without the optical reversal) we're the Great Divide inside the Unbearable Fold with all the charm of a double hernia—but at least we're a cautionary tale—a queer bunch of two and each with a remarkable pair of kidneys. Suppose at this point a micro-needle *seen* by the naked *eye* enters a cross-programming device and produces some pussy *green* vibration that turns us into two separate analeptic facts. *Alchemy* was born of the need for such transmutations, it offered a *ride* on a bursting soap-bubble full of those occult virtues called the Renaissance and it caused folk to *face* up to all those botched attempts at discovering the Philosopher's Poem. To *hide* from the gnomic phrase is no *disgrace* but the constant ability to *shine* forth in such platitudes brings a wrinkle to any *brow* including *mine* or Hulk Hogan's. Speaking of "H" did you hear that Hitler just announced "a further understanding" with Austria? Baudelaire's poet is a decipherer in a world where all is hieroglyphic, these days poets must be wizards to make real facts happen.[2] Yet he wants to speak the truth in saying only evil speaks the truth. In that case why don't you lipstick my blitzkrieg, or napalm my swastika then put my breath on a banderole? Poetry's meaning lies not in its images but in each word's ability to disembowel. John Stuart Mill claims all poetry is of the nature of soliloquy[3] and I'm glad we're not exclusively subject to the unrelentingly antiphonal. Our call and response measured out in rhyme would be intolerable without the occasional monologue, but then again, the soliloquy has its own problems, words poured out in cascades as the sound of the one voice speaking. Imagine silence occupying the first-person pronoun in the screams of the one who doesn't speak. Yet to be *now* and only for the ability to stop *disdains* the law of stable equilibrium reminding that it's time to supplement the tell-tale *stains* on another Dow Jones sunrise.

1. Cocteau, *Opium*.
2. "Réflexions sur quelques-uns de mes contemporaines: Victor Hugo" in *Oeuvres completes* ed. Yves Le Dantec and Claude Pichois 2 volumes (Paris: Gallimard,1973): II 133.
3. A claim, of course, endorsed by both Martha Stewart and Hamlet.

Enter Macbeth, with a Servant and a Torch.
I like the way phylogeny gets immersed in a thread of *deeds* and the analogue expectancy *sheds* a tear for its dissipating vortex. It's then that the albatross in *cross*-quantitative variations finally arrives at consanguinity. By *relief* viscosity the Medusoid drops disperse their titubancy and eventually the little bell begins to ring, at which point the *loss* of a distinctly Scottish viewpoint confirms the presence of either cylindrical *grief*-connector modules or ferro-concrete kink-curve wirings. At which point a morphological *disgrace* enters into complex membrane tension until, urged to *speak* across the *face* of a single segment, it emerges volatile as the error in the system. There's no apparent *break* or malformation in the ground-rat's geometry until *smoke* appears on its nail-claw radius, enigmatic in the *way* the logarithmic spirals serve to *cloak* its overgrowth of teeth. To the left foraminifera guard all affiliations in a strictly graded theorem as group sex with the octopus finally begins and living things announce Cretaceous *day*. Incidentally, I heard your brother died on this very *day*; all through his life he wore his penis as if it were a veteran's poppy in someone else's buttonhole, lurking inside a *cloak* of ignominy and shocked by the *way* you defined life as a permanent state of missing in action. Poor, predatory him, sitting there, the wheels of his Honda turning inside out with embarrassment. He should have spent more time trying to calculate the square root of the soul. But he's gone now and the absence of white *smoke* from his chimney betrays no *break* in the deadlock among the Cardinals over who'll succeed him. His best hope in life was to end up in Heaven (assuming Heaven's where they put you when you're in the Witness Protection Program). Fat chance of that now. Let's *face* it, you can't always realize those dreams that *speak* to you from childhood, sometimes you have to settle for the clicks that issue from the hind legs of dung beetles breeding in the summer sun behind Messerschmitt Cottage a foot away from the New Brutalism. Call it Neo-Plastic Bauhaus Suprematism if you like but it won't help you improve your bedtime manners. It's a *disgrace* the way we have to end each day with "have a nice dream." Good *grief*, what a wish with which to start your sleep. I'm embarrassed too at having to admit my otherness lies in the fact that I'm just the same as you. Imagine a text though, as a scenery of vapor then say "*loss*" is one less word between you and your grave. (At this point a *relief* valve on the

chloroplast explodes on the surface of the *cross*-diatomic inhibitions and *sheds* all the remaining reciprocal mutations. *Deeds* caught for a week in the life of Truth in the plural.)

Enter Voltemand and Cornelius.

You know you've never once offered *me* a Grand Theory of Meaning and you've never fessed up to why you pawned your Medal of Honor. Can't we simply communicate and *be* beyond the little of the single self?[1] But I *hate* to *commence* conversation on a negative note and you were quite right to *advocate* a common *sense* of urgency in this cracked version of the Goldberg Variations but what *are* our odds of successfully evading the Intellectual Vigilance Committee? Things go *amiss* in the quest for the preternatural but you can't beat City Hall and you can't dump a friend for a life. Don't forget you'll always rank as my other and as such my possibility to politicize. [Ed. You might *compare this* last sentence to any jungle of pleonasms making up this narrative, or the fact that in the past palindromic time was always dialectical.] A new *bud* in light from the *sun* casts *mud* on the shadows formed by our Dawn Augmentation Department, but we've still a chance, outside our predilection for uniqueness, to find meanings by losing them in everything we've never been. See, I'm not as stupid as you think. What's *done* is *done* and despite such Walmart semiotics those California *mud* slides still remind us that we built our Jerusalem for refugees. What is death but life in act said the poet Henley, but perhaps life is merely a very rare type of disease, then again such a hypothesis is sure to breed disunity in Galactic Workers' Councils. Better lease that one to the Metaphysics of Marxism and go build a cathedral of erotic misery[2] in the *sun* where we can smell the lemon orchards of Kyoto and watch a *bud* break into leaf. That way we can at least celebrate if not consecrate our impermanence. *This* fact's for sure that everything my ego likes is mine. You might *compare* the drop in our molecular disintegration to the way words seem to lie on their sides showing something's *amiss* at the corners of communication. *Are* you aware of a *sense* of inversion in your hysteron proteron and want to *advocate* your face against its name? To *commence* here, at this point where *hate* and symmetry collide, is to stand where your otherness completes a space until it can't *be me*. Now that's taking urban cottage ontology to the next level: (possums on a wet black bough).

1. Laura Riding.
2. Kurt Schwitter's term for his own merzbau.

Exeunt

Enter Theseus, Hippolita, with others.

It's hard being a conservative when there's nothing to conserve. Stelarc renouncing the pan-sentient and systematically replacing bits of himself until he's finally a robotic toilet that talks, that's hardly a redefinition of the lyric self or the metamorphosis of Ajax.[1] Or is it? And what about Orlan, subjecting herself to razorblades and ricochets of antimatter and having to change her passport photograph every nine weeks?[2] Incidentally, a *report* came in that haptic space gets triggered by a quantum innovation in any message. (Par example, les mots glacé are simulation sites with croissants for each victim.) We *sort* through these gruesome facts and try to *name* the axiology beneath it all, then suddenly we realize happiness is a place called "ethics" somewhere around the corner on its way to another incomprehensible catastrophe. It beats *me* why we even bother to lock the cage at night. It's a *shame* that Ernest Hemingway didn't become a politician and introduce bulls and matadors into the constitution. Did I ever tell *you* that your mind is a strongbox for the ultimate in catachresis and would be a *delight* to experience on a TV quiz game? I remember sharing a can of spinach with Barnacle Bill musing on what new *effect* will lift us out of here in *spite* of our reluctance to change? With all due *respect* our brand new laptops open up a vast world of travel and disappearance—it'll only take 2.5 seconds to feel as if we're on the boulevards of Paris. Twinkling *alone* in his afterglow a dead magician on the Rue Saint Jacques turns a camel into a courtyard in a town called Community, or Tikrit, and we *remain* there after the trick for *one* last indoctrination, two persons each called *Twain* making our quietus beneath a nacreous dawn in the rise of the House of Usher. Too true, my chiasmic paradigm, a Mark *Twain* only happens twice in literature, *one* brief name to a face before it's sutured into the canons of proportion. Yet fate's assured that a turn in any event folds the trace of a memory into the opening scene of Ibsen's Peer Gynt. Riverruns *remain* our central problem here *alone* in the land of the intertextual, where it's always difficult to *respect* a tributary interstice away from Howth Castle and environs. Baudelaire proved all correspondence ends in paranoia and in *spite* of an under-disciplined imagination the Real in his world still seems a glyphic scrawl announcing his terror of nightingales. Fate yes, but the *effect* of sunlight on a syllogism ensures uncertainty in this incredible mirage, keeping us normative and responsive to all the second-hand *delight* one derives from reading Tennyson in the nude. As we pause to cough we're in the city of a moment and *you* have become the soundtrack to my summer. *Shame* enters the relation, but not guilt, and Alain Badiou stops *me* at the porch to offer an alternative *name* for Philosophy, the *sort* that sounds like "Protagoras" before the Great War tended its *report* of an earlier assumption of peace.

1. The title of a treatise (1596) by Sir John Harington elaborating his invention of the first flushing toilet. (The majority of early editions ended up as paper in the said facility.)
2. Paul Virilio offers an openly negative and pessimistic assessment of the body-art of both Stelarc and Orlan in "A Pitiless Art," an essay now accessible in Paul Virilio, *Art and Fear*, trans. Julie Rose. London: Continuum, 2003: 23-65.

Enter Host and Bardolffe.

Pax profunda, frater,[1] encounters like ours are retained not as memories, nor genuflexions, but as handshakes, a mutual greeting thence internalized to carry us through life. Sometimes I look at that face of yours ambivalent to smiling as it looks at *me* with its huge color, full of ripe fruit and cedar wood nose, hints of cassis, elderberry and pomegranate to reinforce its tannins and wonder why (knowing words talk against wisdom) we paused along our separate ways into poesis. *You* constantly remark that all of this was Shakspurre before Steve McCaffery intervened with his revisionist Arcadia. When the Bard was a *live* poet it *sufficed* to leave inter-textuality to herpetologists and let playwrights *give* illiterate folks pleasure by way of cheap plots stolen from the popular literature of the day, confected with a little disguise, cross-dressing and a bit of a blood bath at the end. But these days a simple dénouement's *despised*, people prefer différance and differends in their performance art smuggled in from France inside a vintage bottle of Clos Roques d'Aspes—both of them are available at your local concept *store* commonly known as the Critical Theory Department where professors get paid to *sit* and wonder what the Meaning of Meaning means after the Revocation of the Edict of Semantics and why philosophy knows only obfuscations.[2] I'm sure the Shake would have said there's *more wit* than *truth* in a complacent peripeteia in *spite* of the cogency of the Paris mafia. According to the Earl of Warwick the only absolute is probability and he's probably correct. It's evident in reflecting on my own lost *youth* dancing out life, skipping over each millennia, probably reading this with *delight* to myself in French. I wish everybody took *delight* in your Terpsichorean ventures but the way your good self dances it takes eighteen to tango, a consequence no doubt of your misspent sedentary *youth* in defiance of my signs of age and—notwithstanding all your *spite* and acrimony—aimed at both Donald Duck and the Artful Dodger. What renders a *truth* absent and *wit more* or less sophomoric? We could *sit* for hours trying to answer that one. Luce Irigaray says that in this age of post-Christianity writing clears a path to language and to *store* up knowledge one first has to waste it. These days old adages are *despised* as a form of epistemological dandruff and people *give* little credence to wisdom as such or how to give knowledge back to thinking. It once *sufficed* to *live* a life of peaceful nonrepentence. Nowadays everyone wants their Johnny on the Spots converted into confessionals. Things shed tears alright but when all's said and done all *you* and *me* want is sin with its aftermath then a dry martini at the Yacht Club.

1. A salutationary phrase still used by Rosicrucians and Vatican Security Guards.
2. "Upstart theory" Wordsworth called it, twenty-nine words before the Aeolian cave.

Exeunt

> Death represents a lot of money, it can even
> make you a star.
> Andy Warhol

Enter Steward (disguised as Sister Wendy).
This one's for Mona, my favorite Renaissance possessive, I can't *praise* that portrait enough, whoever limned that gem definitely knew what she was doing. It sure beats Grandma Moses painting the Ten Commandments for the Angels of Contingency. The likes of Arthur Danto claim that art's dead, that we've outlived beauty, but wow, one can gaze for *days* on the smooth flesh

with its color of Spring snow an hour after sunset, the smooth incarnate of her cheeks tinged with orient hematite, her captivating eyes set hauntingly between their false fiber eyelashes until one notes the sly distortion of the left arm enhancing the jaw's orthogonal resistance, the laughter wrinkles holding up both cheeks, the dark, hairy energy beneath her armpits, the missing *date* on the forehead and the subsequent moustache and beard. The Sphinx is reborn in this Anatomical Eve. Note the schistous insouciance of her strategically constipated smile powered no doubt by venom in partial gridlock as her mouth pours *forth* an enigma sufficient to *invocate* any absent God. One imagines her breath toilet fresh in whose exhalations and inhalations Old Time is made young again.[1] Hers is a beauty not discovered but rescued. I guess nobody could kiss her and survive without having a safety-belt on and with designer mascara on her antennae she must be ferae natura through and through. Gautier called her the Isis of a cryptic religion but I sense a premonition of Whistler's mother posing as a medium at a Madame Blavatsky Symposium in Chicago. The quintessential *worth* of background is masterfully stated in the dim penumbra of her eyes contrasting the finger that took Francesco del Giocondo's marriage ring. Innovative *light* folds into her decor puellarum making it feel an inch in front of *you*. The idealized mountains, still Platonic in their hazy materiality, form a perfect anchor for the torso framed by an apex holding those perfect folds that speak of Froissart at his best. The *sight* of it drives *me* wild so why do I prefer the movies to painting? After eighteen visits to The Lion King I know all the songs by heart. What a pathetic way to *rehearse* my mnemotechnia in an age of mechanical reproduction, in fact it's the cinema that precipitates the catastrophe of architecture, converting the wall into a screen of magic movement, sacrificing the very concept of the fresco— and besides the popcorn's so expensive. Speaking of food why are my lunches based on bricolage? After washing out the convent lavatories I could have a super supper to look forward to, those *excellent* organic beets and mache I never eat, after that a *verse* or two from Gray's Anatomy and a midnight chance to *invent* a new saint. But is there anything left to poetically *invent*? Unlike a painting a poem's just an overcrowded room of words and *verse* only took us to topology, contradiction and an *excellent* species of textual cannibalism called Conceptual Writing by its practitioners. Life used to be my favorite monosyllable but not anymore. Mortification's now my Beatrice. In fact in my current brand of eschatology the important question's how to *rehearse* the slow procession into paraterminal decoherence and inevitable loss of being. Which reminds *me* of another thing, was that a spot of euthanasia I witnessed in the convent greenhouse yesterday or something less spontaneous? The *sight* of it was so upsetting I had to wake a nearby nun from incubation to phone 911. But *you* know how it is, the dark turns into *light* and Dawn seldom leaves a TV celebrity nun an orphan. A religious life seemed *worth* it at the time though, until a message came from Sister Mary Srebrenica, embryonic of a sadness, stipulating death is not a fact. Biopolitics can *invocate* the right to life as much as it wants but I remain a Buddhist on the matter of ethnic cleansing. I also choose to let my kind of modernity oscillate back and *forth* between the *date* it started and the *days* I will end. Faint *praise* to the avant-garde.

1. Paul Valéry, *Dance of the Soul.*

Exit

Scene 2. *Enter King and Polonius.*
I still remember those triple rainbows of Brontë country; they were the perfect recipe for writer's block. I could dig that event horizon for miles. Robert Lowell envied me those moments whenever he failed to write a poem. He'd *remain* stationary for hours wondering how Mark *Twain* would have written Wuthering Heights. But don't *deceive* yourself about literary trans-national-ism. In texts as in sports and *love* the interplay is not the tossed body.[1] Any quantitative calculation of our promises would *leave* no time for more urgent questions, such as how can we *prove* that the new literary taxonomies are basic to our lives? Unfulfilled promises *alone give* help in understanding how fate conjugates our verbs. When Oscar Wilde smoked a cigarette the ash he tapped off with his right finger fell to the ground as the powder from a gilt asphodel. As for us, we've only *one* way to go and that's off. But we've sufficient to *live* on and exist in; our one-way part bio-degradable wilderness remains a safe-house where silence evaporates each time *you bring me* a song to *sing.* So *sing me* a song and *bring* along a cockroach to contemplate and I'll create for *you* the grandest rainbow of them all. We mostly *live* life as a background species

parasitic on optimism and nostalgia for the present.[2] Fernando Pessoa thought death a bend in a road, in which case shall we drive along and take that *one* last chance to revoke our own personal Edict of Nantes and *give* up hoping for that bend? When I'm *alone* I stare at the egg-timer Mao Tse Tung broke last Easter and try to *prove* to myself that a revolutionary society of one is still possible. But perhaps we've already passed the end of time and we should *leave* that question for our scientific communities to answer.[3] Still, *love* serves us well as placenta to an extended community named two. But don't *deceive* yourself about life on the Mississippi like Mark *Twain* did, try to *remain* as I do the trivial epic hero we're both designed to be, safe, although sudden, in the concept of the infrathin.[4]

1. Compare William Carlos Williams' "The Visit."
2. If only last year could have been like today we would have been happy then.
3. We could continue this argument in a footnote just like this in which I'd counter-claim that riot is better than revolution (at least for the ones who cannot vote).
4. "Inframince:" a concept of Marcel Duchamp's.

.

Death is here:
Not in another place, not among strangers
Death is under the moon here and the rain.
Archibald MacLeish

Enter Peaseblossom, Cobweb, Moth, Mustard-seede, and four Fairies.
One needs to die in order for Philosophy to begin again and now God's dead I guess it's long live the virtual interface. The lack of tangible *foes* in hyperspace, with its absence of well-defined boundaries, simply enhances the definition of our enemies as abscondite. One particular website *shows* how *injury, grief* and *poverty* make up the collective *thief* of all the few basic dignities that remain. Incidentally, I just adore the miniature cobweb lampshade you designed but how I yearn for the beautiful regularity of a polygonal meshwork to put over my toadstool not my laptop. Those were the days when jewels and *refuse* were indistinguishable, joined together in a froth of analog concepts. Back in the age of the pencil the values of vacuoles and transcendental possibilities didn't *deceive*

us. That was when *use* value confessed itself to be fundamentally exchange value and Karl Marx turned in his grave. Queen Victoria used to *receive more* genuine phenomena from a slice of unbuttered bread than from any current website. The yeast would rise white as snow in its processed cell-formation to finalize the crust on her *call* for the maximum in imperialist expansion. But that was *before* bourgeois subjectivity raised its ugly head and shouted "take us to those teeth called Mount Rushmore!" We can only utilize the past inasmuch as a phylogenetic surplus can force *all* co-opting parties to consume the historical as mere tourism. Experts are terrified by the skilled amateur and it doesn't take much to risk the impossible, that's why *all* the best art springs from a critical anxiety *before* the threat of a temps perdu. Poetry may well be the rhetorical perfection of paradox in a house of language, but the poet's wish is to invent a world, the architect's to reinvent a city. *Call* me dogmatic if you like but the *more* you petition Romanticism the less architects *receive* a mandate to construct the true barrenness of unworkable utopias. That describes our modus operandum in a nutshell, organized according to the current law of dystopia and the *use* of my cognitive functions to *deceive* Early-Modern pederasts into not taking their vice versa. Why *refuse* the call to obsolete causal relationships? Any *thief* of the irrational distrusts both manipulated sensibility and the *poverty* of technical rationality. Good *grief* the *injury* to collective praxis is real enough and it *shows* up in the same old vocabulary: "Minima," "error," "draughtsman," "Cyamus." I've never met a word I didn't google and my *foes* think I'm practical for that.

Enter Ross with an Olde man.

In a film adaptation of Darwin's Origin of the Species, Brad Pitt plays a primate evolving into a balding Stoic philosopher. Festive, in a sad sort of way, the plot threads excitingly to culminate as one day in the afterlife of a Greek God. I like a good film, but I've never been partial to montage. Call me old-fashioned but there's something about it that reminds *me* of body parts and crime scene investigations—besides which thinking about it adversely affects my golf swing. *You* used to complain about the lack of *truth* in anything I said but *there* was a time when *youth* seemed firmly settled in both of us, and a trustworthy *forebear* said I was as transpositional as a cyborg J. Edgar Hoover. In those days the temporal co-ordinates of our face-to-face relationships required the synchronization of two distinct streams of reality. Our radiolarian bodies consisted of a spherical mass of protoplasm not unlike Detroit from the air. That was when good practical rivalry *prevailed* and if a *son* bought his father a pocket guide to architecture the clever parent countered with an architectural guide to picking pockets; it turned kinship into an enantiomorphic vaudeville. But some things remain constant, I mean it's been basic to survival since Australopithecus to know the difference between rabbis and rabies when talking to Jewish veterinarians, otherwise voilà *assailed* by more vituperative comments than Albrecht Dürer launched on Peter Bruegel the elder. To change the subject, what would happen to metaphor if bare truth *won* out? [The editor here again. At this point a bird flies out of *art* and interrupts their view of a full moon scratched by its tiny orthogonal claws.] It *befits* the *heart* to pump this labyrinthine mentality to annihilation in non-thought. The spontaneous poetic image *commits* us to an uncompromising dependency on an optical paradigm, but many say it's the sound of words that matters and quote Allen Ginsberg's "Howl" to prove it. As for life in the real world I prefer the actual atrocities to knowing who *commits* them, although my *heart* always pumps with excitement when I'm wiping bits of terrorists off the window sill—and this *befits* our epoch. The composite *art* of sex and warfare is abundant in Egyptian literature and back then the men always *won* but it's been downhill for guys ever since Thelma and Louise. I'm sure that if Moses had been born a woman there'd be lots more than ten commandments. Look what's happening to the masculine dignity of gerunds and proper patriarchal syntax, we're *assailed* by trans-sexual local appreciations of strictly universal phenomena and every inflatamate comes equipped with an alibi. Even my own *son* tries to force culture down my throat with a fake ceramic offshoot of the late Tang Dynasty carved by some nine year old Princess named Kwan Loo, only this time the partial application of everything to nothing seems to have *prevailed*. I mean how would a *forebear* have reacted to one of Mondrian's insufferable grids? Even in their misspent *youth* people preferred theosophical Darwinism to obsolete anti-perspectival paradigms. *There* needs to be an elementary *truth* for *you* and *me* to cling to, though a little distortion in scale towards an unprecedented synaptic snap will do, such as taking up ballet once again.

Scene 3. *Enter Hamlet* (with Yorick's skull).

"A child will have been killed." In saying this I pass from life to language, but how to transcend that phonetic exhaustion in the ordinary idiom of the mortal? Some speak of new beauty and unlimited aesthetics but I *alone* know horizons can be surprisingly brutal among the pronouns that birth *one* into speech. If only I could think the way Saint Augustine did with eyes the arms around each reader, and—without words—exploit my uncontested ability to *cross* Bauhaus with primitivism and that way corner the market on interior design without resorting to the Cycladic as a secure default style. I was surprised that those *two* complementary tickets to the Slobodan Milosevic genocide exhibition at the Copenhagen Biennale didn't help better my understanding of the true meaning of death, but they sure brought home with conviction something far worse than living a life of laser spine surgery between reason and experience. Moreover my consequent *loss* of belief in a transcendental goodness helped me *gain* a firmer foothold in this slough of despond. That said, I've always had a soft spot for the Graveyard School, I mean the mere thought of Napoleon with a copy of Edward Young's Night Thoughts tucked away in his jockstrap is a guaranteed turn-on, but when I think of Leni Riefenstahl and meditate on *her* indecisiveness around color coordination in the opening scenes of her Triumph of the Will it makes *me* want to throw a can of Zyklon B at *her*. I don't know what I was thinking when I bought this skull as a souvenir of a trip to Cambodia and named it Yorick. (I couldn't believe the family resemblance.) I suppose *you* need the occasional reminder that life is as reliable as a condom on a porcupine, but it makes my war wounds twitch and every time I look at it I *nearly* always jump into another soliloquy. The *chief* problem with being a character who talks to himself is finding an interesting topic to talk about and I *dearly* believe that the topic of being or not being would cause a lot of *grief* to both Heidegger and Sartre. Deep down I'm a shy, reflective Prince who prefers tacit abjection and even the blandishment of suicide to public *grief*. As Julia Kristeva reminds us abjection's something to be really scared of and it's perfect for a male. Normally it's brought on as the consequence of a classical example of homicide. The victim pays *dearly* with his life while the perpetrator howls in a gesture of remorse. On the subject of pain the *chief* glitch (because there's suffering) is the absolute trust put in medical science for a fast last-minute pain-free cure. [Ed. A contingency precipitates a phone-call to an expert on theories of the abnormal and *nearly* all the answers open up to multiple choice.] It makes *you* feel like Mary Douglas in the midst of all *her* anthropological research into the constitution of symbolic systems. She believed defilement is of the order of a boundary, but, should anyone ask *me*, *her gain* in credibility's matched by my *loss* of it. Ours remain *two* compossible but variant theories of the signifying process. Mine of course tends to navigate the *cross*-currents of all the usual panaceas in the form of a sort of schizophrenic common denominator by which the *one* can leave the other *alone*.

Exit

Enter Prospero and Miranda.
It's a funny feeling to be surrounded by what we hold. An orange as an orchard and our clasped hands a city full of people all looking like *me*. Is there a name for this disorder? It all makes one feel rather Complutensian, Spain's good that way, it helps *you* brush up on your Roman Catholic Bible in several different languages. I think it best though if we *stay* in the *shade* of an old Hittite apothegm to help better choreograph our intellects and prepare for the *day* when this unitary urbanism turns into a summary of the above and we're burned in effigy for good. Incidentally, what *made* a girl with your love of athletics take up deipnosophistry, does it run in your family? Such questions sound *so* insignificant in the *light* of this current fiction. Mind plus abrogation equals the destiny of linguistic thought which goes to *show* how *bright* we've both become, our life together growing from its roots in a story *directed* by a perverse will towards slippage and displacement. I'm still curious as to what *you*'ll do when this masque's over, stepping into some new metropolis of the moment, unknown and *unrespected* by the ones who count the ways we *see* our being as amphitheatrical to the end. Some simply say we'll just have to wait and *see* while others insist that irony should govern the *unrespected* permanent condition of life's unpredictable contradictions. I'm such a sensitive plant that I'll be too nervous to die, what I'd like is a principality (or something

vaguely Prussian) and *you* as my chargé d'affaires. *Directed* by the pleasures of imagination we could quench our fugitive vocalities in Tuscaloosa-style margueritas as *bright* politicians on the edge of party protocol. Maybe it's time to *show* the *light* side of my early arbeitsideologie but it's the wrong time for living out its consequences. *So* much for certitude, knitting our hermeneutic circles and hoping for a hoola-hoop of eternal returns. It's time I *made* better use of my corpse d'ésprit rather than trying to make the *day* stand still in the all of the something that's not said. That Zen *shade* of nowadays is less contemporary than it used to be, but yesterday is where we both can *stay* and *you* can tell *me* once again of all the myriad places we have left our words.

Exeunt

Scene 4. *Enter Ghost and Hamlet.*

Remember my description of how I met your mother, the Queen, on a crypto-anarchist chat line and how our honeymoon took place entirely by cell phone?[1] That was long after sex was called intercourse and before that copulation (round about the time sexual harassment was called "putting up with it" and well before education became optional). *Woe* betide anyone who forgets the consequence of that linguistic mutation. Ah the *slow* turn of a partially buried etymology set against incessant iteration! Still, a reader's *moan wrought* from a book consisting entirely of borrowed end-rhymes does not imply that all originality's *gone*. Take for example Walter Benjamin's academically popular Arcades Project, it's a veritable library of other people's sentences, yet, despite the first part of Polonius' famous caveat, it remains so quintessentially Benjamin's own.[2] I had a different *thought* to think but I've seemingly misplaced it on the edge of where I used to *be* among profit margins in a *land* that always looked to discourse analysis for its answers. *You* know, unlike humans, books are built to last but I'd hate life as a volume in your library, I'd feel so alone and neglected, having to *stand* and think what it's like to have never been read. Ah forget about books and concentrate on the art of cooking. We should eat more spare ribs, they're cheap and nourishing (providing they *stay* fresh) and we can build something with the bones, perhaps a personal Xanadu like the Facteur de Cheval's.[3] We can even order take-out à la Parisienne now that I've learned the French word for garçon. I must add, however, culinary culture is purely conceptual to a ghost like me, it formulates a number of proclivities that together spell out "posthumous simmering" incorrectly. In the Middle Ages the corpses of the rich and famous were boiled prior to burial. (Pity the poor old canker-worms with a coffin full of bare ribs and fibulas.) What *brought* us to this *way* of morbid *thought*, some acute epithumia of our infrangibles, or a memory of the days we used to dine out together at the sign of the Scraped Plate? I'm a little too defunct to take death seriously, or so I *thought* until life got in the *way* and *brought* me to that Leadership Convention of Heavy Metal Spiritualists. Despite the high price of those illicit drugs and all the gibberish it did help me *stay* in touch with fringe values and *stand* up for my periodic prosperity anomalies instead of the cause of arte povera. Unlike *you* I always *land* up in a space lacerated by Gnostic anguish where it's a case of killer takes all. If only each instant of clarity offered a hole to crawl through I would *be* free to lose that "all" in a different game. David Jones spoke of "the gnosis of necessity" and all I *thought* about were the gay flamingos of Lake Begoria, pink in their pride. Am I truly the person on this line of sight *gone* sudden, a punctured echo *wrought* in brass behind Saint Peter's chair and the *moan* of *slow woe* if the space still fits?

1. The post-honeymoon coitus incidentally really sizzled.
2. "Neither a borrower nor a lender be."
3. Ferdinand de Cheval, a country postman in southern France, gave up his job to build his *Palais Idéal* from the stones he had gathered while delivering his letters. Work started in 1879 and ended in 1922 after which he decided to build his own grave. He died before completing it.

Exeunt

Scene 5. *A Tucket afarre off. Enter old Widowe of Florence, her daughter, Violante and Mariana, with other Citizens.*
It's *sad*. Old friends are gone, an era has passed.[1] But it's great to grieve and I'm *glad* the past made *me* aware that both eco-science and sociology have proven most of our proverbs to be sound. Rest *assured* having made it this far through the blood bath of idealism[2] our lines of flight will get us somewhere more unpredictable than

this charnel house of interiorities where everything adds up to what it all boils down to in one grand comical thanatopraxis.[3] *You* look younger in that older body unlike myself, with a physique resembling a terra incognita I'm cholesterol's best friend. What are we eating? Parmesan cheese and a horse's head by the taste of it (or is it Spaghetti Al Pacino)? While we're on the subject of bad cuisine (and worse jokes) does *recured* bacon go with refried beans? Both sound resurrected and deposited in the realm of the second-hand or the previously regurgitated. But what if the other we call "indifferent necrotic irreality" was somehow reinstated, to remind us Death makes nothing happen in the kitchen? I think that's why Albrecht Dürer's *Melancholy* looks the way she does, sitting *alone* waiting to be swept up by some law of epic inevitability and taken back to the ranks of the unengraved.[4] Perhaps Death is a place called Barbra Streisand, take a look at that vista of abandoned synagogues and churches with their dead surrounding them! That's quite a topography for necrophiliacs and grave robbers! *You* know there's a lot of profit in death: plunder, coup d'états and lebensraum to name but three. That's why I've *gone* back to the practical philosophy of the Glimmer Twins and take a perverse pleasure in reading obituaries. But no holy martyrdom! I want my death to be the occasion for all the living to get happily pissed. I'm more than happy, however, to stick around, I mean promotion's still easy at court, just glue this pig's head onto that heraldic shield and voilà a Knight for life. However after death the *slide* from a nefarious existence to a posthumous sainthood is never guaranteed. That's why my number one *desire* is that long overdue vacation in the Swat Valley singing *"Abide* with them" over non-existent martinis to the sounds of car bombs and sniper *fire.* I recall them well, those endless weeks of playing Nine Men's Morris at the home of a local sympathizer and, after dark, ruminating what questions coordinate our singularity. I even remember the night Shaxberd caught *fire* and almost burned to death; they built a tavern in his honor: "The Inn of the Burning Bard." I was out at the time in a North Carolina mortuary trading my subjectivity for a tombstone, debating with the Chief Mortician how death, as decay into equilibrium, provides the perfect antidote to chaos theory. But since my latest oesophagus transplant I don't remember a thing, memory's a pachydermous privilege I'm now denied. Truth is I can't *abide* the burden of the past, however if I camouflage *desire* for a permanent present and *slide* into the persona of an absent God, that's wonderful. It's like being both Outer Space and Philosophy rolled into one where I'm everything because I'm nothing and I'm nothing because I'm everywhere. That insight brought home the realization that 100% of nothing's infinitely preferable to 50% of something, but with the *gone* and going rate on entropy how can I ever get to know *you* all in a lifestyle characterized by change and variety? Am I still just one day in the life of a mutant virus? Those two questions *alone* make us all insecure. I seem to be getting good at posing questions that don't deserve an answer. My *melancholy* is best conceived as a long chain of short mutual dependencies, but then again, what if my faded, shy effeminacy was miraculously *recured*? Compared to your verve cliché I wouldn't stand a chance at making a serious impression on that gorgeous guitarist in the Mariachi band from Tijuana, even though *you assured me* otherwise. I suppose I'm *glad* I feel in retrospect a *sad* seeker of affordable plastic surgery.

1. Gertrude Stein on her return to Paris in 1933.
2. From a letter by Henri Gaudier-Brzeska shortly before his death in combat.
3. Georg Lucácks.
4. And who remembers Sara Shade of Stoke Edith once famous for her curry? All she ever wanted was a Papist cremation, nothing lavish, just stripped down to her socks and a service without flowers.

Enter the Earle of Warwick, and the Lord Chief Justice.
You asked me pleadingly what's a fifteen-letter phrase for "bovine predicate" and I didn't have the *heart* to answer. *Part* of me wanted to and *part* of me couldn't, it's what economists call a state of precautionary hypo-investment. I know shyness is not one of my more endearing features but I'm *determined*, however, to mend my ways, that's why I'm off to the Annual International Conference on Self-Confidence. Unfortunately I'm "off" in the way cheese goes "off," elegiac as it sounds in the cheerful factuality of decomposition. The *heart impannelled* with its irregularities makes me think that perhaps poems really are laboratories for life in search of the hysterical masterpiece of an abandoned adjective and what *lies* outside the pale of poetry might be less amenable to scrutiny. Not to *deny* you a few sonnets for relaxation, but Death still has its appointment with us and we mustn't be late in giving birth to maggots. Your *eyes* look rectangular in this light, it would be a *lie* if I said they look disfigured but their smell is indisputably anomalous. You know there are 202 bones in the human body and everyone smells like a crypt. *Right* there in the worsening schism with bread riots breaking out in all the Black Sites they *bar* access to the press and block *sight* of those human trafficking scenarios with sex slaves and

bogus brides that give the *war* on drugs its baritone precision. The *war* is over in topology, and history follows cities back to bed. Moving to leave this room one is sucked into the function of its door—but with my *sight* the way it is my egalitarian impulse to grab a drink might not even make it to the *bar*. I think you made the *right* decision not to join that local cell of philatelists, a good Catholic like you doesn't need a hobby. Give me the futility of the practico-inert anytime, mowing the lawn, shaving, and the routine but conspicuous care of unwanted rocks marks, methinks, the nonpareil of bliss. What's your favorite truth? Mine's the fact that before we're born we're old enough to die. That's a charming thought for any birthday. It's also true that the emolument pertaining to a poetic *lie* is tepid justification for faux panegyrics from a Poet Laureate. With the *eyes* of Inland Revenue now transfixed by off-shore bank accounts it's hard to *deny* the dubious nature of my speculative investments with Fanny Mae and Freddy Mac, coated with cover-ups and *lies* about repurchased loans, and aphoristic sentiments above their modest monthly earnings. But what if a tear fell from one of the eyes of the word "hypotenuse" and landed on a copy of The Selected Poems of Jack the Ripper? Matter is alive and mutters on and on until you stick a stake in its *impannelled heart*. In knowing nothing I love everything. Poems do that sometimes, *determined* to stay as a *part* for the whole when a *part* of the *heart* isn't pounding.

Enter Banquo.
Remember the time I went to Mac Duff's fancy dress ball dressed as a minor diasporic community, got accidentally stuffed in a turkey and ended up being thrown out with the morning trash? Maybe it wasn't a life-changing experience but it sure became the story of my life as a changeling out of Faerie (one of the unfortunate consequences of being born a petroleum bi-product). In fact all my landed and moveable possessions could be put in an egg cup—if I had one. My bruised body is really inconvenient, I know it's my own fault for trying to break up that martial arts demonstration in the Ghaza Strip, but it feels like I've been at death's door for a century and these days I can't tell my alma mater from my dura mater; I also tend to think like a man who's never won a jack-pot. That said, growing up with a man-eating shark as my swimming instructor sure brought home the value of staying put on land. In fact I *delight* in the pleasures

71

of authentic Highland scenery, what a *sight* for sore ears, and such a dose of the "genuine" sublime it causes my recollection to stammer in tranquility: "It's morning. Why get up?" The day asks such important questions, so why do *you* all insist on saying I'm the Derek Walcott of the New Scottish Pragmatism? The *move* from metropolitan to industrial in your jurisprudence makes us all wonder if your modus operandi's changed. Either way the sensualists truly have my sympathy. I've been a life-long fan of sexual intercourse but people like *me* tend to look on making *love* as an obsolete practice of semaphore; for the most *part* the attendant scratching and hickies recapitulate my Post-Culloden Highland teleology, not to mention those wounds I received in the Belgian Congo as a *guest* of a mock-surrealist. But how about everyone else? What with your orbital eccentricities, shrinking diameters and melting polar caps I worry about your collective *heart* palpitations. Moreover the way everyone loves to *feast* on the fact that "the concept of cat does not scratch"[1] instantly raises the question as to why there's a constant complaint about the hegemony of anxiety? In my own recipe for stumbling through living one has to assume, like H. G. Wells and Alfred Jarry, that space and time are binary opposites, a matter of months apprehended in the phrase "not always this sudden." People at the local Good Will Store tell us that to *smother* your petulance and *look* smilingly into the face of the *other* leads to happiness and neighbors, that's why I've made Elsewhere my permanent address and haven't *took* goodbye to mean just the farewell to hellos. It *took* a long time to realize that the only reason people talk to each *other* is because it might *look* better than thinking, or being alone, or trying to *smother* mace all over the School-Crossing guard. What is the sound of one hand laughing? The answer to that question really would be a *feast* to clap at. Yet an event is always an incident before it's an accident and being alive sure beats crossing the Styx, but as always, with good *heart* and gracious in defeat, the *guest* enters, in *part* to contaminate the symmetry of all our soi-disants. They say asymmetry does not exist in the larger scheme of intelligent design, but what if suddenly one's house evaporates? When I say "*Love me* for the *move* not why I'm moving," *you* bruise the ligatures of all that's left to tighten up the windpipe. What a *sight* to *delight* those pessimists of perspective who never knew that to ants my left sock is a landscape.

1. "The concept of dog does not bark" is a phrase attributed to Spinoza.

Enter Servant, and two Murtherers.

I was flipping through the Hamartigenia of Prudentius the other day, with its savage attack on the Gnostic dualism of Marcion, trying to understand the origin of sin until it came to me where it actually is. Look up at the sky and count a sin for every star. *Dear* me, I *fear* there's so much bad in the best of us, that *part* of the human comedy stays the same in any situation. It's when sociologists and cops both tell you crime implies dystopia that your *breast* heaves a sigh at the thought that doing *art* is penitence for enjoying your day off on the toxic landfill. Keats claimed that he derived as much pleasure from conceiving evil as conceiving good. We may be criminals with a mission to "kill our neighbor as ourself" and, like Venus and Serena Williams, fatally partial to celebrity endorsements, but we remain law abiding in our crime, sibling Behemoths destined for death row when the next government gets elected. Incidentally, how's your mother, I found her diligently cooking Catherine of Sienna's heart in a white wine sauce claiming there's much more protein in saintly organs than in a slice of wild boar. I think everyone's victims of the global recession and it's a pity that life's passing us by instead of running us over. I realize Death offers a great means of getting out of the city but there's little appeal to the modern *chest* in such martyrdoms as St. Erasmus's or that *thief* Barabas that they hung with Jesus.[1] So much for Paterian aesthetics, we however prefer the crimes which become vows[2] so we need to take *care* around those democratic rulings that mark us free to be condemned. Do you still believe in the perfectibility of our species? Frankly, I can't imagine a life without vice, the anxieties of others, *grief* and our own odd nightmare. Just look at who we *are*, early-Modern versions of Gilbert and George fictioned into a life of crime to be governed more by contingency than necessity under the aegis of the one who isn't Chacspier. We should all have been born with a sell-by date tattooed on our buttocks at birth. I'm well aware from my reading in cultural studies that "hybridization" "negotiates" "polysemy" but how does that help us carry out the latest Operation Al Capone? To merely *trust* on lucky escapes from the law is only half that matters to career criminals like us; we also need to *stay* in touch with our sixth sense as a final phase as we recollect but don't remember how many victims we've produced. It's quite the scenario, dropped here like Flash Gordon and Captain Kirk, *thrust* into traumas enacting other people's malevolent schemes along the *way* to a shabby destiny courtesy the combined expertise of torturer and hangman. Sure, reality hurts, life's like that along the *way*; *thrust* a clock onto the mantle piece of metaphysics and it'll stop ticking at eight minutes to Descartes at which point the mind-body split will never happen. The secret to successful crime is to *stay* on the blank side of the moralistic where the aporetic remains garrulous. Remember, the resort to praxis always invests itself in the concept of the nation-state, whereas the illusion of pop culture is strictly congruent with the fantasy of the public sphere. Hence, we should both take up more philanthropic activities like going to friends' funerals and putting our *trust* in wearing crucifixes around our necks (who knows we might end up honorary cardinals with a hospital ward named after us). *Are* you up now for a little more covert carnage? The next one promises to be a veritable symphony in sanguine, which reminds me, after this next assassination I must go to confession and get final absolution of my sins. Not that I'd many to start with before I took up this job, apart from tagging the Taj Mahal and putting chloroform in Xmas Crackers as a Christian seasonal jinx, my life's been relatively pure.[3] Good *grief* to think I could have retired early on the innocent profits made from the manufacture of a successful line of faux Neolithic chamber pots and instead I end up earning minimum wages doing this. I don't *care* if it's for the welfare of a despot, *thief* of the living that I've come to be. So what if I have a *chest* tattooed with a Tantric chart reading "my victims constitute my diocese" to guide me from bad to worse. What I want to perfect is the *art* of the hypothesis, a poetics of supposing for the *breast* and mind that never want a certainty. In fact, it's *part* of my five-year plan in the asteroid belts where *fear* mutates a little closer to those diabolic archetypes caught up in the extra cellular matrix we three still hold so *dear*.

1. Not to mention that famous Indian fakir who was buried alive for nine months beneath a mound of Basmati rice.
2. Hugo Ball.
3. He should also have mentioned to our British readers poisoning the odd corgie at Sandringham.

Exeunt omnes

Scene 6. *Senate sounded. Enter Macbeth as King, Lady Lenox, Ross, Lords, and Attendants.*

A funny phrase "we three," it sounds vaguely Scottish like me, a highland propensity to connectivity, no doubt, but in our brave *cause* cultural chaosmos must precede political articuli, but then again if you're shipwrecked with a new-born prime minister under one armpit then the complication in the *laws* of the preceding statement intensify. Speaking of intensity the *part* of Tertullian I like best is where he claims "regnum Caesaris regnum diaboli." Quite the Titanic equation to *uprear* on the white steed of anyone's malevolent despotism—but it's a little too late for that retro-style imperial engineering. Did you know that George III and Queen Caroline called each other Mr. and Mrs. King? We could do that ourselves if we were humans or monarchists but the Gobi *desert* that comprise these scenarios limits us to either tambourine and guitar parties (courtesy the Witch of Endor) or endless cocktails with Chogyam Trungpa Rinpoche and Sir Walter Scott down at the Bonnie Bunch of Bagpipes. Twinkle twinkle *here* we are, thrust out of *gravity* as events in a film that *was* never made. Let the *eye pass* over its field of scopophilic pleasures and pay its *respects* to all the rest of those Structured Settlement recipients. Next stop senility, death and oblivion. I think you're missing the bright side of aging. Dark as it is this human menagerie's got everything and if I could *sum* up life I'd say ontology's a little rubbed with worn extremities yet still without serious *defects*; for most of us it's still a world of limousines, tax evasion and cocaine-spiked champagne by the swimming pool with folks laughing at the thought of inevitable death through their hiccups and snorting yet always remembering to take their last rights in a confessional. I love a thought to *come* from a dead man's mind, *come* to think of it so do we all, although there's no way the surface temperature of your mythology would ensure that *defects* in the cytoplasmic inheritance wouldn't tissue us apart. To *sum* it up, I'm too old to die and with all due *respects* I don't miss the thought of Paradise like you do, not even a tithe of it—Angelus Novus they used to call me, and I would *pass* all history between my wings. A corpse's *eye* might still see that the statistical hour has arrived and from beneath this pinguid earth exudes "the detestable evaporation of herrings."[1] Still, despite the dictates of taste and sanity, it's great having your mind close at hand as if it *was* the last of your species, brought down to the level of plebian *gravity* with me still active in the auto-erotics of young History. And *here* it ends in a cottonelle *desert* for two where the ghosts of community *uprear* a giant penguin of your choice as the missing *part* of the rule of *laws* among clichés and ampersands in a *cause* more sliced than italicized.

1. Mary Wollstonecraft.

Enter Queene of Fairies, with her train.
This is not an occasion for fairy cavalcades, it seems everything local has shrunk, look at that bookcase *behind* the concept I identified with "matter of" in relation to the unknown factors that are bound to come later, it's less ambi-parousial than it used to be. Maybe it's time to start saving up to buy a new doll's house. My *mind* to me a kingdom is under siege by some power of pantomimic minimalism in an epic of the subjunctive. Actually, at this *side* of logic and, speaking as one of Nature's great Tinkerbells, I don't believe there's such a thing as a sentient subject. We *groan* all we like but we can't *hide* the fact of subjectivity's middle-being. Shelly, Novalis, Ungaretti all caught its image in migration through long hours of interbreeding *on* the assembly line for internationally famous writers. But *you* all *know me* better than I do myself. I may be preoccupied with Pixie Politicks and the welfare of the elf-employed (outside of strictly seasonable work for Santa) but I've never shouted *woe* slow down a bit to an active *friend* or a servant. Perhaps we should *say* boo to survival, jettison onto-typology, and take up advocacy of some visible minority such as heterosexuals or synchronized swimmers. Remember, death is simply life without the stress—a secluded journey to the *end*, along the *way* of a life unnoticed.[1] At which point the mail arrives and we survive. Notice the *way* meaning murmurs when it's facing two different directions? Indeed, and recall difference is what gives repetition its object, it suggests we're satisfied now everything in the house sounds louder. I love embalming fluid streaming through the heating pipes, the mere thought of it conjures up the image of all those museum security staff predictably snoring asleep on their chairs every time a visitor wants to ask them the *way* to the cafeteria. It makes one feel like one's in Madame Tussaud's not the MET. How come I only misplaced my virginity and never actally lost it? Why are we always absent to ourselves in a

question like this one, locked into being as the last of the tour guides among sensibilia? To speculate an *end* outside of language? Poetic questions like these construct an emptiness, the silence of a precantation in a viaticum. Recall a word is merely a phoneme's happiness, verbs in isolation however are the angels of movement, furious old ladies canopied beneath adverbial parasols complaining of nouns. Necroeconomists *say* that dialecticians give birth to morticians and the paleotechnic integrity in that claim is amazing. Death by dialectic into language. It's a well-known fact that only the dead give earth its good name, but I've a vague feeling I've talked to a *friend* in depth about this, and *woe* betide our autistic affinities to knowledge, for truth arrives as its aftermath and there isn't a conjunction between this and that. The separate *me* in this equation baulks at the opportunity to *know* the reasons for anything. Lacan's mirror-stage offers an infant encountering its own face but always in a third person; it seems to mutter I'm beginning to be a closer stranger, deleting the name and that way passing into psychology. But following Baudelaire I might claim my imbecility to be the compound state of hysteria and joy. No doubt most of *you* would disagree (as usual) and move on to different questions such as why we hide the fact that maybe life's too short to make friends. Kant thought folks can get away with a transcendental schematism but they can't. So *on* we go with nowhere to *hide* from the *groan* from the mouths of others, projective voices near the illegible *side* of spring's sprung rhythms, that grief in scraps of language, a dictum drawing silence to a smile with a *mind* bruised by the luggage of language, unprepared for the expurgation hovering not far *behind* it.

1. Horace: Secretum iter est fallentis semita vitae.

Exeunt omnes

Enter Lear, Edgar, and Foole.
Ever noticed how an aerial view of a Zambian village looks exactly like the mycological phenomenon called witches' rings? Wow! from megastar monarch to mentor of the African habitat, I just love the way you perform "difference," but you still *go* too *slow* inside that orbiting habitat facility some call your

crown. Try disemboguing your discourse by doting on this little *jade* object wrapped around my neck, or maybe theorize your insights into constitutional monarchy understood as "meat in a dream."[1] We're a proud *race* so what *made* you prefer the anxiety of existence to the Beaubourg effect?[2] Something's happening to the neuroses of being—happening, or listening, that speed of fear, its *pace* a breath turned up on an apple's nipple and quite radical for our specific Wilderness; it was a long story of the summer and we twice deleted it. I suppose you *know* nothing about art and periodicity with the *wind* from the subway vents now blowing up the skirt of Art Nouveau? After Modernism comes modernism, but via the *slow* meander of structural determination we *find* that what we *need* is a new class of variables and from *thence* to readjust the *speed* of the projection of our fictional parts. People take *offence* at the slightest deviation from mainstream narrative. You and your home-style narratology—you sound exactly like Tolstoy on prozac and I take *offence* at such fossilized waffle. First, we have to transform the world of fiction and then interpret it. I mean you could sit and read Clarice Lispector at the *speed* of light all year and from *thence* pontificate causalities or nihilisms and you'd still *need* to *find* a way to explain why, on this battlefield, the dead have not yet been shot. Here we are, stuck in a war of ideals halfway between the ornamental and the pictorial, bored to death in some pastoral capriccio with the Arch of Constantine burning in the background. Some say the *slow* boat never sinks and doesn't get to China and when we're alone I'll explain why we *wind* up with such banal sentiments. [Coughs.] Ah, the topology of the sounding throat! Nicotine plays a significant role in the history of coughing, cigarette? Thanks. You *know* I like the *pace* at which your congenital hedonism converts a love of life into a reinterpretation of the Freudian death wish. Put more academically what *made* mortification become "post-functionalism" in the better colleges of the liberal arts? No doubt there's a touch of existential angst in the question but it's essential to understanding why our faith in the human *race* diminishes by the week. Perhaps I should effect a Chinese turn (like Ezra Pound did) and ask which concept of *jade* you prefer? The *slow* one that attempts to blend possessive individualism into a monolith of corporate-endorsement, or the quicker one that rereads Nietzsche to remember subversive struggle has no other place to *go*?

1. St. Augustine.

2. See Jean Baudrillard, "The Beaubourg Effect: Implosion and Deterrence" in *Simulacra and Simulation, trans. Sheila Faria Glaser. Ann Arbor: University of Michigan Press, 1994: 61-73.*

Exeunt omnes

Enter Friar and Romeo.

In my brand of leper-logic it's perfectly okay to take an annual shower and have part of a thumb come off on the towel if the soap stays intact but it's a shame about the rest of the collateral damage. My motto is "if you can't get a life you can at least change your socks." Still, it's peevish to grumble, being the best French-fry friar at the fast-order counter in the refectory gave me instant promotion to Chief Chip Monk. I also did well to survive the Dissolution of the Monasteries by a strategic use of punning like the one you just read and, after ritual deformation, successfully change my name back to Toulouse-Lautrec to end up on a janitor's salary in one of the better brothels of Bangkok.[1] After that long sentence I *hope* I can stay for supper; we can warm up some of yesterday's dead dog soup I brought along with some cat meat in an Iraqi eyeball sauce I bought at that new Abu Grhaib Delicatessen. Alternatively there's some cheese fonda left over from last week's supper with Jane Fondue in Acapulco. It's a little past it, I mean the best before date's printed in cuneiform, but it's fresh enough to rustle up a firm conviction that I know it's happy being here. Instead of dessert chosen from the limited *scope* of fructal virtualities we can take *pride* in the tekhne mimetike those fudge rissoles turned out to be. I feel I'm *special-blest* with a different talent than cooking, which leaves me in the hope that we can touch each other—like Stein did Toklas—as the communication in our interruptions. Perhaps I could *hide* in a *chest*, jump out wearing a *carcanet* of emeralds that *are set* in Celtic gold. What a *rare pleasure* it must be to *survey* each vicinity of death annihilating what we call its "sense of urgency." Perhaps Ludwig Wittgenstein might join us and reveal the *treasure* of his Tractatus leaving us (as a final *key* to the philosophical relation of word to world) his claim that death is not an event in life as we continue to stop living. But is a *key* per se the alterity of the lock's own absence? The *treasure* trove of our life-events might warrant another *survey* of all known mortuaries available before we take *pleasure* in a *rare set* of tarot cards that *are* carelessly placed on a map of the nothing that's to come. Sure you prefer your Tudor *carcanet* to my own Neue Sachlichneit lavaliere?[2] I think the latter "amuse gueule" would expose more of your *chest* to the radiation belt yet still *hide* most of its erotic expression as you croon out a love song to Juliet in that famous balcony scene. In fact it used to be a genuine Duchamp readymade until my wife (the abbot) started to wear it. As a *special-blest* conceptual flâneur you might take *pride* in listening to more of my monastic paronomasia and check the *scope* of the scary contradictions in the logic of my anagrams. I'm happy to say that I survived a treacherous birth in a forest of dirty jokes and *hope* to have a witty cliché for every occasion. Let's split now I've an appointment to have my nipples pierced in the convent dormitory by that singing nun from Rouen whose capacity for euphrasy remains unstoppable.

1. I'm surprised you don't mention that highly successful male escort-service you ran out of Montevideo, Toy Boyz 'R Us.
2. The New Objectivity or New Sobriety pioneerd by Walter Gropius, an architect born with the soul of an amoeba and the imagination of a pot noodle.

Enter Falstaffe, Quickly, and Ford.

Only a *heart* like yours would need cough drops. Mine takes *part* in the syncope of an aspiration beyond the human: a phart, a moment, then a brief adieu to the sun. It doesn't take a college diploma to *know* what's happening to all those archeologists of progress, and after my perlustrations of the entire gamut of technological break-throughs it would *appear* that cosmic vertigo's returning in a final *show* of sex at the gym. Each *year* brings fraternity in seconds, brother to sister in the factory of *new* problems known as tea-break for the masses. *Set*-theory offers *you* a different solution with a desert made of Cantor dust, constructing some *counterfeit* argument to *lend* microparticular disturbances to intelligence—a kind of opera that's sung yet divorced from the lips. In the *shade* of this coolibah tree I *tend* to display the piety of a St. Chad *made* down-under in the image of a genuflection before the old Hyena of Quinzy. It happened once that an emptiness in the dream-advertisement machine *made* the hyper-script legible: "I am nor am I" as if reversibility always wins. I *tend* to prefer theory in the passive voice where speech remains a crocodile between two parties, edged into the *shade* of the "good life" getting better. As Louis Aragon put it "Everything that is not I is incomprehensible." It's good to *lend* poetry to everything rendering the listener a witness to witticism, but these days a limerick can mutate into a bildungsroman overnight and cause me to break wind. In the current crisis poetry is folded onto its own image in a general instability inside a landscape of commodities: *counterfeit* Listerine, decaffeinated cereal, organic fruit bars, flatware, throw-pillows and late Hildebrandine views on the relation of spiritual to temporal sushi.[1] How can there be three candles in every light? *You* struggle and *set* your brain to a brand *new year* of challenges, but logic lost its efficacy millennia ago. I mean when Pierre Paget sculpted an emblematic seat of Hercules for the Chateau-le-Viscomte, everybody knew what they sat on.[2] The skin lifts literature into history but the question is at what point does history enter as the hideous product of a diseased mind? I wish that old ball-park proverb were true: you don't make history, you catch flyballs. Sperm and other factors *show* that I'm a man in so far as the extent to which the world is human isn't. In which case it would *appear*, according to propaedeutic estimates, that we never were a screen for discourse. But I *know* I'll have no *part* in pessimism around the future, in fact it warms my *heart* to realize that the "nightmare of materialism"[3] is turning into quite a Boxing Day Sale.[4]

1. "This is not the place for a critique of medieval religion. But, unless we bear in mind some essential features of the Catholic system of thought, we miss the key to that ecclesiastical statesmanship which dominates the twelfth and thirteenth centuries." H. W. C. Davis.
2. Historians have now concluded that earlier that month an anagram suddenly transformed Armandus Richeleus into a prototype Hercules admirandus which then mysteriously offered itself sexually to an arthritic security guard at the Academy of Inscriptions.
3. Wassily Kandinsky, *Concerning the Spiritual in Art*.
4. "Pardon me for interrupting again with a fourth footnote but I've no idea why this interesting dramatic piece is turning into an abyss of obscurities. I mean that Hyena of Quinzy? Come off it, I spent a good hour on a search engine looking for that one and came up with zilch. Yours truly, Senator Max Clarity."

All good Americans go to Paris when they die.

W. C. Williams

Enter Puck (disguised as Clement Greenberg).
Please read this line first. Art goes monochrome when war goes polychrome but I've little respect for artists themselves, the ones I write about are more concerned with getting grants and Aristotelian extensions to their phucking resumes than changing the world. Same goes for artists' models, crab-crawling out of their skinny ecto-skeletal apartments to pose nude in some studio garret for $13 an hour. If you're not one of them you're stuck on the left side of *truth* as the accent falls capriciously at the "centre of the silent Word."[1] My ideal artist is the lumberjack-jill caught in those heroic struggles against the resistance of sheer arboreal force. If we turn to art itself instead of lumberjacks I'd have to say that green spit from an off-white cough hardly marks the satisfactory return of Abstract Expressionism. I am fairy *youth* of pixie way the microbe of an avant-garde. I hew through dock leaf and stagger-petal, love King and Queen, shave intercourse twixt mushroom sessions, take tic from cow-petal as I pass bentile into moonbeam-cream, haul wood vetch to coppice dwarf, harness chariot to micropede for turbine power up Pook's Hill. Oops, what *made* me explode into that elfin musical and why do I seem *so* attractive to that pig over there selling pizza? It's enough to make you want to reestablish apartheid in Fairyland or rebuild the Berlin Wall across Dingly Dell. Wow, those mood swings of mine are catastrophically Ovidian, it's probably best to listen further to the word I was writing to hear.[2] Every memory leaves a fingerprint and mine might *fade* away to *show* a final emblematic scenario in which a slit *discloses* an old corpulent castrato *wantonly* stepping on plucked *roses* as if they were human throats screaming "Go to the dead and love them."[3] I'm neither questioning the private right to *die* nor meditating in a formal fashion on what it takes to *live*. I'm not a parsimonious elfin guide but I do *deem* it unwise to *give* a slave a Master Card; it would *seem* to guarantee a maverick consumerism, in fact "please read this line first" may *seem* an odd request and *give* you the feeling that you've read it before. Critics *deem* reflexivity bad in texts written after 1983, but these days who can tolerate a memory for dates? The dominant paradigm demands we *live* and *die* inside a bed of unwanted *roses wantonly*

proclaiming somebody else's jokes. Some driftwood patchwork *discloses* a quilt made from the ridges of a reptile's skin which serves to *show* that more seems less as I *fade* into my Slimmer's Guide to Calories. *So* why not buy a *made*-to-measure breakfast for that lame beggar in New Orleans and place it between the two great April poems as that cruelest of showers sweet?   Go figure it, a *youth* splashed out from a catanemia of all its future selves sampling failure as an hors d'oeuvre. *Truth* is we might never have Paris although it's up to me if me is up to it. Still it's hard to watch Independence Day fireworks and not think of the innocent victims in Iraq and Afghanistan. So let's wobble to Arabia and survive the conquest of the Fertile Crescent and let fireworks feed the poor. Now that sounds like giving choice a chance!

1. T. S. Eliot.
2. Cf. *Corpus Hermeticum* Book I: 18.
3. Creon to Antigone.

Exeunt

Scene 7. *Enter King and Queen.*
If I admit that your *eyes* are the twin drainpipes to my heart would that make us the Mars and Venus of cardiac drainage?   I don't really need an answer to that one do I as we drizzle into twilight across the stock-pile of bad jokes and metaphors this text is turning into. A different theory of capricious matter might *arise* and seal our *doom* in a flash but *posterity* assures that philosophy will always clip an angel's wings.[1]   Still, it sure beats a return to the humanities and it does seem ironical to be the final voice completing this design, there, as yourself, (and preferring to use the Royal Me) the momentary figurehead upon a ship, itself transitory. If there's additional *room* for comment I'd say it's analogous to caressing a kitten in the abstract. Incidentally, I've lost my *enmity* for *memory*. A man on a bus forgets to pick up his legs and leaves them in a minor language. "My eyes are open but they lack horizons" says his face as a chin. You can *burn* all those paper optimisms alright because Melancholia will always be there sitting on a pile of *masonry* looking like Josef Mengler in drag explaining what death is to a tiny Jewish child. But you're the King and with a life-term membership

to the Karma Sutra Club you can turn gynecology into a rampant fetish and lift the ban on laughter by commanding everyone to cheer up. I know, and I alone am supposed to be the return of the impossible as such. Unfortunately whenever I order unexpected turbulence in the provinces all I get is another unbleached wheat diploma from the Fat Chance Club. But I can change it, I can put a crime scene barrier around the entire Republic of Pessimism. At least last year was not the paradox it might have been; those visions of verity in late September didn't *overturn* the triumph of the lie. Albeit a redundant king I could still feel the hump and withered arm of grandeur. *Time* and again I'd pose the same question through some thermal trope: do you prefer light over fire or symbol over reality, but now? Bon après mayday I've drained the *contents* of every hope I had. Even warfare in words where *rhyme* schemes meet relational planes as *monuments* to war zones has disappeared. I blame it all on the revocation of the Gin Bill—(such sad lives after the intoxication wears off). You think their lives were sad? Try reading Thomas Hardy's Winter Words, those lyrical *monuments* to Mother's Day held in abortion clinics. He puts a gibbet in each *rhyme* and the reader dangles from them for what seems an eternity. As for me, I fell speechless once after reading Yeats' "Sally Gardens," the *contents* convinced me Purgatory's more a mood than a place. But it sure beats Paradise with its sixteen annual Grammy awards for transcendental non-existence. Do you remember the *time* we argued with a group of Shriners and tried to *overturn* their logic by questioning the link they made between secrecy and *masonry* by petitioning the Abbé Suger's door at Saint Denis as incontrovertible evidence that they were wrong? That sure made their fezzes droop. At least with scholastic philosophers like Duns Scotus and G. E. Moore you get to shower before they *burn* you with the single question "What are you here for?" Having sex with you last night was like reliving Dorothea Brooke's dream of Casaubon complete with the *memory* of what absolute knowledge might have been if evolution had ignored the primates. What *enmity* one feels toward those transi petrified into a permanent form of becoming-dead knowing the soul's a bag in which you'll carry all your bitten bits of fingernails. Oh Death, won't you spare me over 'til another year? I'm afraid there's little *room* for optimism in such pleadings, and there'll be zilch to give *posterity* a hope from the sounds of the one who wondered. I know we're stuck in the pleroma of a minor species with oblivion guaranteed, but when I'm gone I want to remain unforgettable even if no one remembers me. Given our compositional unbalance and constant need for re-equilibration there's not much left beyond the pain principle and the *doom* attending on the fact that knowledge is self-sabotage. I think therefore I experience an effect as a thought you glimpse in the negative, where solidarities *arise* exclusive of civilities to *eyes* now settled on departure. Oops, must go I'm late again for my lobotomy.

1. John Keats.

Exeunt

Scene 8. *Enter Lysanda and Helen.*
Why is it after three million years of natural selection we've arrived at a species in these parts that's perfectly adapted to uselessness? It's karaoke night on Neptune and we're missing it. I know the chance is *rare* we'll ever want to leave this planet but if we do visit earth again let's take *care* to hijack Imagism and deposit it in Las Vegas. Imagine the *view* of Richard Aldington describing a slot machine in less than thirty words, or H.D. a dryad croupier raking the chips in at roulette. I *see* from your socks that you're a *new* friend of the Bodleian, it'll *be* an august life I'm sure among the dust of old intellects tackling ancient tomes as if trying to master the north face of Mount Everest. I agree with Hofmannsthal that the real challenge is to read what was never written. Do books remember the histories of the fingers that caressed them into curvature by the crease in a dog-eared corner? These days it's rare for me to think so, but to turn a page could mark a fundamentally poetic act. Like Alexander Pope I believe *dullness* is a prevalent species constantly attacking us, attaching its suckers and trying to *kill* our … suspense being the obvious function of this sentence it's hardly worth the effort to complete it. Completion will never construct anything and to shun the radical implications of an uncompleted thought seems a necessary condition for self-survival given Death is the *fullness* of history under the hollyhocks. I believe it was Adam's invention, the man who neglected to name the fishes and what dire profundity followed to culminate in Walton and Cotton's Compleat Angler translated into Melville's Moby Dick. Dying's an ancient ritual in many parts and was elevated to a sport in Roman times, they called it "Saturday Night Thumbs Down at the Coliseum"

but Protagoras knew it as nekron—that's why I'm thinking the hardwood way to coffins. "In a voice irritatingly apostolic you tell me screaming is the secret to a whiter smile and that smile may *fill* a need." To read a sentence like that *might* help explain why, with pleasure *allay'd* these days by mandatory agency, I've lost all *appetite* for reading. We specied out three millennia ago and with that *said* we should bid adieu and tattoo while our skins remain sunny. Listen to this: "Seventeen convictions for sodomy, thirty-eight forced penetrations, [turns page] twenty-eight and a half date rapes plus ninety-seven cases of pedophilia"—and this is only in the Theology Department. Who *said* higher education's the closest thing the mind gets to a nunnery? I've lost my *appetite* for back-to-school specials and my fear of contracting a sexually transmitted Ph.D. is not *allay'd* by your pedagogical assurances to the contrary. Nor *might* my breakthrough knowledge of the difference between aerosols and paint stripper *fill* the gaps in my happily shrinking resumé. Rather than pursuing the possibilities of artificial intelligence in higher education there's an urgent need to re-examine the concept of one's own brain in its *fullness* and then *kill dullness* with some cold watercress stuffed in a jock strap. If you shoulder my parentheses I'll unpolish your quotes and when that's done it will *be* time to catch the non-being of becoming in a *new* sit-com or a TV Game Show. Who knows, we may *see* one of those cave-aged cadavers they found in the Himalayas suddenly shout out "Deal or no deal?" or perhaps before those ads for motorized wheelchairs we'll get a *view* of Democracy in flagrante delecto caught with both the Pope and the President in their stocking feet. However, reconciled to health *care* cut-backs neither resurrections nor erections turn me on in such *rare* instances when they occur.

Exeunt

WARNING: THE FOLLOWING SPEECH CONTAINS VIOLENCE AND COARSE LANGUAGE. READERS ARE ADVISED.

Enter Hamlet reading of a Booke.
Hmm "X tries to beat his enemy with the greenhouse effect brought on by toxic emissions in the battlefield, but X's troops fall *ill* from poisoned

tuna sandwiches and all Y's enemies remain alive and dry in the caves and mountains where they've always been." Tuna sandwiches indeed. No doubt there's a halieutic tranquility in some of the more fishy fallacies of hope. The tuna's corpulence in fact proved crucial to those conquistadores trapped in the production of colonial histories after all the Gods moved back to Kansas. Ancestral volatilities aside, it would be great to move away from here and renew my youth. A gap in the firewall *will* let me through into one of *those* Iranian nuclear-powered perpetual rejuvenation chambers and I'll be Dorian Gray Junior and a size five for the rest of my life. Even if it proves impossible to get back to that spinning Way-Back Machine one jumps through to return, there'll still be cause for optimism by going the opposite route. Moreover self-annihilation's still attractive, hence Death will be my flagship project, just gliding across the primrose puddle to the everlasting bonfire—et indomitaeque morti. My current girlfriend, Carly Simon,[1] opines good Catholics like me come back from death to shake hands with truth and sit down in a chair. I still prefer to sit on one of those unexploded land mines in Bosnia and strategize for the best in the worst of all possibilities. But to soliloquize on something less morbid, I'd have to say I love *nothing* more than the gusto of the antique set against that vegetable scribble some dignify by the name of abstract expressionism, it merely reinforces my longstanding hostility to the non-representational. We all know aesthetic nominalism of the kind now rampant inflects the legacy of the Hutchesonian model of moral liberalism and, thanks to the tachist, aleatory turn, modern painting's become so democratic that even a chimpanzee can paint a masterpiece. (I heard of one social worker who had an accidental nosebleed on an old shirt and sold it to the Getty for $13 million.) I *suppose* to be a painter requires remaining passive before experience and then connecting the consequently induced mood of composition to the enforced homogeneity of viewer response and voilà you have the history of the essential copy in a fake Giotto courtesey the Pre-Raphaelite Brotherhood. The *thought* of such a radical transmogrification of that pious man from Bondone into William Holman Hunt reflects an *adieu* turned cannibal in the sweet and *sour* sauce of bodies and appearances. "I" truly is a universal emptiness, an "it" before death manifests. Ergo Death is a *you* the *hour* I becomes an it. Does a philosophy of language *require* me to *spend* time on claims like these? Can't I just say forget the speaker and enter the indifferent murmur of the one who is multiple, so that as "we" one remains an "I" equipped with operating machines of *desire* ad infinitum? Fact is I *tend* to avoid authentic mis en abymes.[2] I *tend* to overemphasize a *desire* to start work on my own Manhattan Project, at the same time ruminating on that other philosophical conundrum: that to construct a dialog is not the same as to dialogize a construction. Everybody in this phuqingue Palace of Pshit knows that I started off as the official number one soliloquist. "Look yonder, love, what solemn spectre through the copse doth buzz? A bee or not a bee? 'Tis blotter blank, a blend *spend* butter bat but swooning, switched and blind amid the open stands away?" Perhaps it is, but I'll *require* a radical change in my lexicon to convince anyone (other than myself) that I'm the number one Viking Sophist. In fact, this conversation with myself is getting quite thanasimonic, setting off the spell check but offering no alternatives. The final *hour* may come and go but messianic nightmares don't get *you* away from the philosophy of Schweppenhauser. Perhaps I should allow my post-industrial prophecies to shine forth in plain style admitting the *sour* truth that the only viable function for poetry, understood as the least tolerable departure from linguistic norms, is a heterological confrontation with itself. So bid *adieu* to the *thought* of the ones who *suppose* an optimistic sonnet-productivity graph's still feasible. Art happens when *nothing* happens and *those* non-events *will* cause a shiver in the category masterpiece. Vincent Kaufmann told me over coffee that angels, being beautiful children who never become corpses never age, however, what I'll need in my cemetery is revolutionary dissymmetry. It's an *ill* tenet to maintain that whenever a prince becomes a corpse it's possible to breathe entirely in the abstract. Oh oh, here comes the ingrowing toenail.

1. And what a girl she is! I overheard Hamlet telling Lady Bracknell's handbag that each time he kisses her it feels as if their souls are fusing. It's probably saliva exchange muttered the handbag before closing itself.
2. Here's an interesting fact to ponder while you're listening to this garrulous non-entity. Edible Charms were common in Tibet and ancient India. Known as Za-yings they related to the cure of disease. The charms consisted of mystically revealed seed-syllables (biji mantra) and were written with specially prepared inks. The Atharva Veda lists many receipes for preparing edible charms. Now back to that interminable monlog.

Enter Polonius.

Hornstrumpot! It's all *well* and good to celebrate logocentricity but *hell*, you approach a calligram the way a tortoise would a whale, (albeit with a slightly more Aztec emphasis on the physical). Cult or conclusion it's just the same in this middle-world where all the children remain criteria. Turning to cosmetics I think it's a *crime* to throw away those temporary lips after you've kissed Ophelia. However, such an observation on contemporary rubberware does not *belong* to our present plan for more theatrical funerals. By the *time* we've worked those out we'll need a tunnel of Babel to satisfy all our rhizomatic inclinations. I've a *strong* conviction that a knowledge of causality isn't the proper solution and that embarrassing *injury* (or was it accident) when I fell in the royal manure sure left me feeling despondent. I know soap's great but I didn't think I'd become hygienic again overnight and now I truly feel like the new me. That said, I've given up tiling my patio of hope, it's *check*-out time in this old supermarket as you finally find out who shot *Liberty* Valance and Bob Hope steps in at the *beck* and call of some minor deity named Jerry Junior who claims he's the head of the local Ton-Ton Macute. That said, it could be worse than this scary existence in Realpolitik, what this place needs is a political enema and a lot less sophistry. I mean there's hermeneutics and my meneutics (it's always that way with that slut the Queen, when she's around you need the ventricals of a Boris Yeltsin to get yourself heard). Call me paranoid but indigestion is more than sufficient proof that the true enemy always comes from within, and given my own dephlogisticated lifestyle (as a minor politician without survival skills) factored into the rampant Pyrrhonism around here, I'm going to make sure I don't stick my nose behind another courtier's arras. Facsimile fascism aside, the confrontation of nothing with eternity seems an appropriate meditation for a convalescent ex-Jesuit existentialist like me. It'll promote an active life predominantly devoted to *leisure* and sleep. I turn black and cold when I think of current theories of the upper class that emphasize the "life is good" scenario as being exclusively designed for the richer-than-rich. What I really *crave* is a non-aggression pact between zero and nothing and the *pleasure* arising from terminal intellectual exhaustion at the end of the project of knowledge. In Hegelian dénouements the *slave* completes the master, which reminds me of your own astonishing career. From sex *slave* in the basement of the Elsinore Club to Prince of Denmark! That's quite a peripetia di fortuna (to quote my old pal Mussolini) and a sheer *pleasure* to think on. I myself *crave* the stability of some medieval guild organization and the *leisure* of aesthetic contemplation granted by art history to its central protagonist—Clement Greenberg. As it is, I'm constantly at the *beck* and call of my integrated modernism without the *liberty* to *check* out the full range of enterprise retail solutions or to recalculate my massive gains from insider trading. Pain does not grimace[1] and, maugre our malapert alliance, I still think we agree that suffering is the best way Romance stays alive. The complexity of my latest *injury* grants the curious a peephole-show. In fact in these conditions my upper extremities could happen overnight. It's already midnight in my lower back and you stand there looking like the Man from Glad. I remember the time before this white on white when I was as *strong* as the last of the living psychopomps. For the *time* being, however, I *belong* to an apocalypse without transfiguration, trapped in some *crime* committed in the *hell* hole of Nineteenth-Century German Philosophy. But all's *well* that ends penetrated by the same unknown.

1. Cocteau.

Exeunt

"A poet cannot but be gay"
Wordsworth !!!

Enter Prince and Poinze.
Do you have a diversified portfolio or are you homosexual like the rest of us around here? I was actually told that being queer at court was a phase one grows out of maturing into the healthy kind of bisexuality that William Empson perfected and Walt Disney mislaid. In your case, however, given all your visits to professional ladyboys in the Mattachine Society's basement, it seems more a case of "buy" than "bi." In my case, I'm happy to say, orgasm remains a strictly philosophical event—so meet a legend in his own bedroom. You should join me and *praise* debauchery as the continuation of Christmas by other means—and don't forget, these *days* our lives needn't eliminate the *same*

additional felicities that Epicurus enjoyed. It's not the end of the world to part with human rights, so instead of getting beneath those satin sheets as active as a vermilion lump of complacency, why don't we get up, get dressed and cast off the look of two solitary worlds? You can be the blind Samson to my Sean Connery and our joint exploits, like mother's sprout and cauliflower wine, will be tastier than nitroglycerine with double the effect. *They* tell me you're never alone when you're a nomad so why not go it solo through the otium dignitati of it all? In passing from opposites to apposites we might *frame* those desirability ratios in a more humble ectoplasm and eventually learn to obey the smell of others. I once heard Regis Philbin *say* that life will be less expensive when we're dead, but when all be said and *done* to die and enter literature, become a *book* read in the *sun* by a reader whose *look* turns towards the horizon of absolute knowledge as Hegel's was might augur the *child* will survive.[1] God however, has proven to be the complete opposite to Hegel, if you dictate a description to her she'll make it real instantly, her favorite cocktail being nonsense on the rocks. Would it be *amiss* to honor at least an interruption already reappearing in the lattice of words, *beguiled* as we are by the indisputable density that language *is*? I'm afraid yours *is* a love more unrequested than unrequited and being *beguiled* by the increasing infant mortality rates barely pancakes the next meal. So I guess it wouldn't be *amiss* to finally put together that *child* anthology of mortuary verse. Now that sounds original and would *look* fitting in our portrait gallery of crib deaths. I know Martyrologies aren't the best way of bringing up a child, but they sure helped me develop a strong hope in an afterlife. Death seems pure terror in those Endings of the Saints. (How beautiful the labor of a journey in the wrong direction![2]) Mind you, it'll take a bucketful of Neo-Platonism to help me survive in the Paradise to come. It's been so dark in here I haven't known who I am (let alone count the spots on my dominoes) but now that the *sun* threatens to rise we should hurry back to our coffins steering clear of this human birdcage you duped us in. As a celebrity vampire and founding President of the Bram Stoker Society, I've a natural preference for boxes over cages. In fact I've never cared for zoos, they're a little too close to life in the Civil Service. I once thought of writing a Vampire's Guide to Paleo-Gnosticism among the Knights Templar but then I realized nothing dies quicker than a good *book*. These days paper publishing's become the most efficient way to those open mass-graves known as the remainder tables. If truth be told I've always preferred a good used bandage to a good new paperback. I think it cool and okay to be a Dracula gone vernacular if you're a night person but, being albino, I prefer day even though it ushers in the totalitarian nightmare of waking up. Survival proves difficult, I know, but when you're *done* with simplicity as I am you realize that the power of the difficult lies in its catalytic propensity to induce the unworkable. Some *say* that historicity casts no shadows to *frame* the ethics of the antisocial, *they* also opine the *same* about epidemiologists in tracksuits. These *days* History gives dates to faces but what does it mean to face a date? With nothing to *praise* but a decline in detours the time has come to put in our earplugs then plug in our dreams.

1. Aw, come off it! I mean what's Hegel other than Heraclitus plus the Absolute?
2. "How beautiful the labor of doing a job in the wrong medium." (Gaudier-Brzeska on the sculpture of Fabrucci.)

Enter Falstaffe.
I woke up this morning believing myself to have become a fatal accident and I sure wish that had been the case. There's nothing like a grey, damp sky to keep you in touch with your pessimism, more so than night with its glitzy evocation of the Jonsonian anti-masque and the symbolic role of midnight in its courtly agit prop. Oh, by the way, that severed *hand* you sent me from the mortuary arrived in first class condition. I'll let it *stand* in the air to dry for a few weeks before having it reattached and in the interim *mow* down with my one hand a dozen more sociological platitudes such as "Death cancels everything but *truth.*"[1] Think what Mina Loy achieved bent over with a furrowed *brow* writing in the Laboratory of the Word, that gal pulled off mass-scale linguistic hygiene. As for me, I'll take my next bath in the raw sewage of Utopia (from the verb "to utope" I believe) before I take the blind alley to the precipice. But I guess Utopia's better than no place at all. If we each admit that life's become a tragedy in a continuous present and that Death only deals in friendly takeovers then suddenly our galaxy will seem collectible. Don't worry, with *youth* no longer on my side, and being pretty well ballasted with bull beef, I've every right to be wrong. But practical matters still *confound* me. For instance, how to live my life according to Hegel's last words,[2] it's an incurable defect in my biopsychic

92

equilibrium but it offers some safeguard in my *fight* against the Barthesian model of the "writerly." *Crowned* with *light* this pot of tulips belongs properly between truth and knowledge. After such a claim it might be wrong to *contend* that food is a preparation for consumption, but I'll do it anyway knowing accuracy is positioned outside the moment that this is. I can't wait to die and join Josef Stalin and Bob Marley in Heaven and listen to my final words[3] but it's probably better *before* the *end* does come to *shore* these figments against my ruin as Ezra Pound advised. What a ghastly work his Waste Land is, an oily heap of schitte penned during one of his horrible interbellum depressions, it would have been far better for him to wait a couple of decades and then ruminate on the moral role of paperclips[4] at the Nuremberg trials until finally pushing off from *shore* in the good ship Rigor Mortis. His Muse might have improved by the *end* of the trip and opened up a passage to show Sparta at sunrise above three scenes by Alcman. But *before* I depart there's one more thing to *contend* with—that final battle of self-conversion from being a singer of *light* ballads into an independent legend. *Crowned* as an overweight replica of Justin Bieber I could launch a *fight* to *confound* death with "never say never" yelled out of pitch. Good luck, what I want is to end up as the last *youth* on the moon in virtual skin and—with a *brow* turned to proving that a shadow is a solid thing— perhaps *truth* will return and *mow* down the demiurge of the new hermeneutics. In fact it might be gratifying to *stand* head in *hand* in a painting by Artemisia Gentileschi and throw it smiling straight at the Grand Design.[5]

1. Hazlitt on Byron.
2. "Only one man ever understood me ... and even he didn't understand me."
3. "All the elegies end here."
4. A seemingly Victorian invention, the first recorded appearance in print is 1875.
5. Ms Gentileschi's preoccupation with this morbid theme and her related promotion of mytho-heroic female figures may be indulged in Mary D. Garrard's *Artemisia Gentileschi. The Image of the Female Hero in Italian Baroque Art*. Princeton: Princeton University Press, 1989.

Exeunt omnes

Scene 9. *Enter Macbeth's Wife, and a Servant.*

The birth of money and the birth of history coincided in 747 BCE when Pheidon marched to the games at Olympia and coined the first copper and silver money in Aegina, thereby establishing the Pheidonian measure. That said, according to Pierre Vernant, the pursuit of wealth as the dominant paradigm of action appears with the advent of the Iron Age—not that knowing these two facts helps pay the rent. Ever noticed how the city grows much quicker than our salaries? With a little effort poverty can be in the reach of everybody. Having to sell my blood and sperm to meet my alimony payments warrants a soliloquy of philosophical pathos, unfortunately Hamlet's not around. I've always thought this metropolis marks the tension in our fiscal logic but it's a consolation having your good self and your poetics *near* at hand. However an experience of language being language in your latest piece of epic doggerel places yours truly *elsewhere* on the south side of semiology. Non-scientific truth is the indeterminate knot emerging in the interaction of epistemological structures with poetic assemblages—that's how poems know themselves. I used to think poetry was the completion of metaphysics in its catastrophe, the construction of lyrical aporias that repudiate the master themes. Now I know poetry reminds us of everything we'd like to forget, but for the *sake* of argument let's say poetry is only language as it happens. Pre-engineered for maximum collateral damage to its readers it is the infinite child of caprice and departure. Charles Bukowski equates the poet's asshole with his imagination, so perhaps we should snatch victory from *defeat* by writing a poem or two with realistic scenarios pertaining to bowel movements—as I'm told he did—if nothing else it should keep us *awake* a few more hours. When does "I" become a proper name? Perhaps when it's part of making heroes not creating them? But why does one have to die to become a hero? A day never passes without the esteemed heroine of the Scottish play asking some *great* question that she can't answer. I know deep throat interrogation figures large in your dossier of insurgences but *jealousy* provokes *me* to *pry* into your mind and find out why *you* know so much. The *sight* of the tanks in Damascus make meaning fly above Exhedra's rooftops, sliding doors to automata and *broken* promises. However, with sex, glamour and a mother named Donatella I'm sure your *night* will stay the color of caramel. I remain disposed to "magnitude-towards-a-goal-across-dead/effort" sort of things, in other words I'm afraid my hopes are less an *open* door. I'd be *open* to a game of Russian roulette right now but being a nervous reader of Euripides I'll settle for a different pedantic pleasure. I'm sure too that with a little carbon monoxide therapy each *night* we could quit breathing for good. Those *broken* promises of Projective Verse about the ear's duty to the heart turn my lucubrations to the *sight* of some invincible pansy caught up in a ménage à douze. Three cheers for the pleasures of the scopic. *You* can never go wrong with a good Tintoretto or Masaccio's north wall of the Brancacci Chapel seen from beneath the west window. But may I *pry* on your thoughts with another question? Must the fundamental optic order of a conventional bounded image carry the observer to an imaginary relationship with reality orientation? It seems to *me* the central challenge is to fuse *jealousy* and technological advancement with social responsibility then afterwards wallpaper the room with some *great* William Morris Guild Socialist floral pattern. But then what? Death still remains the nocturnal name of the being that is negative excess and nothing keeps a wife *awake* like the hope that death constitutes the *defeat* of the temporal. Less optimistically, eternity might be a jammed turnstile or an empty parking lot, but for the *sake* of being *elsewhere* let's forget about the *near* and familiar and build a sepulcher over the sadness of those November roses in Milan.

Exeunt

Enter Macbeth.

So whadder-ye-think of my brand new toupé de jour with its point de fuite focused on the end of the species? Clausewitz got it right, war sure is the most popular of the world's insanities and after my quick survey of all the current carnage and poverty, I find there's little to celebrate these *days*. It all makes me feel on a par with a Frenchman who's caught his best baguette in his bicycle spokes. *Praise* be to the hegemony of the catastrophic, in fact God must have been a schizophrenic to come up with a world like this. Those guys down south hold me to be the most irritating being north of Hadrian's Wall and, given my own penchant for assassination and *iniquity*, I'm sure it comes as no surprise that I always identify with Satan each time I'm made to *read*

Paradise Lost. Milton's such a great poet and he couldn't see a thing. It's quite an achievement to be blind as a bat and still be able to write—and think of the money you save on electricity and light bulbs or oil-lamps and candles if you're stuck like me in some backwater of Scottish *antiquity*. *Indeed* it's necessary to *surmount* traditional concepts of disability and *define* new uses for decrepitude as it bolsters ontology as the disappearing subject. To take *account* of my own disability I have to admit that I was born with a mind that was never destined to think. I was pathetic in everything I planned. That's why I've always pitied poor Saint Jude, I mean, if you're the patron saint of hopeless cases like *mine* then you can't answer anyone's prayers by pulling off a spectacular miracle. I suppose you get used to saintly failure and call on a resolute *heart* to explain to those pathetic sufferers there's not a *remedy* in sight. A large *part* of hagiography intimates an heroic tenacity to live audaciously, in the manner of Saint Stephen for instance, pleading for larger stones at his lapidation. But shouldn't I really be meditating on morbid genius, Mozart perhaps, composing under the constant fantasy of being pursued by Husserlian killer dwarfs from La Belle Epoque (each one of them named Fritz), or on the insignificance of silence in solar death as seen by Georges Bataille's enucleated *eye*? An equivalent question arises from the sight of the yellow marble disc in the center of the nave in San Ignazio. The *eye* is carried to a *part* of its architecture that offers a sacred *remedy* to the current scarcity of farm houses and plaid windmills in the Highlands. Like God and globalization that nave is everywhere and nowhere. Then, at the *heart* of the all-in-all, an ineffable force offers il grande non-infinito to a faith on vacation. Faith's okay, if it's out-sourced, but *mine* deserted me as soon as my rake's progress was cut short in an Aberdeen massage parlor. My parents were both grammatically correct and theoretically non-veridical, in fact, you couldn't tell them apart. Then came the poetic detonation of their disappearance when I was born before I was born, not into birth, but as the idea of birth. I grew up believing Christ died an atheist and that body and soul were Siamese twins joined at their paradox: the mind. However in my *account* of onto-eschatology I couldn't *define* the way death always calibrates community. Presbyterians like me are taught to *surmount* doubt by believing the body is the soul's hotel, but if Plotinus got it right the body is *indeed* within the soul: plura diafana.[1] [Ed. There are ghosts of philosophers from *antiquity* in this speech disguised as ambiguity and polysemia, they are to be *read* against the grain and never twice and they will castigate the *iniquity* of the prophetic voice in any *praise* of a democratic inheritance that architecturally builds its Hell for other people. Jacta alea est via the thoughts of Mallarmé.] A smile from glittering teeth might help but it seems that dental hygiene is no longer feasible in these *days* of shark-infested mouthwash made by Bernie Madoff.

1. Attributed by Marcus Aurelius to Epictetus.

Enter Ophelia.

Let's see, where am I, ah yes. Pregnant and betrayed! No, that's a line from the next act. Ah, here we are. [Coughs.] The negativity of miracles surrounds a love turned *green*, but *seen* a little differently it promises a matrimonial death to most of the human race. The *life* of the wilder type of primordial germ cell might survive, but if *memory* doesn't betray me, the contemporary fusion of democracy with monstrosity in a suture legalized by biopolitics will bring a new dawn to the deeds of Gilles de Rais.[1] A *knife* cuts knowledge into segments in order to analyze the morality of evil, but does it *fortify* my claim to the transdisciplinary? To *spring* a proverb on you I might say that the freest tree is always hidden in the densest forest. Lenin in Zurich. The brief *sight* of such a past caught in some modality of the moment makes each presence as transitory as the *King* of France's the *night* before the revolution. So go I then this *morn* to the *brow* of some event and sing of cooked meals in the marshlands or other precise culinary coordinates as *over-worn now* as language is. Speaking of which I feel truly sorry for concepts (especially the ones I dated). I mean, look what happened to deconstruction when it turned up on a late-night weather report. "Hegemony" used to be my favorite cliché closely followed by "agency" but *now* it's "diaspora," "no problem" and "whatever." I'm afraid other people's temporary is my permanent[2] and I refuse to be suffocated beneath such *over-worn* pseudomorphoses.[3] In fact, after tweezering my way through twenty-four consecutive volumes of early Aristotle I'm so bored my *brow*'s disappeared into it's a-soul and I'm ready for that legendary fall from grace. After all, the *morn* is not new and so, inept and insubstantially, let's walk at *night* the hodos basiliere together,[4] a *king* and his companion transcribed along a plexus of

97

two opposites: our speech and this earth. The *sight* of a cougar ready to *spring* out upon its prey should *fortify* my recollections of a better life in the analysis of sites not magnitudes. Unfortunately that large *knife* called a guillotine that awaits me is but a *memory* of a former *life* to come again as soon as I admit to being constantly mistaken for Marie Antoinette. Remember, a sentence is not an institution for reference, therefore the hill *seen* in the distance will not be *green* but culpable and erratic in the sleep that's always guilty for the one who dreams.

1. It's not surprising that a pervert like Georges Bataille, with his own brand of vigilant depravity, would be fascinated by the pederastic slaughters that Rais perpetrated. If you're a psychiatrist, you can probably blame it on his being a lieutenant to that other Nietzschean bozo Joan of Arc.
2. Courtesy the mind of Karen Mac Cormack.
3. For more on this poetic term see Oswald Spengler's *Decline of the West*, trans. Charles Atkinson. New York: Alfred Knopf, 1926: II. 189.
4. Royal Road.

Exeunt

> … the lack of necessity that is
> at the heart of the sonnet.
>
> Ron Silliman

Scene 10. *Enter Clowne and Audrey.*
Sweet maid, what grief has changed your roseate grace, and quenched the vernal sunshine of your face? No more your light form sparkles as it flies, nor laughter flushes from your radiant eyes.[1] Yea, yea, I love you too but spare me the crappy verse. Paul Valéry insisted that a poem must be a holiday of the mind, but the ones I read instantly require a tour guide and even then bring on a migraine. Ezra Pound judged Dante's greatest achievement to be his perfecting of the common language, so explain to me why we end up with ass hauls like Mallarmé, Gertrude Stein and that near-sighted Irishman with halitosis and bad teeth who wrote Finnegans Wake? (I can't imagine a life as the narrative voice in that compound labyrinth of verbal pschytt. Attempts at reading it make me feel and look like Marcel Marceau trapped in a food blender and it sure proves to me that the only

means to obtain pleasure is by hating it.) You won't *lose* your academic reputation by arguing that the sonnet is an epic poem after liposuction, in fact claims like that are all the rage right now at Princeton and, on a practical note, with all that fatty narrative removed you'll have a tight, wrinkle-free lyric for your next explication de texte. But *choose* your method with care. The fact that we're caught up here in the shards of sonnets makes me think we should develop our own poetics of deletion. The death of the sonnet, however, is an exhausted subject, we are each and everyone one's own Jokespierre. The shift from stylization to vivissimo involved a reemergent interest in curiosity and mechanics but that sure ain't the case with these horrendous fourteen-liners. What I find most suffocating in his sonnets is the dreary monolog going on for 2066 lines and a total of 17, 599 words, it makes me want to jump into last week's episode of Antiques Roadshow and steal Martha Washington's butter churn from that nice white haired lady from Cleveland. James Merrill actually deployed a poetics of the anti-masque in his Changing Light at Sandover, but he didn't prove God to be an astronaut as most readers wanted. (The failure of poetry resides ineluctably in the contingent ephemerality of the one who walks *away*.) Despite the fact that propositions truly are the serpents in the Grammar of Eden, it's prose alone can put an elevator in this Tower of Babel. Incidentally, we could be less than a day from the advent of post-mortemism and we'll need a new genre for that—a splendid possibility to *ruminate* as we check through the various handbooks on *decay*. Origin is a vanishing point—and every infant proves it; in a collision of chiastic rhymes we're born to scream politely at God then pass away into nothingness. To *state* the obvious we're as impermanent as a virginity in the Vatican. We've gone the way of vinyl records, back to the boomerang baguettes we forgot to eat. Even ambiguity's ceased to be ambiguous, a face slams into the front of a *store* in the final caesura of its *main* window and on a distant *shore* a group of puzzled tourists *gain* a platitude by way of compensation. *Rage* as much as you like, the stakes stay *raised* to maximum collateral annihilation. I think I'll try counting my blessings. That didn't take long, best in this *age* to say a prayer to Thérèse Cabarrus, Our Lady of Thermidor while the defeated are *defaced* by some baby commissar of terror tending the dying with a whip while we two remain the conspiracy of equals at the end of metaphor. I love the way I think, flooding my poetics with the fear of death. In fact, I could be the Albert

Einstein of the Dead if the Poetry Foundation of this *defaced age* endorsed it. All my errors have been my teachers and that's why I've done well for myself in this slaughterhouse of wisdom. I was *raised* to believe in ultimate forgiveness and a practical theology of instantaneous infinity by way of spontaneous combustion. (Faith always rejoices in the nude.) Most Modernists spend their lives in some *rage* for chaos and don't equate their lives with the sinuous formality of the sonnet. I mean you don't *gain* much from fragmentation other than more shards to *shore* against yours and others ruin. The *main* thing to gain from reading T. S. Eliot is a clear understanding of the difference between a fake and a forgery. Let's collect up all our optimisms and *store* them away in that terra cotta pyxis you stole from the Hagia Sophia. There's strata to repragmatize among the numinous innumerable right down to the last incommensurate tick. The demons remain active but at least the monster's gone; that's not such a terrible *state* of affairs, so better leave *decay* to those psychogeographers of compost to *ruminate* upon. Let's pack up and move *away* from that species of middle one calls place.[2] We can *choose* a post-Euclidean landing-site together. Perhaps the preface to The Hampstead Annual, or Henry Olerich's Story of the World a Thousand Years Hence, or perhaps we can dine out for eternity at Lascaux upon the auroch captured there in the Magdalenian ekphrasis. Whatever the choice there'll be ample time and opportunity to *lose* sight of the fact that the breath of finality is finally a language to find it.

1. Venus to Pasithea in Book 33 of Nonnus' *Dionysica*.
2. An interim thought on the districts we live in.

Exeunt

End of Act II

Death is like taking your thumb
out of a bowl of soup;
it has to leave a hole, but it doesn't.
                              Djuna Barnes

Act III Scene 1 *Enter Lady Macbeth, and a Servant.*

You remember the post-historical?   What a *bright* weekend that turned
into, played entirely on the epistemic side of events with our crisis calendars
jammed to capacity. In fact there's been nothing like it since Rob Roy sat on
a thistle. Having successfully eluded all the pro-life prosopopoeia, missed
fornication by inches and successfully bypassing the late Bronze Age, I became
trapped among the more sordid international priority airmail scandals and
ended up being forcefully re-directed through Glasnost into the full *might* of a
British tank division described in volume six of Winston Churchill's Collected
War Correspondence; it felt as if I was entering Saturday on a toothbrush.
Then there were those cocktail seminars with Noel Coward circa 1941 and the
hidden synapse in a dictator's moustache, (in those days death was a monster
out of Germany).[1] Heaven *forbid* that era of maximizing corpses returning via
that frightening chorus of jackboots in Beethoven's Moonlight Gestapo. But
suppose we colonize a different concept than death and think *back* to some
optimistic sentiment *hid* in the bonfires of paganism? From "*alack*" to "ahoy"
it still pertains that communication cannot be authority but only experience.[2]
Burt Bacharach once told me all felicitous experience *decays* if placed in a
non-synchronic adjacency to fairgrounds, but that was before he wrote "Walk
on By" and after my ephemeral headache in the Adirondaks. Disintegration's
reserved for the *stout* of heart (like him) so why don't we talk about the
weather? A Santa Ana would be quite the thing in the Highlands where these
days the not-yet to be is already here. But what about you? Now I've given you
a uniform you've got the authority to hurt people. As custodian to a pile of

worn-*out* insights I'd say it must be humid in your part of the galaxy. You must feel like a daffodil forced to come up in February next to the broken *flower*-de-luce that says it all: one stage, a single spectacle, another coup de plume. I'm heading back to the Eastern Front to avoid all *plea* bargains and I'm never saying "fooled ya" to the *power* of the *sea*. The unpredictability of *sea power* puts me in mind of quantum hydraulics in the middle ages before perspective was reinvented by Giotto.—The Assyrians used a huge water catapult quite successfully at the Siege of Khartoum. Did I tell you that I once came down with a severe bout of Mrs. Oliphant and had to live her life for three decades? And quite the lady: spotty, intelligent and a satanic tactician with negligible description. Membership has its own privileges but if I was caught in some late-Victorian Salon with her I think I'd render a *plea* of dispossession through insanity. She has one image in a novel of a *flower* clutched in the hand of a dying infant that became a Victorian icon,[3] but she never found *out* that Death's greatest pleasure is always to carry you to a final laugh.[4] The obituaries are as fat as the Manhattan Yellow Pages these *days*, but theological doctrine tells us that *stout* hearted people who believe in God shouldn't worry about death as ultimately nothing but the body *decays*. I say alas and *alack* to such a fragile reassurance, in fact it's hard to believe in a next life when you don't even believe in this one. Fear's always there, *hid* and lurking at the *back* door of our hesitations and death induces fear alright. However, Maurice Blanchot frightens less with fear itself than with the solitude of fright. Heaven *forbid* a visit from him in your sleep, in fact it *might* help if we stay on the *bright* side of things and pay attention to Shakispere's last words. "Mehr licht" he said in an age when light meant laughter.

1. A deliberate misquote of Paul Celan (Death is a Master out of Germany).
2. Georges Bataille once more.
3. The flower not the child.
4. I must say the dead seem quite alive in Dante's *Inferno*. What a place to end up. Far worse than a vegetarian forced to work in a salami emporium, worse even than watching a rerun of some classic golf tournament hosted by Tiger Woods—and well beyond the reach of the Red Cross.

Enter Duke and Provost.
It may sound a bit Pre-Raphael "itic" but when I'm *alone* I lose the power to

write the word "I." Solitude pushes my lyrical proclivities into hibernation. In truth, when you're *gone* life becomes a city without writing and this way writing cannot cease to speak what my hand which doesn't write resists. I may be an *ill* chosen leftover from some Trotskyite jazz quartet but the *simplicity* of sadness is best experienced by two, that's why the couplet's *skill* consistently rhymes a dual *authority* in my tenement of *disabled* poetics. I'd feel *disgraced*, however, if I appeared to myself as the place where something is going on[1] like some ex-nun *strumpeted* out to the current devaluation of agency as a product of a *misplaced* nexus of urban sexual necessities. Even if you do leave me I'll still be *foresworn* to kindred *jollity* and laughter, committed to the one truth that ever really matters: that as soon as we're *born* we're old enough to *cry*. I didn't hear you *cry* (with disbelief) when I told you that Katrina is the most popular name for baby girls in New Orleans right now—and while we're on the subject of names only parents *born* in Three Mile Creek would call a child Kermit. (Even NASA named their first space-monkeys Cain and Abel.) As Adam and Dr. Johnson both knew there's a certain *jollity* pertains to defining, but to name a being is a sentence to community. We both knew we were sent here for a purpose other than lexicography, perhaps we're the reincarnations of Buddha and Bob Dylan, *foresworn* to piety and folksongs respectively, *misplaced* in a cab ride to charisma, then *strumpeted* out to the highest bidder who only manifests in sudden happy places. "Nomina sunt consequentia rerum" as Aquinas keeps reminding us, its other names are shopping malls and condominiums and all the other *disgraced* boutique-urban imperatives. But now that we've finally *disabled* the syntax of the sphinx we can evade all the *authority* of the Law of the Father and develop the *skill* of sheer *simplicity* in a highly complex fashion. For instance, although *ill* will is an effective antidote to catharsis it won't be useful when the anonymity of genocide has finally *gone*. It seems our form of the future will be a dead-end start and it leaves us *alone* to take a less than optimistic approach to the retreat of Being as twilight licks the fat from both our beards.

1. Claude Levi Strauss.

Exeunt

Scene 2. *Enter Oberon and Puck.*

Now I'm stoned again on catnip I'm dying to make my bedsprings sound like the Halleluiah Chorus so any chance of a sefirotic intimacy for two? After all, happiness appears to be the most subtle form of revenge, no? I understand we're siblings in flexibility but too *bad* you prefer aphaeresis to apocope, via "the you" I fear the burden of speech has entered the written, but it doesn't alter our credit ratings. We wear Freudian slips the way Sumo wrestlers wear bikinis, one meaning barely covers the genitals while the other discretely conceals our dictionary definitions.[1] But reaction has always been the world I never live in, which prompts me to remember your maneuvers in that text-book tournament to the death you *had* with Saint Pancras just before his beatification. With all those blitzkrieg strategies he employed and, despite the *gains* obtained from *his* miraculous powers and pin-point targeting, he didn't stand a chance against your spirit of passive resistance. That was in the days when martyrdom really meant something—(we all preferred a good crucifixion or burning to a visit to Casino Niagara). You thought because his name was "Pancreas" he was the patron saint of diabetics; all eyes were on that misprision right through the Byzantine era and up to the emergence of early Fauvism. Your errors however are always another's erotics and without life all our mistakes would be music, although we still smell fear through borrowed noses and the *veins* in our nostrils remain clogged. Ahi esta el punto respondido Don Quijote, the trick *is* to make the nasty things look even nastier, for instance it would be a *true* lapse in decorum if you invented a way to gamahouche a gramophone[2]—at which point you might *seek* a parallel way to corroborate my perfection with a little more of your own diachronic uncertainty. The *hue* and cry of its governing epistemes can still be heard in the fractal inducements upon each anecdote. All of this makes poetry simpler than computer programming. I mean if you turn your *cheek* away from the hecklings of polite *society* there'll be nothing that a fairy poet can't *achieve*. You'll realize that poetics give you poems that stay poems and you can pun until your nose drips accidental noise. However the danger of the poet to the poet has always been to erect a transcendental position from which to comment on the indefinable immanence that defines her. It may be sheer *impiety* to *live* a life among the non-intentions of the act that writes it, but to *live* "a life" not as "alive" might be the alliterative way to face le rire savant des morts.[3] Forgive the lapse into French and forgive that *impiety* but I'd love to kill Modernist eschatologies with a short burst of historical unavailability; that said, your idea of the Chinese Written Character as a Medium for Modern Braille sounds brilliant. Think what you could *achieve* in disability break-throughs—all the accolades that would come your way from the *Society* for Blind Foot and Mouth Painters if you could capture the three-dimensionality of Basho's frog, touch the three warts on its left *cheek*, and caress the delicate *hue* thrown on the back of its throat in a three-dimensional ideogram![4] "Mehr wasser!" you imagine it croaking as it plops to its death in the latest translation by Stephen King.[5] If you want to *seek* a *true* way to my affections what you might do *is* place your lips on the *veins* of my left hand, although I'd prefer it if you kissed my evacuation route. Boris Pasternak did three years ago to the day and it won him *his* Nobel Prize. But the poet always *gains* the upper hand he never *had* and always remains the supreme contortionist of language, which maybe a tad faisandé but not a *bad* way to evade the more carboniferous layers in contemporary writing. Oops here comes Homo Erectus between two chess pieces and with a crown on its head.

1. King: n. 1 male sovereign (esp. hereditary) ruler of independent state. Fairy: adv. In adj. senses; utterly, completely, (fairy beside himself); considerably (fairy narrow); acceptably (fairy good); actually (fairy jumped for joy).
2. For more on this subject see Charles Grivel, "The Phonograph's Horned Mouth" in *Wireless Imagination: Sound, Radio, and the Avant-Garde*, eds. Douglas Kahn and Gregory Whitehead. Cambridge, Mass.: The MIT Press, 1994.
3. Why is it that St. Jean Perse gets all the great phrases?
4. Point taken, but imagine what would happen with *Finnegans Wake*? It would be the equivalent to reading a cheese grater in a circle.
5. "I wish that poem had been a little longer and without that disappointing plop at the end. With a little more skill and imagination the frog might have turned out to be a lapsed pantheist or some reincarnation of Empedocles dressed as Matthew Arnold." William Empson, in an unpublished letter to Gilbert Ryle (now in the author's possession).

Enter Richard aloft between two Bishops.
In days of *yore* one read Spinoza in order to fall in love, despite the smell of noise from the camp's incinerator.[1] These days however, there's not much in

store for the fate of reading, although I'm sure some *new* generation will come along committed to the fact that it's only the typos that make reading a pleasure. Facts no longer conciliate because nothing's certain these days. They say that in Hollywood Time flies by wearing a genuine diamond watch, but how do you prove it? Do you really lose weight by vomiting? I'd eat an acre of *green* artichokes and throw up if it were *true*. I'm also told that sodomy normally occurs between two consenting adults but in my dictionary it occurs between a sociologist and a sophomore. There's something odd about a word list *seen* from the viewpoint of a lapsed sonneteer. Perhaps it's best to close all books and stay on the *gay* side of a smile that's moving to that scream of Edward Munch's. Without texts we can *head* back to infancy where the world is everything that is before we are. Granted, that's a positive conceit only for a body without becoming, but at least it gets us *away* from the age of the revival of thinking via internet access and closer to where the *dead* comedian meets laughter in a grimace. Moreover, the fact that separation of Church from State naturally invokes the complicity of politics with theology through the foundational commonality of values and concepts makes me want to catalytically convert to Anabaptism. But when Moses carved the ten commandments he made sure each contained a pun. Who knows, in the spirit of les enfants perdu, we may stay baby Dadaists for life taking poems out of the bowler hats perched on the *brow* of the sestina squad that apprehends us. Despite the fact that we both hate musicals perhaps we'll be *born* again Christians forced into listening to an eighteenth-floor oratorio spewed out by a fat diva from Coral Gables with tonsillitis singing like she had piles and with her mouth detached from her dentures before an audience of unskilled factory workers. I'm happy to enter the Republic of the Deaf, thank you very much *now* that the Sound of Music rings through the palace corridors with its *outworn* family sentiments, sung by a chorus of Swiss mountaineers with goitered necks. Sorry Bishop did you say a "Göethered knock" or a "goatherd Nick?" My hearing's not as good as it used to be, *outworn* by the decibels of organ music you order played in church it seems my ears have quit the civilization of the audible. *Now* that I think of it, *born* into the pratfalls of linguistic disjunction, I've lost all desire for any wish at all. The *brow* on a *dead* species of syzygy light years *away* makes me think of the reason why we always *head* to the latest hermeneutic fallacy, a *gay* itinerary when *seen* from the vantage of Lippo Memmi's infant Christ. It's comforting to know that Death is always happy to help the living, and thereby to the *true* conversion of *green* turf into a brand *new* coffin for words. An epitaph remains the excuse for having lived but what's in *store* for we false prophets trapped in the letter O[2] a year before *yore* in the tables of destiny? Hang on, here comes another weirdo with a crown on.

1. See T. S. Eliot, "The Metaphysical Poets."
2. An example of this curious grouping can be consulted in *Gradual* 9, fol. 33 now housed in the Piccolomini Library, Siena Cathedral.

I will teach you the secrets old men know.

Jack Spicer (sortta)

Enter Lear, Foole, and Gentleman.

At least my old age is in its infancy but is that truly the reason why a superannuated monarch like me suffers from diaper rash and has to stick a post-it-note on the end of his penis to remind him to take a pysse? Now that I'm a full member of the Rubber Sheet Club a question arises: am I getting younger, or decomposing? Quite the case of stat rex indignitatis wouldn't you say? Counting the days until Thanatos, that lean proofreader of his very own Book of the Dead, deletes you with his yellow highlighter marker. Either way to *grow* senile and stay regal sure beats selling bootleg Metallica t-shirts from the back of an old pick-up and it's so much closer to our final destination in that great condominium of incessant sleep. There's quite a tremor to that word and, given the optical effects surrounding it, I'd say we're still recovering from open-heart Caravaggionism. Ah, the odor of success! Can you imagine the smell of Lance Armstrong's bicycle seat immediately after winning the Tour de France for the eighth consecutive year? Victory comes with its consequences alright, as for me, I'd prefer to go down to defeat early and that way avoid the awkward embarrassment of rectal halitosis. To an under-appreciated neo-Heideggerean like yourself this may sound more like the effervescence than the disappearance of being, the upsurge of a vitality in the general forgetting of remembering. Current statistics however *show* that the unproblematic is always the harbinger of a premature disaster. Those *weeds* that insert themselves in pastoral seem closer to the *kind* of lifestyle I should stay clear of. They say the eyes of a cat never reach euphoria, caught up in dreams of predatory *deeds* they function not unlike the Charles le Bruns and Sebastian Bourdons who painted them.[1] My *mind* constantly goes back to the time I first read Blake's Tyger and came away convinced that all predators partake of the angelic. Unlike both of you I still prefer the logic of inaction *shown* clearly in the Dutch still-life paintings of Jacob Vosmaer and Willem Kalf. Living cats like Bojangles and C Diddy *confound* me minding their *own* business sleeping and grooming their balls until feeding time like the human figures in Manet's Déjeuner dans l'atelier. *Crowned* with the laurel of over-interpretation and pulling straws from whiskers I'd say we're caught in some calculus of imbalance sufficient to *commend* us both to move into another polygon of conspicuous absence. Do you think there's sex after death or are we *due* for an after-life of celibacy with those bodies without organs some call angels? I may be old and flesh fails me but the blaze remains. Fate's never in the future so they'll be lots of time to *mend* the present. Your grand pontifications give ten years back to my skin. Cosmetics apart, the *view* from here suggests it's time to bivouac in the new technologies. Taking a *view* of the latest informatics puts me in mind of how much I miss the old cellular telepathy and the little jingle after knowledge. Perhaps we should *mend* our pathos by actively returning to the legacy of Eliot—polyphony, heteroglossia and collage, it would sure beat suffocating under gender studies, identity politics, national literatures, and similar sociological disturbances. I thought we already had when we concurred that the ethical responsibility of the poet is to unleash the savagery of language against representation. That said, and with all *due* respect, I'm more than happy to withdraw to the acedial torpor of pattern poetry. Which reminds me, before we die we should set up that clinic for the treatment of premature problems you mentioned earlier. It would be seasonably "with it" and there's loads to *commend* such a service. *Crowned* as the new archbishop of impossible inventions you might finally get to *own* that dream ranch by a polluted lake where you can kiss the ancient art of husbandry goodbye. Take me along, intermured between asphyxia and dilemma, and we'll continue to *confound* the pundits of instrumental reason. I'm well aware that Post-Cartesian anamnesis has *shown* the contemporary *mind* to be suffering from the President's disease but let's prove our own *deeds* can carry the day. Roaming on some plane of consistency our eyes blink at twilight in the intussusception[2] of the *kind* of dawn transfigured in a widow's *weeds*. Which goes to *show* why science still stammers in its futile attempt to *grow* the right avocadoes for fruit bats.

1. I didn't want to mention it in the main body of the text but I have to admit I love the raw elegance of the predator—one kill, one big feast for you and your family, then no more food for six weeks. At least too, if you're an anthropophagi, you get a balanced yet concentrated diet of protein—an adroit polyglot response to those edible prosciutto mandates. So let the prey come to us!

2. The first recorded use of this word (meaning a taking within) is in the anonymous 1707 Augustan best-seller *Curiosities in Husbandry and Gardening*.

Enter the Queene with her hair about her eares. Rivers and Dorset after her.
Failed as a Queen, failed as a mother, failed as a wife and failed as a lesbian. Quite an achievement for one lifetime and still historicity condemns me to finitude precisely because history itself (since the event of the modern) is a quantum formula. Rimbaud and Bataille both attempt to recover a reconnection with the infinite reconceived atheistically as the infinite indifferent outside the finitude of being. Cool don't you think? Still, History doesn't *owe* us a goddam thing and I've nothing to *show* for being its subject other than an *enlarged* synchrondosis of the lyric and my hair looking like a used Brillo™ scouring pad. But quite the crown don't you think? I mean what an imaginative use of bananas after they've started to go brown. It was Laura Riding, after she'd accidentally napalmed her underwear, who first drew attention to how procrustean masculinity really is. However, you know as well as I do, History is only maternal from the viewpoint of a strictly masculiniste sense of quantity surveying and, as for my part in it, well, I'm sure glad I wasn't that drummer boy of Shiloh, it was the post-bellum troubadour's non-negotiable nightmare. If I'd been him I would have got out quick and joined one of those emergent Dixieland jazz bands for twice the pay and twenty thousand times the safety. (Ironic *praise* indeed from those generals who send you to a muddy Mississippi grave.) Oh Guernica, in a great cry shattering the eardrums of Goya! Such a war to shipwreck the silence of death! Which makes me think of my own

part in the French resistance when I couldn't tell the difference between the mayonnaise and the Marseillaise, no wonder my croque monsieurs tasted so bad and I always sang the French national anthem with my mouth smelling of aioli. I much prefer to keep bravery strictly on my back burner. Rather than having *charged* with all those fools at the Battle of Little Bighorn, died in combat, been scalped and spent the rest of my non-existence in some tomb of the unknown optimist, I'm happy to be spending my remaining *days* in the *prime* of my senility as a mobled Queen speculating on whether Christ was a man like Bismark. "The hero," quipped Emerson, "is he who is immovably centered." In which case I'd *love* to spend *time* in Felujah asking where all their heroes went, but you wouldn't *approve* of such indelicacies with your *air* of political correctness and annual gift to Doctors without Borders. I *suspect* these days it's a *fair* bet that mundanities like waking up, getting dressed, and acting out your genocidal tendencies in day-care centers indicate less the *defect* than perfection of the post- "enlightenment." You might "enlighten" me with a little more of your discount proprioception. It's funny knowing that now both of you are a permanent part of my anatomy effectively neutralizing a *defect* in my monadism. Is it a *fair* bet that if we went on line we'd find one another? Somehow I doubt it; I *suspect* we'd become our own worst unknown majorities. In fact, given the appalling quality of our intersubjectivities it might be best all round to embrace the logic of the proto-umbilical handshake. But one thing is certain: the day I think of you as a kiss between parties will be the year that Christmas never arrives. You know, there's a slightly Muscovitic *air* to your reflections of which I thoroughly *approve*, but when you grin like that you show a row of porphyry teeth reminiscent of an anamorphic sketch of Stonehenge. Ah teeth the bruxed unflossables, it makes me glad I bought a copy of The Flosser's Guide to a Wooden Smile. All of my best friends are Druids, great guys; in their *time love* manifested in the form of nude gatherings for sun worship plus a human sacrifice of Phoenician captives in the *prime* of their lives—and they always made sure there was sufficient blood for everyone to swim in. I also read that mass deaths by stoning (in preparation for ritual cardiac scoop-outs) was the single most popular national atrocity on Summer Solstice weekends. Those *days* were *charged* with good sense and practical suggestions mostly dispensed by drunken bards gulping down gallons of wassail returing from the annual Eisteddfod at Car Lleon. To *praise* some unknown deity in the form of human sacrifice may be a consequence of fear, but those guys realized death's an effective method of escape from all those social pressures to get your penis *enlarged* or put your child in a beauty pageant or a talent *show*. But looking at you and your karaoke exploits I'd say we *owe* it to the Edsel and Social Credit to spend the rest of our lives proving that the works of an age are best represented by its failures.

Exeunt

Scene 3. *Enter Rosencrantz and Guildenstern.*

What ever happened to those great discussions we used to have about speech disorders in western invertebrate physiology before 1482? I loved our arguments and badinage about the Hippocratic Corpus and Saint Bernard's Apologia to William of St.-Thierry. We even found ways to disagree about the Systematists and John of Hexham's theory of the vocal cords. Those transient moments of informality, those days of fecund conversation are *gone* for good, the only things we talk and *moan* about now are God and arthritis and not always in that order. Incidentally, that carcass you brought back from the International Butcher's Convention has started to *decay*, looking more like a portrait by Francis Bacon than the Thanksgiving meal we forgot to eat. Why don't we *rehearse* some major conflict or set to music a few stanzas of Tasso's Gerusalemme liberata; it's a fantastic poem and it sure beats Marinetti's pompous pshitt he called parole in libertà. To compare the two is to compare the difference between gold and *clay*. Wow that *verse* about massacring all the Christians with halberds and scimitars, quite the vivassory rearrangement of the midriff! *Woe*, slow down, you don't want to end up looking and smelling like an e-coli outbreak; I *forgot* to mention the Annunciator has finally arrived, *so* you can talk to him about the Immaculate Conception and the angels. *Not* to anticipate the course of your discussion but you could ask him if it's true that Emanuel Swedenborg kept a pet seraphim he called Caspar and fed it bird seed. Also find out where they *dwell* when they're not guarding us, and whether they molt or get lice in their wings like pigeons do. I've always preferred the fallen angels who *fled* to Hell, like Negursenal "der fürst des Gehinnon"[1] and

Belial "Hell's Ambassador to Turkey."[2] Those two names seem guaranteed to scare the shytte out of the Taliban and to keep on ringing a *bell* in the valley of the *dead* on judgment day. When two friends part it's usually the survivor who dies. However, re-enactment typologies ensure a certain ontological encore. In fact the *dead* are still alive. [A *bell* rings at this point in our narrative in an inconsequential way announcing tonight's cuisine is Spanish.] It's not as if they've *fled* into oblivion. Nobody really goes to spirit, people simply pass over onto the World Wide Web and Wikipedia. For the most part you *dwell* peacefully in a hyperspatial limbo to be occasionally called up on a search-engine or Facebook but *not so* distant as you'd like to be from the digital nightmare of e-mail. Think of it, spam from the dead across eternity. These days my junk mail's mainly discount offers on sainthoods and viagara. Speaking of which, you should e-mail the Earl of Flarf about his recent Google sculpting around the broad topic of the Royal latrines. What a predictable place to try and pick up a sailor I thought, but thought is always a certain kind of forgetting. That's how memory functions like a penis in both young and old, protuberant e'en in its perpendicularity on a flagpole of platitudes. Action too forgets events the way measles don't remember the morphemes that comprise them—at which point speech fails me. What was it called that place in Berlin where I met you? A center for treating Alzheimer's disease named the Vergessen Mir Nicht if I remember correctly. What a catastrophic farce that was, people in a state of intimate disconnection, sitting for hours changing channels on the communal microwave or walking into swimming pools and smiling while they drown, believing they were helping Granny do her laundry and muttering "Adam *forgot* to name me hence I'm christening myself Moby Dick." *Woe* betide the philosopher who tries to place this all-too-common scenario in the ontology of the exception. The Poet Laureate should turn Sumerian and write a *verse* in cuneiform on a *clay* tablet to commemorate all the sad consequences of the mind's growth-onset disintegrations. I want a quick death in whispered vermilion rather than *rehearse decay* before the final *moan* of becoming *gone*. Qui est iste qui venit?

1. So called in the *Alphabet* of Rabbi Akiba.
2. Termed such by Victor Hugo in *The Toilers of the Sea*.

Enter Hamlet reading of a Booke.

Hang it all William Shakesepeer there can be but the one "Hamlet." But Hamlet and my Hamlet? Hhm, sorry boys, that doesn't sound quite right (part of my banana monologue from Coriolanus if memory serves me right), but listen to these: "Rumor if true, spiritous windrows troughed by a rimpling wind teasing whisters from overshanks, weasande, chops and barme. Pill cops cross cabbage garth aloft trines hold wearish teene yet steady for handsel over cod wick snibs." Wow! quite a barrage of anachronisms, plundered no doubt from yet another unread copy of Arabia Deserta. It makes me wish Ophelia hadn't burned that rhyming bible in one of her piques.[1] To me old words are nothing but philological affectations. To call my jacket a wadnel, my overcoat a mandillian, my beaver hat a Castor, or that out-door crapper a pentical hardly resuscitates the soul of Beowulf. Poor him, his naked body shivering with dandruff somewhere between the Library of Congress and Arthur Miller's Death of a Salesman. But let's get back to those angels you mentioned in the last speech; it might be *worth* our while to reflect on Michel Serres' theory that they're actually message-bearing systems, ergo a type of technology carrying divine information back and *forth*.[2] *You* might think that angels are part of a complex theory of cosmic enunciation but in fact they're just like pigeons; they carry messages alright but the messages they carry aren't theirs. Speaking of messages *is* it *untrue* to say we suffer language when made absent from us? Old Mother Hubbub, matron of *this* pre-linguistic clamor *impart* to me a clarity from a word yet to come. Incidentally those black holes and time warps are a real drag. Last week *I* ended up in the middle of the Franco-Prussian War talking to a cavalry officer named Heinz about the comparative social infrastructures of Anglo-Saxon wapentakes and Operation *Desert* Storm before finally arriving at the Allegory of Ideology which takes the form of a fifty-mile high pyramid of televisions all playing the identical channel. The ads are a welcome relief, they're called "Occupations" and in other casinos "revolutions." But things could have been worse. Take the case of Jesus, for instance, no sooner born than subjected to useless presents from three bearded guys wearing turbans and each one calling himself "Maggie." That must have been awfully confusing for a new born savior. It would be a *lie* to say we reached consensus on anything other than the mildly gruesome rhetorical question as to why we can't leave Nature and other people alone? How can we conceive of a Nature any more natural than those corporate demonologies controlling all our pilotless drones. That last sentence incidentally requires a question mark. Emerson spoke of England as the paradise of the first class but who wants such a place? With its four walls, electrified gate and corner guard towers even Paradise was a systematic intervention into the natural order. It goes to *prove* God was less an architect than a *quite* unimaginative urban planner.—That place was more like an internment camp than a lakeside mansion. Incidentally, despite the incontrovertible fact of irreversible global warming the palace feels as cold as chastity. Winter can be a wonderful artist but right now we should be singing "God bless Antarctica" to Nanook of the North as the President's State of the Union Address instantly freezes on his lips. George W. Bush used to *love* to *recite* to Dick Cheney those frank confessions posted on the witness extermination download site and we could do the same, but before that let me *recite* a little known fact.[3] Death's first kiss on a corpse renews an ancient *love* that a child's birth breaks. Such facts are *quite* helpful to know when Polonius next goes on E-Bay trying to add to his prized collection of Romanian fetal death certificates and it sure goes to *prove* idyllic sentiments don't mix with ethnic cleansing. However, listening to me these days must be like looking at a toothache. Best *lie* down for a while and listen to those Poughkeepsie chickadees coughing up their feathers. Close my eyes in the *desert* and let me imagine *I* am Lawrence of Arabia screwing Kim Kardashian or one of the Victoria's Secrets' models. Incidently if the Pope forced me to adopt a vice it would be hypocrisy. Preaching charitable words to *impart* a poetics of common virtue while all the time exploring the suburbs of depravity. And the great thing in *this* would be the fact that it would be so unoriginal. Also terrific would be the lure of the *untrue*, like the kind of promises made at Republican Conventions, or Robin Evans' claim that a corridor offers a "hyphen between departure and arrival." Hopefully death *is* like Mallarmé's bed, eternally absent, so let me meet *you* in the abattoir of your choice from whence we'll go *forth* into the valley of breath and cough the world to sleep for a penny's *worth* of peace.

1. The Central Franconian Rhyming Bible, or *Mittelfränkische Reimbibel*, an early twelfth-century German Verse Homily that now survives (like the Eurozone and Medicare) in fragmentary condition.

2. See Michel Serres, *Angels. A Modern Myth.* Trans. Francis Cowper. Paris: Flammarion, 1993.

3. I can't let the mention of this esteemed former Vice-President pass without a footnote to remember some of his inspirational adages. June 4, 2003: "Except for the occasional heart attack, I never felt better." September 10, 2005: "There are a lot of lessons we want to learn out of this process in terms of what works. I think we are in fact on our way to getting on top of the whole Katrina exercise." That said, the former President is the clear winner. Listen to these pearls: "They misunderestimated me." "I know the human being and fish can coexist peacefully." "You forgot Poland." "Families is where our nations finds hope, where wings take dream." "I just want you to know that, when we talk about war, we're really talking about peace." "If this was a dictatorship it'd be a heck of a lot easier, just so long as I'm the dictator." Need we list more?

Death is best.

Bacchylides

Olympian Ode for Hiero of Syracuse

Enter Helena and two Gentlemen.

My imagination is a mortuary and I its favorite corpse, therefore love me and if me you love I won't be there, at least not there in your absence, that's why the world is full of disappointed lovers. It seems so *long* since you told us anything like that as we go on in our own *strong* version of the vanishing act. Having been subject to the male gaze for the last ten pages it'll feel nice to be alone without you two clutching on to my life membership in the Atlantic City Jouissance Society. Speaking of which did I tell you I finally finished reading that Kantian feminist's latest book, "The Critique of Pure Orgasm" in which she posits a theory of transcendental jouissance that's quite appealing to a Barbie doll like me with my wall to wall smile before the paparazzi. Still, I must say it was a genuine thrill to lose the first of my nine virginities on Superbowl Weekend, just like Monica Lewinsky! In retrospect I regret not misplacing rather than losing it. I mean there's hardly a virgin remaining in the local convents. It's amazing the Mother Superior died intacta and the abbot had her tombstone inscribed with a quote from the Postmaster General.[1] But more to the point how many Verocchios does it take to screw in a limited impact with footnotes *by* the predella? The reason I ask is that paintings instantly raise the problem of where exactly to put them. Museums are prisons of the human spirit and a museum of modern art implies an institute of binding paradox. Before I finally *expire* I'd like to see them all abolished. Just think of Picasso's Guernica as a shower curtain or a tablecloth; or imagine those authentic Leonardo da Vinci designer coasters for your martini glass to *lie* on as you sit feeding more Mantegnas to the *fire*, the door propped open by a genuine replica of Bernini's Holy Ghost; it would be a functional solution to both aesthetics and the entire institution of art. Who needs em? The sight of a common Vanessa on a hosta leaf sets up a rhythm to truly confront chaos; it hints at figuration without figure, its wings evoke ecstasy at *rest* and, for a fleeting instance not far *away*, the corpse of God as a Christian Apollo.[2] They say the *west* is always associated with death because it marks the sun's descent into night. That *day* you *sang* of transience and colon cancer there was a tragic odor to your words that made life sound as cheery as three months in a leper colony. Shall I phone and see if there's been any last-minute cancellations at the mortuary and book us in? At least when we're dead and *cold* we won't be failures; we can *hang* our laurels proudly and say *behold* at least there's one thing we've achieved. When your voice drops like that you become illegible and I *behold* a man who was never taught to laugh. You look like Death's other masterpiece fighting for prestige. In fact I don't believe you'd ejaculate at your own *hang*ing. Turning to the *cold* topic of death again I remember the old Spanish cante hondo you *sang* while we were learning the ins and outs of the corrida. Boy, that song stirred such a lust in both of us for the horror of the Goya of the 1790s! It was the *day* I went to the Prado and saw a masked man pulling a gold tooth from the mouth of a dead security guard. It's an eastern cliché in the *West* that "the dream of Reason brings forth monsters,"[3] in which case you can throw Clement Greenberg *away* along with the *rest* of those art historians into the *fire* and brimstone of the proletariat.—Art is a *lie* in the service of a truth disfigured as the soul of a bullfighter on black canvas and before they all *expire* beneath the weight of their book reviews and press clippings they should leave a few genuine insights *by* which to be remembered. Mark my words, there's a *strong* possibility death will be so quiet that they'll hear the lyttae consuming them with their weighty volumes of useless *long* ideas.

1. "Returned unopened."

2. According to Wikipedia the Vanessa is a genus of brush-footed butterfly with near global distribution. It's also the name of a Boston-based independent Escort Service promising "the ultimate in busty, buxom companionship." Take your pick.

3. Goya.

Exeunt

I live my death.

Michelangelo

Scene 4. *Enter Father Capulet, Mother, Nurse, and Serving men two or three.*
Quote the cold *remains* of a corpse that breathes unquote *contains* a minimum of thirty-six post-ontological possibilities and leaves us still hoping to be happy some day. I'm glad I *remembered* to laugh at mortality this morning before the surgeon sterilized his *knife* and fork and started in on my sex-change.[1] Oh to be *dead*, I mean *life*'s been such a nightmare, I wouldn't wish it on the worst of my enemies including *me*; it's so gripping it should be sold as a sleeping pill. Tennyson found the idea of personal extinction unthinkable that's why I never read him. Hey, it would be easy to convert this living room into a mortuary, just think of the convenience and the money to be saved. To give probability its *due* I'm sure my happiness is temporary or at least sufficiently logical to be merely theoretical, but it's a happy thought to share with all of *you*, living the impossible death as an event of life not lived through, in some magnificent fountain of pure asparagus.[2] I've a wonderful sense of stupidity but I thought I'd play it safe in case there's judgment after death and have myself buried wearing two t-shirts—one reading "God is Good" and the other "I love Lucifer." I hope my death has a little more excitement for other people, that's what's so seductive about high-rise suicides in cities. Simply stand conspicuously on a nineteenth-story penthouse balcony and in an instant the TV cameras are there. Then splat, the perfect pureed body off to sing in the Choir Invisible! Then again it might be more effective to wire yourself up to the National Grid and turn it on. The problem with suicide, however, is that a person can only do it once. I'm told the Annunciator left town, went back to *review* those mortality insurance bills we never paid. (Unlike Ann Frank who paid hers in

full to the Gestapo.) Has everyone followed Nurse Khlebnikov's advice and taken their tablets of destiny for this century? I'm sure they'll be necessary if we're to *stay* intangible after a couple more of these universal cataclysms. (The world seems a case of a God who failed.) But perhaps the universe is merely God's notebook and his best entries are yet to come. Contrary to both Sarah Palin and Epicurus, I structure my own happiness entirely for the *interest* of others,[3] but I don't get too carried *away* with altruism and I never *arrest* my more mordant possibilities in the opposite direction to the vice versa squid. Speaking of vice versa how about Gilles Deleuze and his philosophy a tergo? Stuffing Kant from behind? Kant's not even worth a kiss on the cheek and with all that transcendental apperception he's worse than David Hume with his own constant worry about the uncertainty of sunrise. Still, given the fact that Hume came from Edinburgh it seems a genuine, if regional, epistemological concern—Scottish weather's almost as bad as Scottish whisky. They should *arrest* all three and put them *away* in a maximum security facility for monks and scholiasts, I've little *interest* in philosophy, I prefer to *stay* far away from the informal fallacy and the eidetic reduction. Besides, metaphysic's become so expensive. My chief delights are a book *review* or the cryptic crossword over a cup of coffee and *you*, dressed up as a Calvinist version of orthodoxy giving sobriety its *due* by reading choice strophes from Caesarius of Arles' Purgatory Eclogues. As for *me* and my *life*, as the sensual germ that Whitman speaks of, I've just one question: Could the *dead* be utter formlessness, or will death's high-modernist affiliations squeeze some hyperfiction around its defining contours on the cutting edge of cool? Some believe the *knife* to be a pygmy invention first intended as an instrument for writing, an origin *remembered* in the image of the ivory box that *contains* in camera the entire *remains* of little orphan ethics.

1. "Most people I know undergo a sex-change at least once in their life and usually by the sovereign law of prosopopoeia. The patient starts off as a hairy lifeguard then suddenly becomes blindfolded, endowed with breasts and scales in one hand and referred to by everyone as Justice." Dr. Montague Slute, *Times Literary Supplement*, June 15, 1942.

2. Vide Stein's "Rooms" in *Tender Buttons*.

3. See Aristotle, *Nicomachean Ethics* 1097b.

Exeunt

Enter Regan and Steward.

If you take *away* a *day* in the life of an open formula does it still remain a sentence? [Finger nervously on buzzer] I'm sure you *took* a masochistic *delight* in posing that question (and I'm doubly sure it comes from being named after an ex-president and Hollywood celebrity) but I do *look* forward to my answer even though the *sight* of you and the after-effects of your cognitive omega values lends authentic *pleasure* to Gottlob Frege *alone*. So here goes. The *treasure* of an indeterminate loop situated in the open texture of an infinitely catalyzable sentence does not preclude per se the possibility of variable-binding operators quantifying *anon* the parallel occurrence within the scope of the relevantly employed formula *found* to produce ipso facto that kind of *strife* among the non-calculated breast-fed new born net operating profits Heraclitus terms polemos. That should at least establish the *ground* for a conversation with a little more relevance to *life,* it certainly describes breakfast together to a tee and yet to be a part of you is to be a foreigner to my own *life* in language. Are we merely two examples of "possibility" projected on a *ground* above an abyss that was never there? Putting aside the *strife* between us I've *found* the unmitigated prurience of our relationship removes all possibility of a conventional anthropogenetic conclusion. A weekend cruise with Machiavelli and an emancipation from a tedious sex-life (courtesy those notorious Gay Welsh aboriginals with their noses tattooed like the Vikings) can teach you a lot about the advanced techniques of Amor. I've been so bad I've won the World Misdemeanor Pageant for fifty-eight consecutive years. But *anon* will come the *treasure* that is death, conceived as the finality of going out of print, and you *alone* will write my epitaph in lingua franca. I'm sick of the rule of the third person but what a novel our lives have been. The balance of *pleasure* and eschatology in two lives lived through the contemporary Plagues of Egypt is quite the *sight* to *look* at from the left-hand margin of a sorites paradox. What *delight* I *took* the *day* I realized you contain every standard interpretation of formal logic and that a few blocks *away* the Third International of the Universal Thomist movement sat drawing up its latest five-year plan without even mentioning Aquinas.

Exeunt

Enter with Drums and Colors, Cordelia, Gentlemen, and Soldiers.
Has anyone here ever been in a state of mis en abyme? Quite appalling actually, it seems to be a consequence of post-structuralist vocabulary and certainly something for us stage characters to worry about. I'm *told* that worry is the dark-room where negatives are developed but those *old* proverbs we *spent* time applying to practical philosophy demand a *new* approach. The current *argument* requires that our escape from fiction involve certain vectors of illegitimation. However, for *you* to *proceed* in this beside me will involve a subtle intellectual challenge. So let's start with a question. Does the *name* Erwin Schrödinger ring a bell? It ought to given your new-found passion for quantum gynecology in the fourth dimension. Apparently he had a cat named Duns Scotus who argued in fluent Latin meows that a *weed* is nothing but an unwanted flower and that the very *same* plant helps formulate the *strange* right cheek in Archimboldo's portrait of Spring. Putting that *aside*—and to *change* the subject somewhat—I take intense *pride* in the way I described to Bernard Berenson the delicate symplegma of the bodies and draperies in Poussin's Camillus and the Schoolmaster of Falerii. It's true, I really do have a way with words (unlike Jane Austen in her *Pride* and Prejudice). However, I still lack the three-dimensional tour de force of eco-criticism to make me the perfect Renaissance miss. The *change* from pristine to polluted in the clouds around the Villa d'Este makes me want to put all aesthetics *aside*. The next best thing to a natural desert is a human jungle, just take a look out there. I remember the day fresh air came into existence, it was imported from the Galapagos Island and didn't stay around for long; these days corruptibility's the only oxygen we breathe. It's *strange* though to realize that this very locus is the *same* home we left. We should speak of the uncanny as we speak of home, it comes by not arriving and evades consuetude. Still, to eradicate a *weed* in the *name* of golf-course horticulture seems an ineffective way to *proceed* toward a spiritualized form of botany. *You* tell me your God is my aboriginal instance of destructive catharsis and the *argument* seems convincing among the rear pews of the *New* Church of Our Lady of Perpetual Misfortune. I respond by applying the old antinomy effect caught up this time in Christ's second coming via the internet. I think it's better if we *spent* time away from religious doubt and

leave this *old* Department of Insecurity for a while. Let's go home and enjoy the garden. I'm *told* by a world expert on Yiddish limericks that a perfect summer day is when the sun is shining, the breeze is blowing, the birds are singing, and the neighbor's lawnmower doesn't work. A lucious thought on which to end this season before bludgeoning more sparrows to death.

> I know of no other bomb but the book.
> Stephane Mallarmé, *La Journal* Dec. 10 1893

Enter Juliet.

Mallarmé believed the *book* is the Orphic instrument of the earth and if you're searching for a great one as a birthday present (something other than the Boghouse Miscellany) I would strongly recommend taking a *look* at the Poems of James Thomson especially The City of Dreadful Night—it'll curdle your *mind*. He sure knew how to de-romanticize the *brain* of the middle-class reader. Abraham Lincoln dubbed him the Poet Laureate of Pessimism and you won't *find* a greater epic of despondency than that poem—(other than this corny Masque we're in right now). Thomson didn't write to win prizes (unlike Paul Muldoon) and if he hadn't drank himself to death I'm sure he would have become the Walt Whitman of Despair. Boy, could he conjure up an image of the worst of all possible worlds, a veritable Dark Night of the Word. The scenes in that poem are remarkably ghastly. You don't find it *contains* descriptions of bourgeois child obesity or type two diabetes, or even happy apple-cheek urchins playing in mud, instead there's the full gamut of Victorian hard-labor, homeless (not to mention noseless) syphilitic hare-lipped cripples thinner than Gandhi begging for sustenance, a whole army of knock-kneed and scrofulous four-year old chimney sweeps (all called Tiny Tim), penniless families huddled around the winter hearth, their starveling fires but a mockery of warmth, and gin-soaked unemployed single mothers forced into trading their bodies to pay the rent to purblind and perverse absentee landlords, then sending their illegitimate offspring into a rag trade sweatshop; it drove countless Victorian readers to suicide by sticking their mouths up the exhaust pipe of the closest passing omnibus, and Thomson himself to drink. On reading it Dante instantly turned Druid; thousands joined the Society for the Suppression of Anatomy and some even took up crochet and converted to atheism convinced that *eternity* is the least desirable thing you can possibly imagine. The only question readers were asking was from which cliff do the local lemmings throw themselves? It proved to be one of the better letter-bombs of the 1880s. Did he *know* how to bring a tear to the eye, unlike those Spasmodics, such as Sidney Dumbell, with their corny medieval castles in the Tyrol, replete with bats and cobwebs and other trite objective correlatives, and such predictable themes as child molestation, abduction, abreaction, revenge, loss of *memory*, rape, a heroine princess called Miranda, and dire specimens of cumulative male abjection ycleped Festus and Balder. It goes to *show* you what nadirs bad *taste* can reach when you *bear* down on the comparative benefits of the pointless loss of life versus the utter *waste* of living. You sound a little worse for *wear* by having read it, but it's sure helping us understand that there's some things worse than the Great Depression. As for me, I've always adopted the everyday belief that death's one of those unfortunate things that happens to others, such as family members and pets. I'll continue to *wear* a big fake smile on my sleeve and go golfing among the grass and bunkers of sans souci. I never *waste* my time with a book, *bear* in mind that the body too needs exercise, but given your *taste* for the morbid you'll no doubt want to jog through Père la Chaise the next time you're in Paris and hire a guide to *show* you the main attractions. Parties of American intellectuals go there on guided tours around Gertrude Stein's grave while Queer Theorists lament Epstein's damaged monument to Oscar Wilde.[1] If *memory* serves me right you can actually buy crack wrapped up in a New York Herald Tribune at several of the dingier mausoleums threading their way through that necropolis. Which reminds me, I should be planning ahead and thinking about my own coffin—I *know* you already have. With my doom and gloom around the thought of a felicitous *eternity* I'm having one built that's low in sodium and designed to *contain* me and two bathrooms with an extra large room in case I put on weight after death. There's also an appeal to sky burials like the ones they have in Tibet where the corpse is dissected into thousands of little pieces, exposed to the mahabhuta, and used as a tempting snack for carrion birds. I know you *find* the thought of cremation increasingly appealing, the brevity and compactness of the whole affair satisfies your Bauhaus sensibility. That said, I still think Viking funerals are best: a corpse set on fire on a burning ship sailing to Valhalla across a lake of flames—they kept the Baltic dockyards busy for centuries. I'll no doubt have my own *brain* preserved in formaldehyde as Stalin did Hitler's. *Mind* you, I'd want to take a *look* around and choose the right setting to be scattered. A seacoast perhaps where the ashes of what I was can mix with the clouds and ocean waves I will become, closing out the *book* of life while living out my new utopia of old obsessions, thinking Death's always morning to the School of Night.

1. The tomb (now enclosed in glass) depicts a flying nude angel. One eager souvenier hunter not content with merely lipsticked kisses on its thighs chipped off the actual genitals. Sic transit Gloria penis.

Exeunt

Scene 5. *Enter Buckingham* (nude) *and Clifford.*
Thank God for easy aristocratic promotions. I was pleasantly surprised to find out that pissing on the palace floor instantly made me a Peer of the Realm, I'm also aware that fashion defines itself these days as strictly floating capital but since the "double inscription" changed to the "remainder" I've stopped wearing clothes altogether and no longer read The Cambridge Companion to Portable Knowledge. So now I'm ready for sex among the Eskimos. People in their *ignorance advance* reasons why it's important to *be* dressed in the *style* of the times but *you* and me are different. We know today's news wraps tomorrow's fish and chips and that's why all our revolutionary ideals always end up as the status quo. So what if Walter Benjamin proved that a little Gnosticism makes one a better Marxist and perhaps Communism was God's great weapon against real estate, it still doesn't explain the lack of novelty in the way we both dress. I mean why does everything we wear bear a grudge against us, to *compile* a catalogue of rainbows in our wardrobe wouldn't get beyond basic clerical grey. I know we wear the ordinary with *majesty* but if we both rose to the challenge and became two radical Hegelian gardeners suitably accoutered in rubber boots with hessian hats, sucking on clay pipes with a sheaf of wheat behind one ear, we might emerge as two new negative Capability Browns, the scourge of the ferme ornée. Instead of a leg to stand on we'd have a *wing* or two to *fly* with to our very own hortus conclusus where we could perch and *sing* the adventures of the new botany. Not to *disperse* your optimism but what's the *use* of gardens

these days? Best leave them to diacritics and the Wenner Gren Foundation and return to *verse* as it's happening without the *muse*. Funny I bring in the *muse* again en route to *verse* but fail to mention Terpsichore's complicity in our own meta-narrational servitude and the absolute injustice in the *use* of tenure-track hurricane survivors to enhance our modes of social reproduction. I'm sure it's naïve of me to inquire but how do we *disperse* a politics of immediacy without returning to the inscrutability of the internal subject? What an untidy quiddity to *sing* about: the un-ventriloquated doubled-voice of language itself, and what a way to *fly* into the twin towers of narratology before it happens! But I'm certain some left or right-*wing* cadre will make sure that particular scenario never unfolds. In which case, given the *majesty* of my current force-field, I'll help *compile* that hermeneutics of Enstellung that *you* have long promised the world, with all its distortion and disfigurement and written in such an impoverished *style* it'll *be* the worthy rival of Samuel Beckett's prose.[1] His kind of exhaustion of thought at the end of what's human shouldn't trouble us however, so let's *advance* in our *ignorance* with three cheers to the clients of the cycle, it's bound to pay off now innovation's been catastrophized.

1. Or the mind of Sylvester Stallone.

Wer zeigt mit Fingern auf einen Geruch?
Rilke

Golly, what a Shite's altar?
Matthew Arnold

Enter Falstaffe, Pistoll, Robin.
That do-it-yourself colonic irrigation kit arrived just in the nick of time. I used to believe the best solution to constipation was a good dose of the philosophy of Thomas Hobbes but not anymore. My chronic early-Modern, early-morning wind breaking didn't get me very far beyond stained wet diapers. Despite Artaud's conviction that the anus is terror I maintain a general academic interest in what comes out the rear end and I know it doesn't *pay* to hold it in. It feels good to have got that guano out of my south-west passage. Thank you Prospero

for that magical stool softener with its secret recipe of ingredients and, after a world-class defecation like this one, I must be back down to a size 78. (Active bowels active mind as Einstein knew so well.) It's at times like this that I like to mumble a prayer to the Patron Saint of Dung Beetles and reflect on Leibniz's claim that force is always a potentiality, it's helped me endlessly in my battles with weight gain and constipation. I'm glad I put all my genius into my excrement, in fact it was the biggest pshyt since my Paleozoic era, I thought a family of tiger sharks were dropping out of my anus mirabilis to the accompaniment of a thirty-two gun salute, but sitting on that wooden toilet felt like krapping into Pinocchio's mouth. My body truly is the supreme achievement of Cartesian extension. Last week in Atlantic City I was booed off a speak-your-weight machine and, getting my calculated biomass into my nightshirt, was equivalent to squeezing a zeppelin into a condom; I'd grown so enormous I had more chins than teeth, frequently rented out my supine body as a speed bump, was beginning to get mistaken for a Sumo wrestler and on one occasion (in drag) for the Venus de Lespugue. She sure was the most calypiginous of those stone-age beauties, quite a bodice-ripper with a figure to die for[1] and, with her broad buttocks wobbling from side to side, packed quite a punch on the super-model catwalks of the early Aurignacian—far more pulchritudinous than Paula Abdul or Britney Spears—and her pharts bent space into time. It's amazing the amount of pshytte the human body can accommodate, with all those miles and miles of winding intestine I'm surprised there's not more traffic jams and car accidents. In fact I once nearly flushed myself down the toilet, so now when I dephecate I always take my own "Guide Book to the Cloaca Maxima" with me, bearing in mind that "Qui hic mixerit aut cacarit habeos deos inferos et superos iratos."[2] What was Bernard of Clairvaux's euphemism for this humble act? Laying cable, crimping a length, or dropping the monks off at the well? Whichever it was I think everyone should get life-time achievement awards for their crappings. It's a funny thing pshitte, when it's in you, you never think of it, but as soon as it comes out it takes on the status of a radical alterity. I'd *say* it's the quantum opposite to childbirth as I've learned about it in the variorum edition of Florence Nightingale's Diaries. What a gal she was, big, blotchy and born with a voice that could knock a hundred budgies off their perches from thirty blocks away not to mention cracking an anvil at five hundred yards—plus a temper when vexed that could inspire the invention of the bulldozer. She was the first woman to make it to the South Pole bare-legged and wearing only a spandex tank-top and matching mini-skirt. Her dying words have been a mantra to me.[3] Meet her and you meet the future's contemporary and what a way to *live*! She started out as the doyenne of early-Baroque swaddling techniques then moved from nurseries to battlefields. Her manic ebullience was unsuppressable, in the Crimean War she kept everyone happily supplied with bedpans, painkillers, urine bottles, holding their mouths open with used toothpicks and acupuncture needles, spreading happiness just by spitting on the floor. Entire regiments were lost in her bosom, never time to wash herself, she didn't care what she smelled like so long as she didn't smell like herself (or the guys in the chemical toilet brigade). Her life was one long love letter to mortality. To get any sleep she had to be shot with a tranquilizer dart and spent most mornings at Scutari autographing the plaster casts on the necks and heads of dying casualties. All her Sundays were spent cleaning up the Black Sites for more uncharged detainees and top risk suspects. She even performed a perfect Caesarian Section on Mark Anthony while trapped half in and half out of a parallel universe that should have won her a Nobel Prize. I constantly think of the thousands of patients she treated and the half dozen she saved. With pubic hair the texture of Wheetabix I often wondered what life would be like in her underwear. And good in the trenches too! She was lethal with a toenail clipper and her crusader diet of fudge and pepperoni served up to the Light Brigade almost won them the Battle of the Bulge, while those incredible edible kosher swastikas helped relieve a lot of the racial tension in the trenches during the Battle of Yom Kippur (although one bite of her shepherd's pie effectively destroyed the entire pastoral tradition). Passing gas in the spirit of a NASCAR pit crew, she was the greatest nurse that ever broke wind. I remember her entertaining the troops one Christmas dressed in sequined tights and holding a trapeze between her teeth while singing a medley of Andrew Lloyd Webber hits. Her living leprechaun transplants were an instant hit in Sligo, while her stethoscope was recently evaluated on Antiques Road Show and valued at par with a first edition of Sir Gawain and the Green Knight. Like Norman Bethune in China, she couldn't *afford* to *give* up working or go to sleep and she never yawned once. She was always polite, courteous and (on the rare occasion) actually found time to change her knickers. And such an optimist, I'm sure if you

126

cut off her head she'd continue trying on new hats. I bet she would have been a veritable Mother Theresa had she served in the Third Anglo-Dutch War.—And what a name for a nurse! The first *word* provokes an unmistakable allusion to a beautiful Italian resort (popular with all except Italians) and the second to a poignant bird immortalized by mostly Romantic poets. I tell you that babe knew a lot more about the world and its deaths-in-abundance than Keats ever knew about nightingales. She deserved to have her face put on the world's coins and banknotes, so feel free to send her your applause in an envelope. As for me, I've always felt the human face to be a toilet seat for the Divine to squat on, but it hardly makes me a Post-Renaissance theologian. You might want to blame that last comment on my germ packed colon, and after that intrepid frank confession I think it's time *again* to *invent* the ode, take up the *pen* and develop a complex *argument* in rhyme to critique the relation of myth to *place* and *decayed* urban spaces to petty crime and the ecumenical fall from *grace* without the *aid* of Grecian urns or songbirds. Come to think of it, why doesn't anyone come to our *aid*, we who move with all the *grace* of three dislocated elbows? It would have been better had we not survived that recent geodesic survey and left for another less morally *decayed* planet where we'd be free from these objective correlatives to war zones. You know, life on earth's the perfect *place* from which to measure the distance between a bad dream and a minor nightmare. Go sentimentally through this condition back to the *argument* that dreams comprise our lyricism's heterology. It's still possible to put *pen* to paper and *invent* some new philosophical enthymemes before we read *again* the Hitchhiker's Guide to Oblivion and finally, as death consumes the *word*, let's *give* a thought in passing to that grave for three we can't *afford*. Being compelled to *live* on I'd *say* it's time to *pay* our last respects to those unpaid electricity bills and tread into the phonetic light turned off.[4]

1. 42-27-38 and her other leg was the same.
2. "Whoever here pisses or shits angers the lesser and the greater gods" (attributed by Hugo Ball to Martin Luther).
3. "Fuck off and let me get the job done."
4. Osip Mandelstam.

Exeunt

What is more to be feared than the making of death a sort of masterpiece?

Paul Valéry

Enter York and his Duchesse.

Increasing deaths plus less body bags yet more and more morticians. I find it hard to remain optimistic about the political economy of *decay* when graveyards grow suburbs[1] and I'm sure relieved I've got my season tickets to the local crematorium plus my hunt for cut-price burial plots continues.[2] Personally, I have no bones to pick with graveyards and I'd like the two of us to be buried perpendicularly in a miniature replica of the World Trade Center as a fitting comment on the times. Still, I find it reassuring to know some things never change. Take *away* your theatricality and *pride* and the sepulchral style really suits you. What with your metaphysics of untidiness and my macro-linguistics of the upper case that *boat ride* over cataract catastrophe might offer a novel solution to how we stay *afloat*. There'll always be a special place for you in the Grand Canyon of my imagination. Still poor and dirty after your brief career as an Afghani war-lord, then interim adviser to Nicolae Ceausescu and now, with a million-dollar incentive to die before me, you're the living proof that life looks better from Salvador Dali's dustbin. Grand Canyon? More like the Valley of Death. It would *appear* our polemical vivacity now operates on a reduced repertoire and organized about your testicles that way it makes me want to take up kick boxing. Valéry thought the ship not the coffin was the perfect architectural form, but *his* insight didn't *bear* the weight of historical consensus. *Is* there a cosmic necessity for our being alive? Somehow I doubt it, for *fame* does not pertain to the evaporation of self in its auto-kinesis so I always reconcile reality to its proper place. Imagine, however, Confucius in a long silk gown, an overgrown moustache, white beard down to his ankles, and a geriatric baldness to his head, standing, slightly nervous yet trenchant, in a martial arts demonstration, the wind whistling through his hernia, set against the entire *might* of the Tet Offensive, with the *name* Matthew Arnold tattooed on his forehead as he meditates the movement of a W upon the architecture of an X where I sit and *write* out the soundscape of Manhattan. The white lumbricus of burials return[3] and we must *write* and *name* en passant the obscene beauty of the cadaver, (although we *might* want to question the governing dialectic between the corpse and the *fame* accompanying the non-survivor). It *is* an incontrovertible fact that to *bear* a grudge against the desirable effects of the macabre will lead you to deny the inseparable modernity of death and the Renaissance man. Take Pope Clement IV for instance, *his* utter disillusion and open embrace of the concept of the living dead proved inspirational to several hundred tortured midgets in Portugal; they would shout in unison "no pain, no gain." To *appear* aware of this state between life and death, *afloat* in some late-twelfth-century iconography, might be the best way to *ride* the slow *boat* to its correlation-testimonies. Alternatively, we could sail to that land where the Matildas are forever waltzing knowing *pride* always leaves a culture that sees its fruition in anxiety and penitence in the flatulent tense from down under. Remember, it will be pharts not prayers that summon the dead from their graves, and if you do *away* with such anal dreams of resurrection you'll make the soul in its *decay* seem like a wet flannel from outer space.

1. A phrase from Khlebnikov's "Palm Sunday."
2. Then again you might be a tad more optimisitic and claim we're saving the planet one corpse at a time.
3. Alfred Jarry.

Enter the Ghost of Banquo, and sits in Macbeth's place.
Only mystics, fundamentalist cracker barrels and five-year olds prefer to sit on the floor when there's perfectly decent chairs available, like this one. [Rude sounds from a whoopee cushion.] I know I'm about as genuinely Scottish as Compton Mackenzie's Monarch of the Glen, but they say the best way to kill Walt Whitman is with a pronounced Glaswegian accent. (Ah, sae few fokk e'er kenned sae mickle thocht as that ain.)[1] Imagine it, Leaves of Grass recited by the fifth Earl of Sterling wearing his sporran as a toupee in front of a chorus of drunken *men* from Arbroath bawling for Hugh MacDiarmid (whose fiery commie bombast stands as a bad example of third-degree Burns).—That would be the Edinburgh Fringe Festival in a nut shell. I used to believe I was born into history in order to rewrite it in compelling verse, but that doesn't seem to be the case right now. In fact you don't need a *pen* to write poems to get your daily dose of eschatology, nor do you need to pass away like I did; you can see the *dead rehearse* their end on the walls of Rheims Cathedral and you

don't have to pay a thing. You can actually *read* (entirely without words) the dire consequences of Last Judgments or thrill to the glitzy glamour of a dozen Beatific Visions, but the latter seem so phony, like Projective *Verse* with that *lie* about the breath's connection to the heart—try selling that one to a poet with compound asthma and angina and you'll get a kick in your trouser furniture. Meanwhile, back in the practical world of pets (not poets), the cat drinks its milk by way of nonteleological expertise. Pleasure, as we're both aware, is not involved in aporetic ekphrasis and with the paint behind the paint you draw the portrait of the finite father. It's a *grave* proposition to assimilate but to *die* is to *have* entered a specific modality of relocation, constructing the problem of what precisely remains to be done once one has traversed death. Go home I suppose. Personally it's the quantity not the quality of death that worries me. All those mounds of *forgotten* heroes, inventors, and astronauts in the corpses d'élite, like Yuri Gagarin, no longer with us, who used to *take* earth's *rotten* garbage as a calling card to leave on other planets in the solar system; it's enough to *make* you cancel your subscription to the Graveyard Gazette. You don't need the likes of the late Walter Cronkite, or lateral thinking to persuade you that war, as the purposeful distribution of death, is remarkably similar to a birthday, assuming that death is a gift and not a deposit. Even so, such profundities won't *make* it to the next G7 nor get me out of this *rotten* mess known as permanently "off duty." It doesn't *take* a cognitive linguist to explain why death is a noun and dying is its singular mode of movement. So many graves surround us in this locus; the *forgotten* tumuli at Bourges and Magdeburg (once thought to *have* offered the dual and perfect explanations of Pauline eschatology) are long removed from the Christian Encyclopedia of Death and deposited in the unmarked shrine to the lost painting by the one with the missing ear. It's reassuring to know that after we *die* there's guaranteed a *grave* to *lie* in without the fear of sunburn and melanoma or bad *verse read* to us by an aged relative of Robert Frost. But the lure of medieval dying, and the puissant charm of the Early Modern corpse, wow! They used to *rehearse* being *dead* by wrapping up in periwinkle satin winding sheets, a pleasant change from being-there as it emerged when Heidegger put thought to *pen* for those *men* who faltered at misprision.

---

1. Geeze that last speech makes me wonder why we stopped massacring the Scots. Yours truly Wlliam Augustus, Duke of Cumberland aka the Butcher of Culloden.

> Better murder an infant in its cradle than nurse
> an unacted desire.
>
> William Blake

Scene 6. *Enter Rosalind and Celia* (disguised as the Earl of Oxford*)*.
Howdy pardner what's your name? My name's Maiden China. Coincidence
so's mine. What's two maidens to do in a place like this, swap make-up tips or
trade hairsprays I suppose until the nano-formats break down and guarantee
the systematic failure of this self-*abused* species we call "us." I don't think
rationality's one of homo sapiens' lasting inventions do you? Phrased more
mythopoetically what will Kronos-Saturn have for supper now that he's eaten
all his children? Thank God we were meticulously remodeled according to
the latest paleontological retroactivities, dinosaurs like us should eat more
humans and stop barbecuing statues of the Virgin Mary. There *used* to be
an intimate connection between commercial cannibalism and pre-Capitalist
formations, a *friend* would prove his conviviality by offering his own body
for dinner and those more lazy found auto-cannibalism appealing with the
predatory and stealth uneccessary. I once *sympathized* with those emaciated
heretics in Gaul with legs as thin as a grasshopper's, burned alive on the Celtic
fringe and I would always *lend* an empathetic ear to a discount prayer to the
Master of the Havard Hannibal (when surreptitiously *devised* for the use of
unexorcised children). These *days* you make laughter and death sound so
rhetorically simple, especially when you cross-dress for our annual vacation
in a nudist colony. I am reality and I demand a name, but together we are
the unknowable Ding an Sich thought *anew* as the critical division between
satiric poetry and vaudeville.—(Faint *praise* for the little door sliding back into
concordat provisionals.) But before we get into all that I have a question to
pose: what marks the place where word and taciturnity are one? Why is it
that you and everyone else treat me as if I'm the Palace Encyclopedia? I'm
afraid that's not a question an Elizabethan secret agent from Stratford like
me can answer, but it's a question that haunts my history plays anticipating
Coleridge's final plunge out of beauty which shattered both the *hue* and the

ethics of silence. [The poet interrupts: This *book* remarks the dream of a new *use* for poetry; steganography assures us a certain privacy and to *overlook* the *muse* guarantees the fact of work. So word, now you're here, invent your own reality; forget the *muse* and *overlook* the consequence of poetry.] It look's like the rabbit stew's come back to life. Why don't we kill and cook it again and have it with a glass of vintage bull's blood as we contemplate the monstrosity of infancy? I'm sure glad I didn't sell my eggs to an internet sperm bank; it took Julia Child a mere fifteen minutes to show the world the versatility of the meringue while we've had half a billion years of motherhood and we still haven't improved on the baby. What a waste of time being alive without the *use* of language or the solace of a *book*. The initial problem for a parent comes from the fact that you can't choose what the baby looks like, it lies there on arrival unrecognizable as a blood-stained terrestrial creature. Take me for instance, the moment I was born my mother instantly died of embarrassment. I exuded the *hue* of an addled omelet garnished with screams and pisse yet still garnered the *praise* of my remaining relatives and neighbors to finally be awarded a Nobel Prize for rebarbativity. Granted, Balthus made a big improvement to the image of the baby, bloating it up to look like a blown frog, while Hans Belmer made them resemble dismembered dolls, and that line of infant accessories from Toys "Я" Us designed by the Marquis de Sade came in handy at bedtime. But none of this alters the fact that it's more pleasurable to read *anew* the latest article on Chrone's disease or a variorum edition of an anthology of Swahili diatribes than change a diaper. They should hire the Boston strangler to sing them to sleep. Jonathan Swift made a modest proposal that babies are best cooked then eaten which sounds a great idea to me. Still, it's a relief to know that today's baby might well grow up to be tomorrow's mass murderer or born-again pedophile. It's all well and good for you to complain about the non-utility of babies but these *days* looking after you at 58 is like looking after 29 two year olds; you're a veritable kindergarten of grumbling malpractices. It's time you *devised* a scheme for living out the poignancy of the Northern Lights or *lend* me a hand in deciding what qualities might organize our remaining days. I'm sure the *sympathized friend* is a relic from some defunct Wordsworthian wardrobe but it takes a wicked mother to bring up a good child. I *used* to believe Structuralism (that *abused* child of Saussurean linguistics) might open up the space in which eschatology could emerge as mere sunlight stumbling through a daytime factory for victims. So let's buy Time a drink and say goodnight to her.

Exeunt

Enter Clowne.
Should I feel guilty about those disruptive passions I *devise* to subvert the aspirations of others? An answer to that question would be as useful as advanced snorkel equipment is to active goldfish. Just look at my *eyes*, they stick out as two transcendental failures in self-deprecation before a *tomb* for defunct comedians. Even Socrates showed reticence around his own philosophic irony, remaining *mute* on the ethics of an inconsistent dying, while I'm here, having gambled away all my burial money as a teenager, stuck in this inferno of court cuckolds courtesy the Elsinore College for Advanced Adultery and their cornuto e contento philosophy (it was always that way with that skank the Queen). I'd welcome a catastrophe right now, perhaps I should try a goblet of hemlock tisane (I'm told it's a veritable hangman's noose in liquid). It's hard to keep faith in an ethos of touch-tone enthusiasms, that's why my anticipation of the non-existent is my numero uno right now. I have a vague recollection of my first visit to this planet, landing among the binaries of speech and writing, but now, language fails me as a threshold. In fact my manager, Momus, turns out to be less a savvy business agent than a commercial disaster. It's so *dumb* to *impute* the dianoetic virtues such as bed-wetting and nail biting to an intrepid fear of death. And another thing, each time I feel I *grow* I actually shrink and, *short* of the image of a pigmy John Stuart Mill descending onto the promenades of eulogy (to *show* his sympathy and shed a tear over the urn of the untold joke), I feel too small to be worthy of mortality. I received a *report* from Woody Allen that death has outstripped jocularity in the entertainment ratings handing over its *debt* to the International Monetary Fund. Yet to *exceed* life is to enter poetry via posterity and *set* in place the perfect reason for a sunrise. But I'll *need* a lot of faith to get me through this job of being; I'll *need* to *set* aside my sense of place in a floating voice not speaking and that way *exceed* the possibilities in van Gennep's theory on

transition via tributes to the dead and rites of passage.[1] I've thought a lot about death and representation and owe a profound *debt* to Archbishop Chichele's polychrome tomb at Canterbury.[2] I also read a recent aesthetician's *report* claiming death to be the best reason for moisturizing cream, which goes to *show* why the Egyptian Book of the Dead adds an exotic dimension to the basic subject of cosmetics for the posthumous. Yet science still can't reassure us death is only temporary or there's eternal bliss in a future life—in fact, the future's where I've always been. There's probably lots of *short*-cuts to non-being if you let your necrobiosis *grow* into a full-fledged properispomenon—or am I confusing things? Either way to *impute* the problem to the negativity of the spirit is plain *dumb*. These days logic really is the kingdom of the unexpected.[3] As a devout exponent of the verfremdsungseffekt I stand lost and helpless in some hydroponic poetics surrounded by *mute* metaphors the size of melons. If a man is funny place him in a *tomb* after closing his *eyes*, and put a penny on each lid, then *devise* a way to change the world by erasing it.

1. See A. Van Gennep, *The Rites of Passage*, trans. M. B. Vizedom & G. I. Caffee. Chicago 1960.
2. Erected circa 1426.
3. Osip Mandelstam in his "Morning of Acmeism."

Enter Orlando and Adam.

Excuse us for butting in, we just called round on the off-chance that your clown's nose might be on fire, which reminds me it's bad enough to be burned alive at another's behest but a far *worse curse* is the one brought on by yourself. I was ten seconds into Shelley's Revolt of Islam, at the point *where* that blast of thunder-speech from the Erdgeist rips apart the speaker's ears, when suddenly I realized what's needed is an intellectually funny genealogy and heraldic history of the extinct and dormant. The point of *wit* is less *clear*, however, when metaphor is understood to be a Borromean knot tied in literary space; it's then that the real interrogations start. Did Adam and Eve ever pheart in Paradise? Why, in the entirety of holy *writ*, doesn't the *story* of the first pig appear? And you won't find it in Virgil with his predilection for neatherds over swineherds. What a phony he was with his false prophecies about the birth of baby Jesus and you can't *tell* me that his Aeneid is better than David

Cecil's Portrait of Jane Austen; with its numerous illustrations and fold-out color-gravure frontispiece it's a *glory* to *dwell* in for an hour or two; it's almost as good as Phyllis Hartnoll's 1951 Oxford Companion to the Theatre now available on Kindle. What a read that *grew* to be through my adolescence; with its *store* of information, plot summaries and useful terminology it's totally unnecessary to actually go to plays. Being with *you* is the same as meeting a hermit on his lunch break, what's *more* it's obvious that poetry's never spent a night in your bed. I should write that down but first here's a condom to slip over your soul, it's much *more* effective than a guardian angel, *you* simply wash it out thoroughly in soapy water after each life and *store* it away until the next. Incidentally, ever heard of Nehemiah *Grew*? His Experiments in the Consort of the Lucation proved a near-best seller among the half-dead Dons and sex-offenders of Gresham College. But let's not *dwell* on the *glory* of his minor chemical experiments, these days we can't *tell* an Anglican pastor from an empty hallway. Remember that *story writ* by Sister Mary Enzima[2] about the death of Villon, in which space meets world in a *clear* paradox of lucus a non lucendo[3] close to a Paris where "not even the lark sees the open sky."[4] Let's put *wit* aside and recount to me the enigmas of your world, declare them solvable when hope's suspended at a point *where* allegory passes into the *curse* of a general semiosis, or *worse* into a Phaedra fable set in urban signs.

1. Owing to multidenominational pressure now known as the Holiday Infant.
2. *Memoirs of a Virgin Madam: the Pieties and Profanities of Sister Enzima Bates.* O.M. n.p. n.d. (ca. 1890).
3. Sorry to sound cantankerous again but I do wish they'd print Latin phrases in italics instead of merely the rhyming words—everyone knows they don't belong in prose. But while we're in another footnote let's get back to philosophizing and start a new debate on the current ecumenical poverties and, stuffing cryptomorphism aside, let's set out to prove the old claim that "frustra fir per plura quod potest fieri per unum" i.e. the famous philosophic razor of William Occam: "entities are not to be multiplied beyond necessary"—an axiom stated a century earlier by Odo Regaldus in the quotation above and totally ignored in this footnote.
4. Heidegger.

Here a daunce of Shepheards and Shepheardesses

Enter Falstaffe and Bardolffe.

What results from mixing a corpse on ice with a flatulent dog in a kiddy pool hidden away in the back of a pick-up truck, and here's another quick question: what's the sensory *effect* of an omphalos placed middle-distance on a gibbet répoussoir, or the quinquagenary meeting of X and Y? With all due *respect* and *before* going any further I have to say talking that way makes *you* sound like Stephen Hawking on a quiz game. Best put aside your theortical physics and witty formalisms there's *more* we need to discuss about a life without art because *true* worth always manifests without it. Did Karl Marx think about Petrarch or the early symphonies of Michelangelo as he bought himself a refill for his *pen* and then wrote the proletariat into its historical destiny of staying poor? It ill *affords* the vomit of bombast to situate its *Amen* in poetic *words*. Even Don Peyote that man from La Mancha *filed* his tax returns in Madrid while thrusting his dialectics into a windmill. His nom de plume was Shaxkespere whose *quill compiled* those sonnets that we used to be and might *still* become again if the death of the author sounds as laughter on the other side of this literary event. Whitman claims "the prudence of the greatest poet answers at least the craving and glut of the soul," however to name us "poetically mutant" answers nothing and *still* leaves the pair of us impervious to any revolutionary problematic. I wish I'd *compiled* those sonnets, with a *quill* like his I could have been the Salman Rushdie of our galaxy. The only writings I've *filed* were for down-payments on a blank tombstone. Did I mention Richard Branson, founder of Virgin Airlines and reincarnation of Howard Hughes, thinks I'm the great cryptogram in his own Paradise Misplaced. I've thought a lot about anthropogenesis among the garbage and on our expiation through *words* toward the ultimate *Amen* of non-knowledge. We might accomplish a destiny separable from the latest chronology between us by imitating the mating patterns of the death watch beetle. The thought of Babel *affords* us the image of a room called absence, while the *pen* in its lift-off from the page alembicates the *true* ennui of this terror infirmary. Better return to "le paradis des amour enfantines" and have it painted Danish blue or pale camembert. Immolation also comes to mind as well as cheese but *more* to the point so does my Baudelairean zest for living. But then again *you* construct a solid argument that if the dead did not exist then they would have to be invented. More to the point *before* concluding can we *respect* a French poet whose sole *effect* becomes too agreeable for credence.

Exeunt

Scene 7. *Enter King and Guard.*
Maybe *mine* is a life that lends itself to cheap Freudian analysis but what makes me truly sick is the pathetic certainty of poetry. Each *line* détourned from some Parasite Museum threatening with the pseudo-rubric that "If I do not write I never was" *thence* destined to reach the ears of all the dead not listening. I actually like a good strophe but what I genuinely *boast* of is a fine *intelligence* that never visited the *ghost* of Shackspire & Co. Ltd. Inc. In fact I thoroughly support literary euthanasia. Get rid of all those scrawny sonnets, villanelles and Sapphic fragments and concentrate on living out those great epic sagas stitched together by the Vikings. I'm impervious to all those lies that poet-critics pedal, in fact the entire Renaissance was a hoax that conned us all. It's a recently discovered fact that Leonardo da Vinci was entirely battery operated and preprogrammed by three teenage internet hackers in Taiwan. Such truths aren't found in Wikipedia. It's not poetry but style that brings word and flesh together as writing interpenetrates the world, that's why there's a crisis in representation—including our own. I'm *astonished* too how stability shrivels in these times. At *night* houseflies intertwine according to the dominant law of their genera to emerge as homeopathic synchronized trans-sexuals in a Cowboy Poetry contest somewhere between Tombstone and Wichita Falls. By contrast the *dead* present an effigy in stasis and speak to us in an honest, constant way: "We are many but the living are few." If I were forced to *write* I'd do so in prose about the end of man as the agent of destiny, enjoying a last drink with a syphilitic Oedipus in a singles bar called the Marriage of Heaven and Hell. Unlike Georges Bataille I'm exhausted by all this inner experience. I *grew* up with thoughts like his until I looked like a shirt worn by Death in a film about speech disorders. Best concentrate on the false pretensions of an Anti-Christ and capture the stability of solitude in its campaign to *inhearse* appearance neck deep in a swirling matrix of Dr. Herpes' Lip Balm. *You* really are three gods in one person, a smile becoming lips on little red militia men,

captured as *verse* is also, anarchically yet principled. Shaykespeea wrote a lot of *verse you* know but his "ripe thoughts in my brain *inhearse*," to make their tomb "the womb wherein they *grew*" captured the zeitgeist. That's a noble sentiment indeed, it says it all, but it doesn't explain why, in Death's mini-series, meaning is always the afterlife of the materiality of semiosis. And that's the thought that I didn't *write* given my sensitivity to fits of baptism and *dead*-pan humor. Each *night* my bed becomes a foreign country and I wake up *astonished* that I'm actually there. Schopenhauer distinguished between immanent and transcendental knowledge, but a *ghost* with a modicum of *intelligence* might ask "what is it to have been thought in a sentence?" and no one can *boast* death's sentence in a phrase on a parapet above fulfilled knowledge. *Thence* I wonder if we're both a joke conceived as the latest penny gaff in which no one's come up with the punch *line*. Sometimes I feel I'm possessed by adieus—it's evident in my neck when it expands—and with needs like *mine* I'm as much use to the court as hooping cough.

Enter a Messenger (convinced that he is God).
Bedazzled by the sight of a severed ear amongst sunflowers I awoke to realize today is Death's birthday and I haven't bought it a present. It doesn't really *matter*, in fact, there's no need to *flatter* myself on my own importance. Am I *making* sense or is this argument *growing* tedious? Am I *mistaking* practical ethics for negative theology again, *knowing* full well that if you kiss the lips of the abyss the abyss will turn you down? Echo to interim are you exceeding me? Am I *swerving* a little too far from eschatology? *Wanting* to sound like Hamlet among all these feminine rhymes am I soliloquizing too much? Is this question already a rhetorical question, or is that she-male nun I placed in the category convent truly *deserving* of a trip to Lourdes? Should I sign up for Linkedin or start my own blog? Does *granting* laceration, conflagration and anguish legal status as blood sports help towards achieving a *determinate* roll for our occupation forces in the neutral zone? Am I now sounding like Clausewitz *releasing* his sexual frustrations on a map of Prussia? Is Purgatory a temporal rather than a spatial concept as Jacques Le Goff contends? Am I correct in my *estimate* that evil belongs to the logic of economy not morality? Does *possessing* a God without a God imply a Deity with vertigo in a sky

upside down? Is it finally time to hibernate in my Zeno affinities? I know I love my own inquisitiveness but rest assured I'll never be accused of not *possessing* a sense of wonder about the world I created. However, in my own divine *estimate*, life is always configured as a consequence of two oppositional forces by which I invent reality and humanity attempts to understand it. I like *releasing* my enigmas and little deistic puzzles in a *determinate* manner to baffle scientists and hagiologists alike. Incidentally, thanks for *granting* me a place in your thoughts, not many embryologists do these days; I admit my radical thaumaturgy needs revising although most humans are fully *deserving* of the more destructive of my miracles. What I'm *wanting* to ask you all, as humans, what I'm *swerving* towards in this monolog, is how you endure life on this planet *knowing* I'll be waiting in the afterlife fully armed with zero tolerance, cognizant of all your deeds before they actually occur? It's a little game I like to play, *mistaking growing* entities for shrinking events. I bet you didn't know that a ternary dialectic always requires the *making* of a fourth premise. The analogy is to a lavatory occupied by you and a stranger—call the latter me but don't *flatter* yourself too much with that scenario. Moment and memory and do they *matter*? Open an epoch so knowledge will disappear? It was Paul's great promise. Paul my apostle, the one who knew nothing.

Exeunt

> Pain has but one acquaintance,
> that is Death.
>
> Emily Dickinson

Scene 8. *Enter Multitudes with halters around their necks.*[1]
"That's a helluva nasty stage direction, it sure as hell complicates our relation to projected long-term goals." "Our plans for metagenesis just met a problem." "It's amazing how some people pay no attention to the Camp David Accords." "Human Rights are yesterday." "There's still time to apprehend, reproduce, then realize." "Let's fix those vertigos once and for all."[2] "Too little too late." "But perhaps there still is a meaning to life." "I once thought that a stick figure was some kind of adhesive Cossack constantly pursuing his enemy on

horseback, finally aware of his being a fading portrait of Aleksandr Solzhenitsyn. Now I'm told it's a person like one of Giacometti's nudes, frequently found emaciated and hanging on a stick gallows or lined up with other sticky figures as part of a sticky abacus counting the world and its terrible atrocities by means of sticks, sticks to match and light the world's last cigarette for the Cossack now riding into a final sunset calling his 'I' an 'it'." "This is where the rubber meets the road." "I must say that these are the happiest wounds of my career." "That prussic acid ruined your complexion but it still looks nicer than your face." "So much for the prophets of gaiety." "My sans souci has suddenly become dialectically unavailable." "A little help sub rosa from some Luddites wouldn't go amiss." "My sentiments exactly." "It's easy to lose weight when living on possum broth." "That trans-fat in my final breakfast tasted fabulous, but the state of espresso after Euclid leaves me asking for less." "Let's try to split up and make contact in Peru." "Method acting didn't help me at all in the end." "This is not the ontological Shangri La that I expected to retire in." "They say 'him whom inquisitors hate angels may love.'"[3] "Touché, but whatever happened to the presumption of innocence?" "I think I'm seeing but in reality I'm being seen." "Every wound inflicted will be a victory." "I was simply trying to get out of the way." "Soon my neck will wander into an executioner's geography." "Pain's gone when the heat's on." "Death is an orgy scheduled for Saturday." "Seems my bubble world just burst." "When I am dead let the earth and fire be jumbled together." "I will survive through time and correction." "This really is Last Hope House." "Remember the man who survived the Nazi concentration camps only to be strangled to death half a century later by two Manhattan teenagers?" "It's people like us give Death a bad name." "So much for diplomatic immunity." "That Veterans Crisis chat-line didn't help much." "We're ad portas inferni and still without the key." "My chains are my charms." "We've got bigger problems than gingivitis." "I'll accept death like those virgin frogs as a victim of the Rites of Spring." "If only I'd entered that Fidel Castro rule-alike competition I might still be in power today." "It's definitely laudable to give self-knowledge its prerequisites but it would be *wrong* to raise the time-space compression in the Beauty-cum-immunity system via a superficially thin case of genocide like the one about to happen." "That class action law suite didn't get us very far." "We truly are Poverty's lost chickens." "But perhaps death comes slower on two dollars a day." "I think my alpha's soon to become my omega." "I see today's going to be a bundle of laughs." "Those 'Arbeit macht Frei' striped jackets look really good on us." "I'll be glad when peace finally breaks out." "These days reality substitutes light bulbs for sunlight." "Fine, we've replaced 'stranger' with 'terrorist' but the strangeness still inheres." "We shall die in the isolation of our semicolons." "When the holiday's over the camp remains." "Parcere subjectis."[4] "Wait till they start taking batting practice on our kidneys." "I blame it on the failure of immigrant integration policies." "Welcome to the Paradise of Fundamental Difference." "The only thing missing for our execution is a chorus line of trainee managers leg-kicking to the film script of Last Tango in Paris." "Happy, happy they that in Hell feel not the world's despite."[5] "But it isn't even Paris." "When I think of all the children that came out of my bowels." "We are Sestos and Abydos, Fate's bookends, iron cupids next a concrete saint, Death's windswept geraniums." "We've always identified with both the victim and the executioner and look where its got us." "All of us here *belong* on the incorrect side of tomorrow." "I wonder if we'll meet the prisoner of Zenda, or the Man in the Iron Mask?" "The scene of the punished sinner is common." "We're the new effects of asymmetric warfare." "At least conflagration will end community." "I really should have opened that boutique in Islamabad." "They say it's New Year's Eve and it really feels like it is, such a balanced contradiction is indicative of our life in signs." "Happiness is a neat recompense for ignorance, but I'm also well aware of what's in store." "Sweet to the wretched is the tomb's repose."[6] "I'm fessing up to nothun." "What is a world and how do we come to it?" "Our world believes it stabler if the soft are whipped to show the face repentance wears."[7] "No retreat. No surrender. (To quote my marriage vows.)" "Kandinsky still believes that even dead matter is living spirit." "Remember just name, rank and serial number." "It makes *me* wonder what went wrong at the Council of Trent." "*Do you too* remain an obscurantist desire behind someone else's openness?   I know it's difficult to answer with that gag and blindfold on but there's actually a power in abjection that resonates in the triumph of the negative. So *glory* in the *tainted* blood that's dripping into your left arm and never suture that wound. I know, it's the same old victim's *story*, introspective in your complacent peripeteia, but it would really help to get *acquainted* with some of the other torturers. (After all alterity is closer to ethics than the dialectic.) Take Officer Samuels, for instance, although he's *forsworn* to secrecy try and get him to explain between the shocks administered how he measures the digestive rate of his victims' food by opening their internal geographies; he even arranges after-suffer full-spa treatments for his victims. Or Mr. Ferris, the Warden, he came up with a most ingenious method of torturing Saint Catherine that he later sold to the local fairground, and his patented ducking-stool for the Salem witch trials led to the invention of the Boston tea-bag. Then there's Officer Astaire, his idea to place hot coals on the shower floor proved a very effective way of bringing the fox-trot back to popularity. Rest assured, no one around here ever complains of Grievous Bodily Happiness. There's a lot more potential to raise the fun quotient in our Master-slave relationship. Any *fight* to the finish will be just the beginning. Heap *scorn* on the *light* at the end of the tunnel, we are justified by everything we are: microbes, traffic jams, Mickey Mouse Surrealisms, deadlines, cancers, gluten free miracles, cabarets of hibernations, and a dead chihuahua named Sir Fopsbury Faceache to complete the happy litany. So enjoy your bastinados and water boarding, there'll be more of them today (oh, by the way I'll need a couple of large bricks for your vasectomy tonight)." "Thanks, but no thanks, your torturer's optimism is leaking through the cracks in your every mumble, it's truly depressing. Can someone around here shed *light* on the fact that *scorn* recapitulates humility in several of the minor miracle plays? And if that's overly 'akkehdummick' for a torturer why not explain why we don't *fight* all the time? But perhaps that's overly 'dummestik' or else all prison guards are really Freemasons and *forsworn* to secrecy." "Alleluia or NOTHING doesn't leave much of a choice." "But supposing Death is God—that introduces a nice Nietzschean reversal. Who knows, I may prove to be the martyr who dies *acquainted* with the most advanced techniques of torture." "It may be an old *story* of the *tainted* wish but I've always hoped for salvation, death, and debauchery in that order." "Not to *glory too* much in that hope but *you* should know that advanced resurrection studies indicate that the Heavenly Paradise might prove to be one endless brothel of defecation,[8] fabricated like the pulpits of Donatello to depict a slow, inexorable death by sex." "*Do me* a favor leave now, and let's rendezvous in a few millennia at the essential zoo among the remnants of thinking. Perhaps I can inherit your female traits, mix them with outside activities and, if nobody claims 'We *belong* to the chosen few,' then it wouldn't be *wrong* to say that all the rest is merely radiation."

1. "A satisfactory psychological explanation of the histrionics around early Baroque dissection is yet to be produced." Lady Seymor H. Titus R.N., *Rethinking the Body from Neolithic to Posthuman*. Coral Gables: The Sentinel Press, 2003: 316.
2. Rimbaud.
3. Leigh Hunt.
4. Above the gateway to Dartmoor Prison.
6. Robert Southey, *Joan of Arc*.
5. John Dowland, *Lachrimae, or Seven Teares figured in Seven Passionate Pavanes*.
7. George Meredith, "The Sage Enamoured and the Honest Lady."
8. A thought conjured earlier by William of Auvergne: "maledicta Paradisus in qua tantum cacatur!"

> Love in its means is war; at bottom, the deadly hatred of the sexes.
>
> Nietzsche

Enter the King of Fairies at one doore with his train, and the Queene at another with hers.

Sorry to look and sound like Mae West in miniature, but is that a permanent boil on the back of your head or are you happily wearing a clown's nose back to front? Incidentally, aren't your knees a little low for breast implants? I really dislike Patriarchy in miniature. So what do we do about it? I thought the answer obvious, everyone should start becoming taller women. You mean form a pan-global Amazonian Lysistrata Committee and work towards a monosexual universe? Precisely, I've already secured celebrity endorsement from Aristophanes and Aubrey Beardsley and I know you *hate debate*, insisting everything I *tell* you is *wrong* but if I averred Totality to be the goal of history culminating in the United Empire of America would you believe me? Sounds as if you've been chewing barbed wire again; what this country needs is a good political enema up its constitution, but I prefer to stay away from politics and *dwell* intellectually in advanced seaweed research and the history of the popsicle™ in frozen knowledge, or reflect on the wonders of the hydrostatic paradox while drowning in the royal bathtub. Incidentally, I threw away that book of poems you loaned me, all those *tongue* twisters proved a little too hard on my lips; there's something in the sumptuous duration of alexandrines that reminds me of the *strange* spectacle of Franco-Prussian Coronations or Emmy Awards in Atlanta. Give me the lesbian bombast of an Allen Ginsberg anytime, superb in its *will* to *change* the poetic status quo, or that cadence of dying captured perfectly in Charles Kingsley's Song of the Little Baltung. Ah, the *ill* desert of oblivion! Who remembers Kingsley now apart from his Water Babies? That said, the *defence* of poetic popularity by a cheap appeal to information theory has always been a lame stratagem for canonization. Should we *halt* at the stop sign or go through it? Please don't take *offence*, but your kingdom is a mind to me equal at least to a Declaration of Independence prefiguring some Gettysburg address in a painting by Hokusai signed "aboriginally yours." It's not my *fault* that you're shorter and a little narrower at the neck than yesterday and it's not my *fault* that you now make a perfect companion piece to the miniature portrait of Bess of Hardwick that hangs at Chatsworth. No *offence*, but life does have its parallels to art. For instance, a squatting figure of the Anti-Christ with a moveable mouth made by Claus Oldenberg or one of his ilk would make a splendid garbage shoot and rival our famed Mannekin Pis balsamic vinegar dispenser. Jarry claims that famous fountain in Brussels represents the Infant Jesus showering his blessings on the world and that wherever his urine drops a branch of Walmart miraculously disappears.[1] Why don't we *halt* the limousine by this car bomb and ruminate upon the infinite sadness of the finite in decline? I know you're full of fear and trembling and to bring a little Kierkegaard to your *defence* would not be *ill* advised. Cardinal Richelieu told me over cocktails the other day that God speaks in nudges, so why not move into some special relationship with Fichte or Schelling? The mental *change will* do us good and at least we'll be closer to the spirit of the *strange* leap back to faith. (I'm told life's one long rave in the Church of England.) I also think that a *tongue*-tied Archbishop of Canterbury would be the closest approximation to the music of the spheres. Not to *dwell* on the horrors of anatomy, but would it be *wrong* to claim that the nose is the least romantic of our seven protuberances? Not if you're an Eskimo or a Doberman Pincher, but it's impossible to *tell* if we ourselves prefer revolution to *debate*. The corruption of man is followed by the corruption of language.[2] Maybe, but

I *hate* to admit that I'm happy to be dying on one of Philosophy's metaphysical trams conversing with the lost homunculus whose mouth's connected to the main drain.

1. See "Virgin and Mannekin Pis" in *Selected Works of Alfred Jarry*, ed. Roger Shattuck and Simon Watson Taylor. New York: Evergreen Books, 1965: 127-29 and Walmart's *Annual General Report* 2003-04. Appendix 7, sub-section Iib f.n. 7: 732.
2. Emerson.

Enter King Richard (disguised as Shaksper).

Hey there little people, that package you dropped off at Anne Hathaway's cottage, was it from Sir Francis Bacon or the Earl of Oxford? These days you never know what you're receiving thanks to the postal effect. Sending a parcel's a little bit like death don't you think, a mode of departure in which you seal it up in its paper tomb and drop it in a box with the hope that it finds its proper destination in the great unknown. It would be more practical to reinstitute pigeon post throughout the entire kingdom. Sometimes a package drops behind a wall to remain hidden for centuries and, take my word on it, even a cadaver smells better than a pile of disintegrating manuscripts. Take Aristotle's Poetics for instance, rotting away in some Byzantine cellar for centuries, or that heap of songs and epigrams Planudes found among the offal of epochs.[1] Some Irish critics hold that the manuscript of Finnegans Wake was buried beneath a pile of dung to be eventually found by a hen named Belinda reading Gilbert and Sullivan's explanations of the Book of Kells. As for Bibliophilia, that incurable disease you pick up in used bookstores, it's as comforting as a cold hot water bottle in Ninuvik. Have you ever smelled a first folio Shakespeare in that cesspool called the Folger Library?[2] It's worse than performing CPR on a camel's ah-soul. Apparently the Bubonic Plague and that pandemic Spanish Flu outbreak of 1918 were both started by somebody opening the identical first edition of Mary Shelley's Frankenstein. I'd be happy if all the world's antiquarian books went the way of Guy Fawkes and Giordano Bruno. But enough about cadavers, books and manuscripts, let's talk about me. Ah, a life *so* sad as mine is best conceived as one of morality's voluntary handicaps. Granted, its great to have the same name as God and that communist theocracy I set up during the Peasants' War turned out quite profitable—but only for me. That admitted, to follow *woe* to the brink *might* be something I could easily give up for Lent. [Ed.: There is a sigh from nowhere and the *taste* of bitter almonds greets the tongue. Counter-moves dissolve in the enigmatic aura of anachronisms and *spite* stays relative to its fissure-point.] Did you pick up our DTECs[3] from that castle in Transylvania? With the *last* historical break into ex-subjectivity just around the corner they're sure to come in handy. But right now our mission is to *overthrow* the political interior of the imagination—I mean, it's been bugging us for centuries. We need to develop advanced analytic simultaneism like those guys in Paris during the Banquet Years, reimplement client service focus reorientation programs (as the Zurich Dadaists did) and bring back those refresher courses in being vile that Johnny Rotten and Sid Vicious implemented during the Reagan and Thatcher years. Come the *morrow* I'll no doubt be thinking that thought Adorno had on the philosophical Eros of the old cosmologies.[4]   *Woe* betide the scoffers of concepts and categories, I mean without them how could we specify our *sorrow* and *loss* let alone our more noxious unpleasantries? And if a poet needs to *bow* down obsequiously before the lyric muse and do everything in order to ensure that the poem he/she writes has nothing to do with knowledge then what do we do with philosophy? I dislike poetry's embrace of dianoia, it seems counterproductive for the muse to have a pure language of certainty. But that's a cultural bridge I don't have to *cross* right *now*, I'm more concerned about better access to sensuous geniality and companion care *now* the First Crusade is over (what a rehearsal for the Vietnam War that turned out to be). Christ shooting a *cross-bow* built by Beethoven would be inferior to one constructed by Hegel, but let's not get caught up in the phantom of the subject-object relation, when it's the lack of difference that makes a history between us all. Despite our identical baggage of *loss, sorrow* and *woe* there are immanent possibilities for all of us as the final tourists of mortality. Come the *morrow* on the Via Nuda Vita, in our shared caprices, we'll understand why our void remarks in the negativity of the infinite[5] an event without heroes. Given that we're limited to official philosophical platitudes all we can posit is a time-lag in the *overthrow* of the Peoples Republic of Plato. With an insight like that I've at *last* earned the right to die, and in *spite* of that observation I still smell and *taste* of rotting rationales. In fact you *might* want to reconfigure all my extra-territorial probabilities but *woe* betide the one who tries to postulate the heteronymity of death in its oh *so* human disempowerment.

1. The famed *Anthologia Graeca*, the original in Greek deriving from a manuscript compiled by the thirteenth-century Byzantine monk and scholar Planudes, who abridged, rearranged and expanded the anthology of Cephalus, (subsequently lost), thus forming the only known collection of Greek epigrams before the recovery of Cephalus' work in the seventeenth-century (and who cares). Mention needs also be made of the subterranean fate of some of Dante Gabriel Rossetti's poems. Driven by remorse at the death of his first wife Elizabeth Siddal, Rossetti buried a manuscript of his poems in the coffin with her body. Seven years later in 1869, and obviously now drinking a new brand of English breakfast tea, he dug up the coffin and disinterred the poems, many of which appeared in his 1870 *Poems*. A little known fact is that on recovering the manuscript Rossetti noted to his horror that the manuscript had been carefully proof-read and revised in Ms Siddal's hand.

2. They use dead pigs as air-fresheners in that musty establishment.

3. Discount terminal entertainment coupons.

4. "True thoughts are those which do not understand themselves" in *Minima Moralia*, trans. E. F. N. Jephcott. London: Basic Books, 1974: 192.

5. Parmenides.

Exeunt

Scene 9. *Enter Friar and Romeo.*

Saint Peter once told his buddy Saint Nicodemus the Hagiorite, that God has long suffered from cerebral palsy, which explains a lot about la condition humaine and since we've blamed God for every other disaster that's occurred this year why not blame him for this one? I remember when ethics was called etiquette and this monastery was a thriving brothel and before that a madhouse and now that madness has become an object of knowledge perhaps it's time to invite Melanie Klein over to analyze us—apart from that I seem to *make* sense in the strangest of ways. *Take* my latest claim that "the voice that is disempowered still belongs to everyone" or my *boast* that "word and thing are merely two sides of the same rupture." Sex may prove to *be* no more than a lost rottweiler sniffing in your previously unexplored kennel-of-love, but what will such a speculative endeavor *cost* the two of us? I only have sex when the head Abbot's watching, but if you ask *me* it's probably *best* to *measure* my exhibitionism against my fear of a giant ant climbing up my reredos. Phuck your phobias old friend, today is the epoch of priapic power, the reign of the One-eyed Trouser Snake, and sin will prove so abundant (with huge amounts of sex accompanying it) they'll have to hire a permanent Em Cee

147

in the confessional booth. When copulating we become the beast with two backs (and you won't find that in the Book of Revelation). Passion absorbs us in a pyroclastic surge until lust exhausts the two of us and, when we tire, drenched, our mouths full of Cupid's toothpaste, we collapse breathless in beads of perspiration and *rest* as usual in the chair (a little cramped) in the background of the Cavalcanti Annunciation, imagining with *pleasure* being kissed goodnight by Daffy Duck. So much for sodomy, but my life in your head is not a pleasant place to reside, it should go out on a *horse* like Roy Roger's Trigger and ride itself into the History Channel. These days I'm *ill* disposed to spend Christmas in the negative or in the *force*-fed uncertainties of structural anthropology (now that it's been seriously questioned)—it seems infinitely preferable to practice my *skill* of waltzing the cogito in all possible directions. Notice the *skill* and adroitness by which the muse deserted my pathetic pate? But perhaps that question will actually *force* us to break in a new tranquilizer. Now that I have Lenin's address I can send him Sister Mary Trotsky's prayer for the perpetual revolution in Braille if he happens to be blind and in lowercase nicotine if he's a smoker. Given your *ill* tempered disposition I think it best to *horse* around a little in Stratford and take *pleasure* in the fact that I'm a negativity with nothing to do.[1] I wonder if the *rest* of ethics will begin with a transposition of self-knowledge into a consensual *measure* of the other, or whether it's *best* to believe like *me* that writing shatters the ethical, or to ask yourself how did I move from death to writing and at what *cost* when it says "writing to end to never cease to *be* again" reduces ontically to the phrase "I never knew it?" Theologies *boast* the promise of an afterlife to *take* away the smell of corpses littering the physiognomy of dead civilizations, viewing a face as a fact through all its social layers to *make* of one's eye a fugitive.

1. Georges Bataille's description of himself to Alexandre Kojeve in 1937.

Enter Polonius and Reynaldo.
Hornstrumpot! I forgot to memorize the doctrinal message from the celestial maiden with the bad breath and hairy armpits—something about the study of human origins as I recall. Anthropogeny never excited me, I rather think it's the question of where we're going *not* where we came from that really matters.

After I *blot* out that sentence let's go to Damascus in the boredom of expectancy; who knows, perhaps that bad shepherd of being will reappear and the same things will happen as they did in ancient times. Before you *die* you should *find* time to come over and check out my edible disarrangements, fossorial in their guidon formulae they're quite the new "foutté." I'm actually relieved that our identities *lie* in the same ontological sphere as two strictly experimental projects sharing one identical *mind* in two separate heads. Albeit we look like a pair of old pyjamas recently returned from (unsuccessfully) wrestling a crocodile[1] and it doesn't make much for conversation. But it's nice that we both *depend* on intense Eurodynamic qualities, it kept us defiantly bohemian throughout the entire 1962 Cuban missile crisis[2]. Dialogue *belongs* to the ones who learn to read by living, for living produces a process of world we can inhabit—and durably too—notwithstanding we may *end* up as a tooth-ache ramified to infinity. To write like this is to remain a terrorist in bed. Ah the *wrongs* we suffer for the triumph of the still-not eventual, I'm so glad we settled in the "ever so slightly intolerable," sitting on the seat of John of Patmos' very first bicycle, knowing life's still left us with our wishes, especially *yours* which *stay* more permanent than *mine*, bagged and labeled, placed one scream *away* from cycloanalysis. We seem light years *away* from genuine inventiveness, placed somewhere between Ariel and Caliban in a dream of *mine* in which we find that we've entered an existence of discontinuous retrogressive assimilation. Let's *stay* just long enough to exacerbate the play of our fate among predicates. Voices disappear into that solitude of *yours*, overtaken by a listening to no one, at which second, or interstice, breath appears in the spectral form of a handshake and community is completed. What *wrongs* of language will put an *end* to the project of poetry? A poet is a path, no more, and *belongs* among a polyconception of the third person, wearing a necklace of dead nightingales[3] flying in a lucent trajectory from Babel to Auschwitz. After that nice intimidating explanation of the crisis in verse you can *depend* on the fact that the bleakest of all our jeopardies will be a prerequisite for any style of life to come. It's also advisable to keep in *mind* that the most effective form of colonization continues to be TV song competitions. So let's *lie* in wait for that bi-polar pickpocket named Libby and let some other characters *find* their own sit-com to *die* in. *Blot* out the brief reality of summer and try *not* to hope for much in the steel hail and bowstrings coming round the bend.

1. Unsuccessfully I might add.

2. October 1962. (What a fortnight for a daydream.)

3. In his "Remarks on Chénier" Mandelstam describes romantic poets as "a necklace of nightingales," remarking further that "a dead nightingale cannot teach poets how to sing."

Enter Ophelia.

That was not one of your better self-vaporizations, but I did enjoy that quote from Mandelstam, and it goes to *show* why life is so inorganic when its heroes *grow* up impersonal. To *tell* the truth and to *be* quite frank, I really wouldn't mind a job in Death's Soft-Toy Department. I don't want to *dwell* on the subject of dying, as you've always been my coach on Heart Walk Weekends, but the way you organize prophecy to summarize today's *decree* on vacant supermarkets is as beautiful as it is *strange*. You likened the lure of malls to that Salon of Aftermaths designed by Albert Speer. Funny, how *history* gets defined as a constant *change* in commodity logic yet it never stops being a springboard into the same old social reification. Incidentally, keep an *eye* out for those bacteria from other planets, they usually arrive about this time of year, a little before the reappearance of mid-nineteenth century pessimisms via Dickens' Bleak House, they tend to interfere with where we *place* our *new* optimisms. Let's *face* it, we were a doomed species from the start, a bunch of experimental filmmakers trained by Leo Strauss to transform the politics of the Oval Office into the land of the *true* and gullible. It's *true*, I love an old failure about as much as I love to *face* up to the eating habits of militant Vegans, failing as I do between a sociology and a philosophy. What a garish *new* interstice, I'm less than a hyphen but more than a blank space, a *place* equivalent to a microscopic piece of stale linguini. Don't you feel that the *eye* of some malevolent deity is watching all of us *change* into obituaries on Trajan's Column? That's a timely intervention into the general *history* of the rhetorical question, but it'll hardly win you a millennial hand-shake. Ah, the *strange* sound of the one mind not answering, approximating some Annie Sprinkle of redemption. It's a wise *decree* to *dwell* on the more felicitous reflection that at the best of times we enjoy that state of being not quite happy. It may *be* that laughter remarks the depth of worlds[2] sent to *tell* us how to *grow* out of our pompous platitudes, and *show* how at the heart of thinking isn't music, but a thinking head deflecting this.[3] But here comes Lear in his smart car, looking like a bionic Beowulf, let's vamoose.

1. But allow me as the first footnote to congratulate you on successfully reducing your verbose prophecies into fortune cookie mottos.
2. Georges Bataille.
3. An obscure and ineffective allusion to Fed Wah's poem-sequence *Music at the Heart Thinking*.

Exeunt omnes

Scene 10. *Enter Lear in a chair carried by Servants.*

Prithee tell me where I am? "Urinna urinal your highness and much too verbose for an oread set in mythic crème fraiche." Are my *weeds* yet in readiness perchance? Pray bringeth out the fetch candle to be lighted.[1] Item, prithee let the measure by pack-thread be taken to the Northern Gate its brigg thereof, thence carried to a Cheshire acre of eight yards to the rod, and the statute verily and all former *deeds* of *dignity* re-effected by the southward wall and in like form from the east side yet dexter it not unto the west so as to *meet* within four days at the destiny gate. And verily effect with good speed my carriage o'er frore yaffles onto yonder pebbled rut. Prithee maketh eftsoons and untappiced of all trillibubs by means ensuring you my benisons and gifts be given to the Beautiful Woman who never says thank-you.[2] Say thou to me in sooth how hail fell on glebesward a flood that almost to an ideogram pressed kindred onto modern eyes. Please it i'faith you to weet that if I *die* communed with the vestment maker it be declared a death of *sweet excellence* and be it Pod-cast prithee via streaming video to happy, pious *faces*. Speak always something other than a salamander's waffle and prove ensured there be erected and forthwith a tomb at my *expense* with images of timber work and item, with my poniard placed not in Bedlam nor the Bodleian, but in proud beodaleana[3]. Also I prithee, let *graces* be showered all around and compass the height of the funeral arch and faileth not to mark in *slow* carving thereof some sundry letters hewed in *stone*. Wherein also I beseech to *show none* the livery about my effigy immured in silks and let *none* be punished save those that *show* how *stone* is not a mark of my *slow* dying. Nor will *graces* be endowed in the copiousness of language at any separate *expense* than that to me. And hide i'faith good evidence of *faces* breathing the stale air of airport terminals amid the *excellence* of iridescent four-fold thinking. As a decrepit father taketh delight, so to my wife be granted my second-best bed, yet sell thee the pillows for the highest price unto my daughters three. How *sweet* and grammercy this way perchance to *die* and *meet* the lasting *dignity* of after-life beyond the tribulations matutinal and the wretchedness of this bleak world where my good *deeds* remain imprended in my heart as soft cowslip and sweet marigold grown forth from the veriest work of *weeds.*

1. In Welsh tradition the Fetch or Corpse Candle is lit to announce the imminent death of a person. See in Richard's *Welsh Dictionary* the article "Canwyll, Corph, Canwyll dyn marw."
2. La Belle Dame sans Merci.
3. An Anglo-Saxon compound word or kenning meaning "sword" (literally "battlelight").

Enter a Gentleman.
Boy, give that old guy a coconut, he's sure as hell's got a natural gift for bathos and he sure knows how to take the *edge* off the contemporary muttering the shards of a lost vernacular. Walking around like a lump of limp celery with a speech impediment, face as worn as a walnut and wearing that crown as if it were an aerosol cap on top of a cornucopia of geriatric and circumlocutional malfunctions; quite a milestone in senility, in fact I've seen dead Japanese on the beaches of Guam looking healthier than him. I'm proud to be gay but that man has the sex appeal of a worn-out toilet brush. I bet he hired himself a taxidermist to stuff all his vocabulary before mumbling it into his beard. I'm convinced he was the guy that gave the Keynote Address at this year's National Dementia Conference at the Pentagon. I'm sure he had fabulous sex during the Jurassic period and I wonder what he looked like during the Ice Age. I also wonder if his mother knows he talks like that, it sounds like there's a frog in his throat singing the Marseillaise with the distinct accent of a Swiss yodeler with a goiter on his neck; it's time somebody made him drink a glass of glue. My guess is he's either dying from late onset puberty, speaking in dialect, or cribbed the whole thing from either the Paston Letters, or Polonius' Compleat Concordance to Piers the Plowman. Either way it's a *privilege* to *see* an aging king with runner beans growing up his Zimmer Frame and fungus round his ankles from the rising damp of centuries *blot* out the new with a good dose of patinated lingua franca and spoken with the eloquence of Saint Potentia.[1] But *you* should never postulate over and above a quantum logic. We've *got* to face the fact those pachydermists *report* to us that camels are not just

animals, but also surface flows in any multiplicity of possible sense-events. *Praise* be that my own referents are usually oscillating mirrors and make *sport* with all the short-cuts to reality. From Narcissus to Alice it's the same old autonomy effect. These *days* however it's those catastrophes within a world of falling stocks and bonds that *enclose* a *name* within a destiny too bleak to contemplate. I remember when I *rose* from sleep after the Thermal Revolution after squandering 30 million Martian dollars in Galaxy Administration and found myself caromed off the edge of a local anagram society meeting into the age of the revival of stuttering; it was a *shame* to wake up. It's also a *shame* I wasn't a practicing atheist at the time I met the devil. He *rose* to the occasion all right. "Call me Left-handed Ludwig" he said, as if Beelzebub wasn't his real *name*. I asked him what does evil *enclose* for the living and for *days* he didn't answer until finally he replied "evil properly belongs to the logic of economy not morality" and then he added "where I come from, Death is a catalyst to the sex industry, but the *sport* of copulation doesn't garner any *praise* from the Council of Hell." Perhaps I should have asked him if he'd read my latest *report* on the disappearance of Shinto, or whether he'd *got* a yen to eat fresh neon? But enough of him for *you* remain for me both a friend and an interruption in a conflict, and in the *blot* upon the scutcheon of this fluctuating logic I *see* I have the *privilege* of being the rotten tooth at the *edge* of Cinderella's final smile.

1. According to the Metz lawyer, Sebastian Rouillard, in his ill-fated 1609 *Phathénie*, this saint "spoke with such eloquence that rocks broke and oak trees fell." Yea, yea.

Exeunt

Scene 11. *Enter Olivia and Viola.*

Ellen DeGeneres was telling me that she read in a recent Yoga *report* how you can gain eternal life by sitting in the most uncomfortable position you can find for a week beyond the limits of your tolerance—but that sounds like the *sort* of behavior that leads to an eternal *state* of severe Presbyterianism. John Calvin, its inventor, claims life is most commoditized in its most degraded state. I'd stay *away* from Calvin if I were you, two children of Lilith like us need him as much as a carrot needs Bugs Bunny, in fact today is Black Friday and the Commodity Goddess beckons her duet of mini-skirted druidettes to be unfrocked in the car-park of a nearby shopping-mall and re-clothed in sequins and cat suits—for where there is no extravagance there is no love.[1] Incidentally, that Darth Vader Welcome Mat went over really well with my latest date—it even helped me make new friends among the local teenage neo-Nazi gangs but most ended up in Bible Camp parsing bits of the Old Testament. Do you recall the time when Lazy Susan™ fell in love with the Dumb Waiter in the kitchen at Camelot? That was long before the Grand Age of Cuisinart and his Merry Blenders slaughtered all the pacificists at a feudal rally in protest of the Second Crusade. Holy copyrights and patents! You introduce supply-side Capitalism into historiogaphy at every opportunity, let's just face the fact that despite some Pleistocene hoarding and saving propensities, we were born to shop and spend. I must admit I'm really turned on by bargains, in fact, I only achieve orgasm during the Boxing Day sales, so let's *translate* ourselves into wasteful consumers and *betray* all those caveats of common-sense *deemed* to be the philosophy of the cautionary. Isn't unmitigated potlatch *seen* as the most sordid of mistakes on The Price is Right, or does our *esteemed Queen* think it best to *resort* to a quantum epiphany? There you go again, throwing crêpe over a sinner's relics with the oddest questions. Can't you be *less* enigmatic and *sport* with me a little? To change the subject, that can't be Botox enhancement, with lips that thick you must have fellated a beehive. Don't forget what Chaucer taught us about *wantonness*: that an inn is never a castle but always a church with a brothel inside it. It puts me in mind of that new night club we visited which turned out to be three revolving toilets with a condom dispenser plus a doorman. Remember that picnic together in the clouds at the summit of Mount Hiroshima? We could see all history below us moving in tiny events until your *wantonness* put my ovaries into veritable overdrive, but then you sneezed on your strap-on and blew your nose and turned sex into the *sport* of topless darts, and what disembogued from your right nostril was *less* mucus than the liquefied ruins of a city taking the shape of an island on your handkerchief. It was so disgusting I had to *resort* to an emergency escape through Pound's Cantos back to those tree pruning classes in San Diego we both loved. Unfortunately I ended up in a cage in Pisa getting a sun tan in my veins from Mussolini's sunshine. But a lizard in a glossary remembers not to cast its shadow. Do you have a favorite *Queen*? Mine's the white one in chess, a veritable fast nude in her potential trajectories. They don't make monarchs like that anymore and it probably explains why the *esteemed* Marcel Duchamp took up the game in the first place, no doubt using an inflatable doll as his opponent. Have you ever *seen* his ready-mades? Apparently he got the idea from the Hitchhiker's Guide to Tips on Originality and they're *deemed* by some aficionados to be the greatest artworks of the entire twentieth century. Mind you, there's not much work goes into them, one's a urinal he stole from its previous owner named R. Mutt, but his Large Glass is something else, it's also called The Bride Stripped Bare by her Batchelors Even and successfully appropriates the picture frame for a purely avant-garde sensibility, yet nevertheless seems to *betray* a meta-aesthetic gesture towards a post-Kantian, non-transcendental life-art interface so as to *translate* courtship into pornography via window cleaning. It contains a bride and lots of bachelors, something called Malic molds that you can make crème brulee in and loads of mystery. He's considered by most art critics to be far and *away* the most sexy adult thinker of the nineteen twenties and, apart from six letters, his name forms a perfect palindrome. As you know a *state* of prolonged postimpressionism can lead to boils on the eyeballs but Duchamp's type of conceptual art is guaranteed to drive you to dominoes or even Chinese checkers. We'll *sort* out your own problematic preference for hard-edge conflicts rather than Fontana's famous slits after we've finished our next *report* on the rhetorical potential of A when it's the final letter in both our alphabets. Oops, gotta go, time for my carrot juice and yoga then I'm due for body piercing at four and I've already killed my allowance.

1. Oscar Wilde

Exeunt

End of Act III

Sex and death are the only things that can interest a serious mind.

W. B. Yeats

Act IV Scene 1. *Enter Isabel and Francisca as a Nun.*

Historic "depth" requires short cuts between its segues. Plant a plant beside the plant and see it radiate dead fish in a different pool of public language—kind of thing. What's that about "public language?" I admire your sporadic social conscience and ecological concern with pustular clarity, but given that the price of healthy gums is eternal vigilance your kind of instrumental technology's going nowhere *near* my teeth. I'll make my own return to the oral tradition via a visit to a genuine dentist. I'm also aware there's a soothing complacence about irenical ecclesiology, and it would be nice to haggle over the relative merits of sin and grace instead of root canals. It's hard for me to take a nun seriously when she's dressed up to look like one of God's penguins; personally, I'll take death over sex anytime (although intercourse by proxy is better than no technology at all). I prefer to put a love poem to my lips and whistle my favorite elegy, remaining entirely indifferent to the looting and *cheer* of the local death squad. I remember that squad well, caught in the circuitry of *mute* emoticons too evanescent to register even a single simile from those hypocrisy guards interpreting meanings as solutions. It's a sign of the times, some contrite Mggletonian from the seventeenth century trades his millennium for a year's supply of marijuana. So it's not surprising I tried to imagine *you* as a narcotic *fruit* and *me* as some emergent problem in Keynesian economics (albeit I'm a staunch adherent to the Gold Standard). Sometimes I feel I'm an apple caught in its destiny between transportation and consumption, dropped naked in a garden to read Milton aloud in imitation of all the lives of William Blake. Harpooned into existence an inedible spectator moans the Kaddish of his life for an unborn foetus. But before I finally "*decease*" I hope to find out exactly what I am, for all I know I could be the afterglow of a drop in the *prime* interest rate or an *increase* in *time* spent among allied blockades of the Galapagos Islands, or even a tin of chewing tobacco named Dry Shag. I suppose it's the peril of being a linguistic shifter but, given the current condition of this world, I'm sure God has doubts about his own existence. By the way I've looked *everywhere* for a competent surgeon to give me a severe charisma by-pass, I thought I'd *seen* one creeping around the Human Parts Emporium trying to fit amputees with wheels instead of artificial legs but it turned out to be a lost conscientious objector from Doctors without Borders. It seems to be a *year* for particular sacrifices but I'm happy truth is too abstract to be totally demoralizing. I've a vague feeling that we've *been* here before or could have *been* had we known the meaning of arrival. The instinct for effect leads to the crystal of pure consequence and it's a pity Walt Whitman ignored the gap between desire and effect, but you can blame that on the Civil War. By the way, this is the last *year* for us to plan our corpus linguisticus or make weekly sorties into state-of-the-art vice.[1] Despite feeling like some volatile hormone bomb after my vaginal rejuvenation surgery, and realizing I'm the perfect role model for indiscretion, I find little opportunity for acts of moral turpitude these days, events are now *seen* through the conflicting heresies of either euhemerism or epistemology and *everywhere time* marks the compromise between two forms of corruption. Given the *increase* in our life expectancy we might live as long as God. Ever wondered what the *prime* mover looks like? An old woman perchance with a long white beard who just won't *decease* from punishing *me* along with the rest of the world's sinners, or the Chief Executive Officer of a Catholic corporation with a Mont Blanc pen stuck in the top pocket of his Armani suit? Or perhaps he, or she, is an it, some vitalist flow through the galaxy and beyond. My own concerns are a little more down to earth such as ascertaining why that *fruit* juice tastes of striped mouthwash. I have an urban curiosity about such unnerving phenomena, it happens a lot when *you* live in subdivisions, but to be trapped in scaled-down pantomimes of death and resurrection? It must be a bit like the Viennese performance art of the sixties: *mute*, self-lacerated human bodies hanging from meat-hooks in an independent gallery, sponsored by a government grant, waiting for either the audience of three to *cheer* then leave, or the janitor to return, cut them down, send them home and lock up the place. I prefer to stay *near* to the songs of those disability boogie-woogie singers such as Blind Lemon Pledge Jefferson and Crippled Clarence Lofton performing for charity at a celebrity AIDS ho-down reassuring you it's sad when your only friend's the blues.

1. A little word like "us" so easily drowns in a world of referents, sucking it up into detective novels and sci-fi fantasies, but better that than being capitalized and followed by an A.

Enter the King, Scroope, Cambridge and Gray.
Ours has been an errancy abandoned to writing, an extraordinary multiplicity entangled in prefaces, mis en abymes and critical prolegomena among the *play* of politics far *away* from *those* sordid arms deals with Columbian drug cartels. It's a *delight* each time I remember your centrifugal introduction into life, the way you *rose, white* marble in the vertical trajectory of Mary Poppins from the ashes of the Monument to Those Who Fell in March, quite different from the mundanities around my own birth into signs. You *grew* up to become the leading collector of Asian meta-narratives and took care of ostrich overpopulation in the lesser principalities. However these days, you can't *tell* the difference between the *hue* of protagonism and that *smell* emanating from the hip neuro-therapy we find in Walter Pater's later essays. Have you ever read Pater, or better, ate *him*? I'm afraid his Earthly Paradise is long gone, victim of a Marxist theory of demographics. Or was that Dante Gabriel Risotto? Either way it adds up to the same *thing*: a literary masterpiece disappearing into the *trim* fit of the totally ignored. These days many problems *spring* from the continuity of piecemeal solutions, such as your own parasitism on my monarchy.[1] They tell me *spring* has arrived in the Chamber of Deputies but all I see is the shadow of the Grim Reaper. It's a *trim thing* quasi-celibacy invented just for *him*, the one called XC3a, who became famous as the fugitive chess player frozen between his moves. He certainly knew how to distinguish the *smell* of an endgame from the *hue* and cry of a check-mate, but I bet he couldn't *tell* the difference between the literary canon and an internment camp. I thought I could until Beatrix Potter's Tale of the Flopsy Bunnies *grew* to be an adult cult classic. I turned *white* with disbelief then, from a medley of mythologies and in clouds of after-shave, *rose* the Blessed Virgin Malcolm, floating like a lead balloon. These days prophecy requires a rear-view mirror,

but miracles can still take place (on the rare occasion) and bring *delight* to *those* who don't believe in them. I'm still blown *away* by the thought of the collotype in the age of mechanical viewpoints. If we put faith over form and not in it, then we get closer to the chromatic *play* of community, caught in the embodiment of light extending from the Sermon on the Mount to the east façade of the Fifth Amendment, where God finally manifests in his perfect simulacra. Hang on, here comes that Joseph Grimaldi look-alike, no doubt a recent escapee from the Royal Clown Museum.

1. Excuse me for being chronically under-informed, but I don't think being a hermit-in-residence dressed in rags made of vegetable bark and wearing sandals made of moss in a cave at the back of one of your remoter castles in Derbyshire makes me a parasite. Besides, all the hermits I know are on Facebook.

Enter Clowne.

You see now why the detection of a reaction to the event of the exception always leads to an ideologically calculated state of alert and that's why I relish the role of eternal opposite and why it's never too late to make a friend. I'm sure *death* won't be as bad as that last sentence and certainly no worse than in the Middle Ages with its tips on how to bury your own corpses, that way cutting out the middle-man, and how to handle the *growth* of more saintly humiliations and self-mutilations. There was more food for pigeons than for pan-handlers in those days. With the high price of candles and no TV it must have been difficult to be a night person. I always hold my *breath* when I ponder on the relics of the Battle of Crécy or the archaeological implications of Eddic slaughter rituals after a victory. *Both despair* and a north-south orientation overtake me as I imagine I *stand* there horrified by a satin-clad poursuivant announcing the local morts du jour. It's enough to make the *hair* on the back of your *hand* stiffen into a cluster of Kahnian skyscrapers with all their windows *dyed* sepia. That said, I still appreciate the achievements of the Dark Ages over the catastrophes of the Enlightenment. Saint Ambrose (of all people) invented silent reading, there were half a dozen sightings in the Netherlands of Jesus dancing on a duck pond, the quality of Belgian beer improved (thanks to the Abbot of Liège), one monk at Bolton Abbey ran the mile for Saint Ignatius in three minutes and fifty-seven seconds with his ankles chained to a set of enormous iron rosary beads, and the leaping anchorite of Anchorage regularly jumped over portcullises to entertain turbaned tourists from Tehran. In fact the entire ecclesiastical history of those days reads like one long series of athletic events. Not many know of the Papal Olympiads held in Reykjavik and the utter domination by the Franciscans in field athletics—seven managed to pole vault to eternity and join the Mile-High Club without a plane ride and then built the entire Burma Railway as an encore. Another ran the marathon on half a lung, (an achievement matched only by Bernard of Chartres who won the Kentucky Derby by three lengths while carrying his lame horse on his back), gold and silver medals in Sumo wrestling went to two anorexic trappists. The freak-shows were fabulous, there was one hirsute stripper so intense no one could tell where her beard stopped and her pubic curls began. And then there's all the miracles and relics like the holy armpit of St. Cuthbert, the blessed foreskin of Eli of Antwerp, the still-working gonads of the Blessed Origen[1] and a bell jar once owned by Sylvia Plath. President Obama now owns an ancient beer can labeled Caius Junius Budweiser that was gulped down by Saint Agatha of Sicily prior to her excruciating martyrdom. (To top it all the Archbishop of Canterbury owned both the signed credit card receipt for the Last Supper and a genuine turd dropped by the donkey that carried Christ into Jerusalem!)[2] But it's hard to come to a rational opinion about relics when presented with a dozen identical heads of John the Baptist and thirty-seven quarts of the Bessed Virgin's milk. I don't think the traumatic zoning envelope in which my cultural form *dwells* gives me any special power to be a worshipable relic but it helps me take a morsel of *pride* in the *smells* emanating from that baby retirement village and *chide* others for their failure to even sneeze. Shall we *chide* organized religion for the collapse of affirmative self-destruction? That question *smells* a little too fishy. I take *pride* in all of my neuroses: happiness, xenoglossia, didacticism, the way my fear *dwells* in the thought of voyages to places where I've never been. Still, I'd love to shake the *dyed hand* of a freshly slaughtered terrorist, it would make my *hair stand* on end, but morphological deformation of this kind makes me *despair* of *both* my production assembly protocols and my intellectual commitment (along with the IMF) to world-wide poverty. To change the subject somewhat, where will we take our final *breath*? I think it might be Berlin or Minneapolis, either way

I want to be stuck inside some clapboard coffin and buried like Robin Hood in the dense *growth* of forest where oak trees *grow*—after I've had a tidy *death* with a telecast funeral. Nuff said, targets evaporate at these altitudes of comedy where Leibniz really is Tiresius in a Paris preserved by Hitler. Then all reality dissolves and the spectacle I *see* of *you* emerges from the life-supports inside a test-tube the evening before all of this was a dream.

1. Eusebius reports that Origen castrated himself after reading the Gospel of Matthew 19:12.
2. The multiple is a product of laterality's disruption of linearity (Badiou).

> The dead decompose themselves under the clock of the cities.
>
> Jack Spicer

Enter Petruchio and Grumio.
Did you think "grab a *knife*" or "get a *life*" in your moment of gravitational re-entry? Personally, I thought about perdurability versus transience in all those bodies we found littering the Comédie Française. Lowell, Forrest-Thomson, Berryman, Plath, such a cornucopia of corpses, lives caught in a detour toward poetry, a danse macabre of the intellect to a point where death might be conceived as an aristocratic form of emigration.[1] I caught a related sense too of how becoming is a hesitation between being and death, an interstice *where* ineluctably erosion and *decay* take pride of place. While we're here and not *there* perhaps we can *survey* the current state-of-the-art hibernation packages and check out that old Byzantine *argument* that *esteem* is best *spent* on those whose souls we can't *redeem*. Would it be a sin against ceremony to entertain ourselves for a while? A *light* ale and a *song* at this point *might* take our minds off the u-turn exits from Dystopia. As *long* as we're the same we can't be different or can we? I've *long* suspected that we *might* not be the best of logicians, but we do know the difference between good and better-than-good idealisms. Yet when we've relinquished the power to say "I" how will we phrase our singular utterances? Shakspeere never tackled that problem with all his tedious soliloquies and the occasional *song* by a minstrel before a plagiarized dénouement. Taken in the *light* of current systems analysis I'd say

reading all those twenty-three plays presents a profoundly boring option to off-shore brokering. I mean it's hard to *redeem* those hours *spent* in deciding if *esteem* is due to the *argument* that the key to Lear is the covert deployment of a schizophrenic impersonal tense—and there's even rumors Shexpere didn't write them! Some say they were written by Christopher Marlowe under the pseudonym of the Earl of Oxford and one German critic claims the true author was Albert Speer's adopted brother Sheik (a prostate magnate from one of the emirates). A *survey* of all the current Spanish polls indicates that *there* is unanimous belief that they were written by Cervantes during his Stratford honeymoon with brain *decay*. *Where* will Early Modern studies go if that turns out to be the case? They'll have to recanonize the Bard of Avon along with Ern Malley and Kent Johnson in the Hoax-poets Collective. [Ed. "The capricious *life* of poetry has a deadly effect on language, the syllable is born between a pulse and a void projected by a rocket of sensibilia at the moment a *knife* cuts through the umbilical institution of the canon and out pours the infinite plurality of words" Araki Yasusada. The world is everything that is the fake. Nothing is reached as seen because of the din—supper produces.]

1. Gottfried Benn.

Enter King, Warwick (convinced he's Shexpere,) *Clarence, Gloucester.*
The relation of configuration to constellation is the relationship of a slice of bread to a plate of olives so we're *now* at the point where nothing fits, croaking away like frogs having sex. Voice and syllabary meet at a bullfight, voice asks what's so post-colonial about reggae, syllabary answers *how* can pity and eroticism coexist? There's nothing worse than a bad-tempered turnip with its super-charged popply anfractuosities that speak to a total collapse in our order of knowledge production.[1] However, it will *be* a great feeling to have emerged from the *tomb* of bibliography unscathed as an undetected plagiarism. But *you* seem to have lost your place in the history of art. That carbon dating of your *dumb* bohemian lifestyle puts your majesty somewhere between the Neolithic and Art Nouveau. If only the dissociation of the ego were *intermixed* with the diminution of specific being then we could reach agreement that our future *lay* in a *fixed* parallelism of consecutive waves, reminiscent of a

life spent inside a painting by Victor Vaserely. During the thirteenth galactic war I styled myself the first post-expressionist poet. I'd like to *say* that after Cymbeline I felt *dignified* with such a historic responsibility but genius and administration inevitably remain incompatible. So much *depends* upon a red wheelbarrow beside the tie-*dyed* memorabilia and it's time I made *amends* to that trollop the Queen's five-year plan to turn this kingdom into a republic. I make my *amends* whenever I choose adventure over assignation; it's much less clandestine than those *dyed* rubrics of Freemasonry; there's no time for a secret handshake when hanging over the edge of a cliff held precariously by Zelda Fitzgerald in a steep Victorian biography. Bugger the poets of kosmos,[2] a bard's life ultimately *depends* upon a *dignified* suffering and the conviction to *say* "I write on behalf of all the dead mosquitoes that never got a chance to bite me." However, we're more ambitious now we're *fixed* in the post-biotic soup— we can finally complete the Great Instauration in the School of Night. Then the *lay* analyst of the interim, *intermixed* with advice from a fellow voyager, might truly stare in *dumb* amazement as *you* remove the sempiternal from disequilibrium. But if the *tomb be* the sign that designates our termination at arrival *how* will we secretly transmit ourselves to somewhere else, *now* . . . my kinsman, the platitude? There it ends, I guess, five minutes into the ultimate Lindy Hop.

1. For more on this fascinating condition see Robert Lyall, "Of the Irritabilty of Turnips" in *Nicholson's Journal* xxiv, 1809.
2. Whitman.

Exeunt omnes

Enter Hamlet reading of a Booke.
"Everyone gradually becomes a one who chants a sad *song*. Everyone who is to become a jolly one chants before a jolly one who used to be a sad one. Every jolly one who chants before a sad one comes to be a sad one and not a one who gets to be a jolly one." Hmmm, sounds like Gertrude Stein's answer to the Joy of Sex, which reminds me of why I always get on better with soliloquies at the castle when they're accompanied by ladders going elsewhere. But to continue and finish before the opium wears off: "Dood poop floolf spitips" those anagrams

have suddenly turned into Flarfian palindromes but what's this? "The *tongue* twice in a twilight-having-broken-it touches a nuthatch sunning in the cantilena we sent out from the fourth floor landscape where a corpse lies rotting in its syntax." Thank god for poetic license, however when propositionally deployed this artistic sentence gives *delight* not unlike the one between a peach *bough* in blossom and two volcanic ranges in the Hindu Kush. In another six or seven sentences, a little after the words "*night*" and "sunsets," the passenger I've become will reach the first stage of his final narrative. "There are echoes *now* that last for *days* throughout the village where Shayke-speaere lives eight paragraphs below." "After an hour in a monk's library an unknown traveler decides to *sing* the *lays* of that dead minstrel now known to be Blind Harry the Arbitrator." "Out of sight, in the book he closed, is the recipe for *spring*, a pen still pointing to the place *where* the words '*esteeming*' and 'analogous' *appear* once more in a lengthy footnote." "The ghost and the child are always allied in a war of independence." Hmmm, that must be me and my dead dad the king. Owing to a *seeming* botched attempt at a *seeming* counter-strike by agents of an unknown party, it would *appear* that all of the above is merely the interruption of an illogical narrative into my grand soliloquy, but without the *esteeming* grace of the transparent to render it palatable. So *where* do I go from here? I might *spring* the coop and revisit an age of resentissement, but then again there's the morbidezza of it all. Are there *lays* I can *sing* these *days* to reassure me that I *now* need to pay attention to Ethel's point of view?[1]   Or am I committed to staying up all *night*, mousing through some on-line catalog devoted to the revival of thinking via internet access? (Polonius became such a web geek he got a speeding ticket on the information highway.) Or perhaps I should become a voyeur and ask mom for a keyhole for a birthday present? Or should I stay on a *bough* in the bower of *delight*, with my *tongue* caught up in one of those mutating palindromes before finally exploding out of *song*?

1. Lots could be said about Ethel.

Exit
Scene 2. *Enter Lovell and Ratcliffe with Hasting's head.*
It is truly amazing how things change. Did you know that the swastika used

to be a good luck symbol? You can *sit* and ponder that historical mutation until the planet's had a third Grand Mal seizure.[1] One can't *tell* for certain but I'm sure a resurrection would be really something, however I'd hate to speculate on the horrors of eternity—what a destiny for temporal beings like us. I *tend* to feel that all the hunger and incontinence among the martyrs of ecclesiastical history might *well* be due to overly-strict monastic regimen. Under the former abbot even a loud phart in the chapel during complines constituted breaking your vows of silence and led to a harsh command to *mend* your ways or be whipped. Give me flatulation over flagellation any time, what a *disgrace* being alive all the time in a state of self-laceration. In fact the stone that killed Saint Stephen seems more intelligent than the saint himself— un-neurotic, free from arthritis (unlike him), easy to house and feed, fixed in the vista of almost endless existence, and never moved to anger. You can shout at a lump of granite and that stoic chunk will never shout back. Now that's the mid-life crisis evolution intended![2] *Quite* a dream ontology if you *face* up to the matter. What a pity Chacspeir never found the time to *write* a sonnet or two on the subject, if he had he might have taken his rightful place *beside* the great geologists of the early modern like Thomas Burnet and Kenelm Digby. Do you think there's any *worth* in hypothesizing that the stone per se is a sonnet more endurable than writing? Probably not, so we'd best take *pride* in the fact that rap is simply Fluxus after political correction, then sally *forth* to write that long-awaited treatise on the effects of asbestos on the lungs of great literature. While we're on the subject of sallying *forth* perhaps we should find out the average life expectancy in this part of the dungeon. I take *pride* in our preferring evolution to revolution and keep on delaying the chatter of a death without serenity.[3] For what they're *worth* our predicaments are a little like the Sino-Armenian dilemma in snooker tournaments, do you ping-pong along *beside* your best friends into the closest hole or carom off the cushion back into existence with your Guide to the Waste Land on $15 a Day? I'd be ashamed to *write* a poem like that and capture the dysfunction of a dying city. All that pastiche bleakness and the careful deployment of fragmentation mixed with incomprehensible passages in foreign languages spoken by some geek called the Fisher King makes me *face* up to the fact that I'm happy catachresis is my identical twin. I know you're *quite* proud that you've already got that detached head fluent in French but there's no culinary *disgrace* in equating a human pate with good food: no pesticides, no herbicides, no GE ingredients, no preservatives, no additives and best of all no irradiation. From stone to skull? Sounds like the triumph of the negative again and a good way to *mend* the paradox of living. *Well,* you always do *tend* to *tell* things as they are while I *sit* silent, the other skull behind *it.*

1. Alternatively you can check out this footnote which informs that the swastika originally represented the sun or fire and appears in many cultures other than the Aryan: the Navajo, early Christian and Byzantine art, and is extensively deployed today in Buddhism, Jainism and Hinduism. The word derives from the Sanskrit word of the same sound and means "conducive to well-being." The poet Rudyard Kipling used it on the covers of several of his books.
2. Or how about a giant meteor, cold, inanimate and silent, but with the capability to wipe out the human species with one kiss.
3. My apologies, Whitman again.

Enter Jessica and the Clowne.

I know I'm *dead* to sophisticated lifestyles, boorish and a tad *unbred,* easily *deceived* by false flattery and *stand* to lose my reputation as a being from another planet if I'm *perceived* to be a command save on a bible screen, but I know from the itch in my left *hand* that a grim fate awaits me, one not unlike the fate of the *green* woods and meadows with the onset of the Industrial Revolution. I'm *burned* out by the fact that however we approach it, whether with recipes or nostrums, lampoons or tampons, this is an estranged harmonium. Yet, sub specie aeternitatis, i.e. *seen* from a different perspective, it could simply be that I'm seriously influenced by Saturdays. [Ed. *Turned* on by the thought of an early painting by Dali a foot leaves without a shoe in it to wander lonely as a shroud of intertextual set-backs, taking *pride* in being part of a strictly aesthetic failure in logic.] To the *cold eyed* anarchist this is a Humpty Dumpty effect of the *old* maieutics of the midwife. I've long been an apprentice to the *old, eyed* the archaic for its treasures and plundered the minds of neighboring peoples for information on origins and destinies. I also take a *cold pride* in the fact that I alone solved the enigma of the formulaic pattern in Homer's Cyclops episode which *turned* out to be a cryptically encoded tourism advertisement for the Canary Islands. *Seen* as conventional narrative it marks the implosion of myth and cartography in a double-triggered metonymy *burned* upon a memory screen that's as allegorical as those *green* coelocanth we used to catch in the ponds around the Castle of Anachrony. I miss those ancient festivals, those Pyanopsias and Cybernessias, as much as you miss effective Cubist pantomime. Granted, the transhistorical is not without certain risks, but I have to *hand* it to those pagans, they sure *perceived* the essential correlation between wine, dithyrambics and sex. I don't know how you *stand* on the matter but these days there's not a lot to celebrate. Constitutional governments and organized religions provide several days on which to pull out the flag, but this doesn't mean that I'm *deceived* into believing ground hog day and the anniversary of the discovery of flesh-eating disease are worthy statutory holidays. Still, that way the uncouth and *unbred* (like you and me) get a day off work to enjoy the techno-felicities of the modern polis in all its gaudy triviality. It's enough to put you off *dead* meat for life.

Enter Prince, Old Montague, Capulet, their Wives and all.
I dig the way Truth hijacks intelligence in the process of which it precipitates the finest of all our intellectual crises: how to excuse thinking for its consequences. Look at me, I haven't much to shout about for being the Prophet of the Eternal Ponder save a lengthy pose before Auguste Rodin as a man on a rock still thinking. Thoughts are the shaving cream destined for Occam's razor, and of all possible thoughts the *one alone* that *affords* me consolation is that old as we are we're still a calenture of experiences and rare survivors of the malice of murmurs. However, given the time we've *spent* as *words*, the *argument* arises whether or not our *difference* is *confined* solely to the linguistic plane? We are trapped as placenzia, paper people and it's hard to achieve communicative *excellence* when Language eats you as it wakes you up. The world is full of social reformers but from now on I want to put an umbrella up against the realities of life. I have to say you're rarely perfect in your assigned role as cater-cousin, owing to the fact that the *kind* of hexagonal structure necessary to our intimacy implies a corresponding "dialogic" relationship on the communication axis that rarely happens. Despite the potential sexiness in these endgames they rarely manifest as those high octane fantasies we aspire to. *So* it might be preferable to think of Death as the dilation of a life into

a single sentence and you as the I in a We seen by others to *be* Them. It's difficult to *show* the origins of *idolatory* in such things as shifters; they're the pigeons of deixis and, despite the possibility of turning up as an ephemeral pronoun in some Shakespeherian sonnet, brimming with *idolatory* of some unnamed person, you're ultimately condemned to being a second person singular in the triangle of Dante's Hell. Non-fiction may *show* you how to beat negation with information but to *be* the I *so* pure it predicates the silence in the dative, renders a *kind* of architectonic *excellence* no longer *confined* to a merely aporial *difference*. There's a lot we don't know about grammar and the enigmatic enunciative Muse. I'll have more to say on that in the afterlife, but setting linguistics aside let's focus on what precisely constructs our fears of the last event. Accepting there's a solid *argument* for atheism's repudiation of an afterlife, there's a lot worse things than departure and oblivion, it sure beats that influenza of pleading *words* that constitute fundraising on PBS and its mission to persuade us that a dollar towards commercial-free entertainment is a dollar well *spent*. Frankly I like a good ad, it *affords* me welcome information about dieting and chest pains, it leaves me happy when *alone* at night, the *one* survivor of reception theory.

Exeunt

Scene 3. *Enter Sir Toby and Maria.*
I used to *praise* those *days* we both believed description to be the fact of an obstacle plus the process of perceiving it. That credo caused us to *sing* across millennia, our *eyes* tracing a ballet of sense data, each *prefiguring* the arrival of events on the wrong side of their *prophecies*. That condition is *now* best *expressed* as a centrifugal force that changes all the information nuclei. Explicit on a *brow* or cheek phrase-precedents cut into the nerves of even the *best* of heroes and from the glyster equipage of all of this we step forth as two Arthurian *knights* promising *rhyme* to reason, and proffering *wights* a former *time* modernity fails to recapture. That's a tricky anachronism to deal with, but this *time* you handled it well: the word "*wights*" carries a vague suggestion of the broadest of chronotypes. They named an island after one of them, I think it means "persons" but when I ran it through the spell-check I got a dazzling

array of substitutes: weights wrights sights nights lights rights fights and tights. Each read like a *rhyme* scheme for some Oulipean inspired epyllion. I know a Rule is no Bar, but a Perfection of Freedom[1] but in the days of Walter Map *knights* knew *best* how to cudgel the *brow* of their enemy with weapons other than formal constraints. *Expressed* in the strict formality of courtly love an unrequited kiss on a lady's hand facilitated daily suicides and the future could always be spontaneously predicted by some haggard court-jester. *Now* we're left with zero *prophecies* beyond global warming and sub-Saharan mass starvation. But I'm through with my attempts at *prefiguring* the post-ecological, I'll leave that to the *eyes* of the few giant pandas and Bengal tigers still extant and reflect instead on some horror from the past: the burned books of Kristalnacht like so many charred bodies. They say that birds don't *sing* at Dachau and these *days* we should carry that absent-presence to events inside each tiny crypt and *praise* the continuity of the quod erat irritation glimpsed as a retreating origin.

1. Thomas Baker, *Reflections Upon Learning*, 5th ed. London, 1714: 68.

Enter Friar John to friar Lawrence.
They say a moment *spent* in reflection on the unfortunate transitoriness of life is the best *monument* to human rectitude. *Tribes* of theologians have argued this one in prose and *rhyme* from Saint Bonaventure to Bernard of Septimania, but whoever *subscribes* to it commits themselves to a politico-economic disaster. I mean what ever happened to nihilism? It's high *time* our *age* looked towards an *assured* exit from such not-for-profit-motivated medieval humility. I mean if I wanted to have a dead halibut as an advisor I would have hired a firshmonger. There I was, happily chanting a few dozen pater-nosters when suddenly I had a *presage* (given all those Masses for the Dead we've both *endured*) that we've earned the right to turn attention from *doom* and finitude to rash 'n wrinkle *control*, affordable hip replacements and a perdurable beauty yet to *come*. Origen of Alexandria claims a *soul* may be freed from the Hell beneath that Crucifix by homiletic intervention, but in my narrative the *soul* requires a bilateral symmetry to even negotiate a sidewalk let alone a car park. I prefer something a little more consanguineous than a rescued spirit, *come* to think of it why didn't I mention this before? The coalescence of *control-*

enhancing demons and *doom*-determining angelic agencies should not have *endured* that quasi-mythological era some call the epoch of Charlemagne; theologians should have sensed a *presage* of the shift into "dual assimilation" iconographies as we both did at Chartres, that way avoiding the danger of mortification in miniature, while still successfully forcing a spiritual narrative onto pure material form. I'm *assured* that our *age* will be no different in a *time* that *subscribes* to the victory of the pixel over *rhyme*. So if the death of God really is the freeing up of the temporal and the consequent birth of real history then we should ejaculate the afterlife as the grammatical promise after the sentence ends. But perhaps I'm sounding like one of those lost *tribes* of Israel updated from a *monument* to a moment of *spent* critique.

Enter Sir Hugh Evans

Hey boys can you be, as Charles Dickens would say, a little less "architectooralooral" from now on and talk about the *dead* on their own terms? How about that medical embarrassment known as the afflatus posthumous? They say a corpse will pheart if you roll it over and you know as well as I do that wind is hard to grasp. Can you imagine an entire chorus of afflatic cadavers performing Gilbert and Sullivan at Bayreuth? It would drive even the better *bred* Bavarians into rampant Petomania.[1] We find the identical precipitate documented on the occasional *page* of books dealing with medieval theories of metabolism, and the veritable "durchfall über alles"[2] that plagued the entire Carolingian dynasty. Observe the peristalsis of a humble nematode in its barely noticeable move from *place* to non-being in that *age* of exsanguinated rigor immortalized by Hugh Saint Victor. I wish Thomas Carlyle had written an essay on the subject, a sort of Phartor Rephartus. Mick Jagger assures me that the Gods once spoke in belches but this is becoming another *case* of your scatology against my *name* dropping. Great thoughts rise up from the ground so we should look towards the acorn's pattern in the earth; the seasons hold the logic of the leaf, its conception in dense syllogism advanced through thermodynamics in preparation for the clouds of Mao. If it hadn't been for Methodism and all its false hopes we would have had our own cultural revolution years ago patterned according to the symmetry you find in Racinean tragedy. As it stands, destiny is *yours* to choose and mine to bear in the *same divine* afflatus you spoke of earlier. Would it be of any *merit* to roll back the nano neutrons to the space the bomb gave us in a second's aperture? Probably not, but to *register* our profound disgust at the current concetto of fog and mist we call The Cosmic Society of Optimists might raise our *spirit* to the level of Sebastiano del Piombo during his stay in Rome when the public *character* of his life seemed more a backstage feature than a foreground scene for the plague. You sure take on the *character* of an Edwardian art critic at the first opportunity, it must be part of your regressive *spirit* and low-carbohydrate attraction to the *register* of eerie vacuities frequently found in Californian health food stores. I still think there's *merit* to be found in our present lifestyles that favor sacerdotal moderation over diminution. The *divine* flâneur so dear to Benjamin makes that *same* assessment the core of his pedestrian code. *Yours* however strikes at the epicentre of the following enigma: "to be a *name* is not to be a place, yet to be real does not entail being comprehensible." It's a *case* methinks of the Platonic mise en scène once again setting up the real as an ideal above the actual. But this is an *age* of neither *place* nor *page*. *Bred* in an era of *dead*pan humor we can kiss both topology and reading goodbye, join that Cistercian reading group and turn our thoughts to the complications of being two Rastafarians stuck in an elevator going up.

1. Joseph Pujol (1857-1945) a.k.a Le Pétomane trained as a baker but turned to exploiting his natural talent as a "fartiste" during national service as a crude entertainment for his comrades where he drank large quantities of water a posteriori and then expelled it in the form of an enormous fountain. His better gaseous emissions led to the discovery of eight unknown galaxies but felicitously he later substituted air for water in his orifice and performed his first artistic flatulations in Marseilles in 1887. With the outbreak of war in 1914 he returned to baking and opened up a thriving biscuit factory. [Information courtesy John Barber <articles@johnbarber.com>] Karen: "Who would have bought his biscuits knowing that?" Steve: "I would have ate them but not bought them."
2. "Diarrhea over everything" as they sang in the Wehrmacht.

Exeunt

Enter Hamlet reading of a booke.
I finally decided to convert to Judaism in the Sector Galactica, seventeen days after losing my testicles while hand-gliding in the Rockies and nine and a half

light years before the Last Supper. What a debacle that was, Christ without a credit card unable to perform some simple fiscal miracle and Judas polishing off an entire jeroboam of Chateau Petrus by himself. Those were the days when "happy" meant "stigmata." At least for me felicity is not a precondition for the future, it's more the film I never saw but always talk about. Should I wave to another condemned soul across the Styx or look Extinction in the face and that way greet the impossible? Mallarmé thought death to be a boundary to the infinite and dying a page on which life structures its departure, but *all* I want to know is how Death is spelled when it's just about to happen? I know this obsessive *call* to correct orthography is symptomatic of my allegorical emergence as World Existential Theosophy that night I played Ouija with Madame Blavatsky. It's not *good* enough in those corny séances to shout out "is there anybody there" and get a rigged reply on some brandy *stained* mystic board, but I'll happily assume the handicap of royal *blood* and press on with PRAXIS until Death tries to tickle me to sleep. Things could be worse, I mean when Nero *reigned* it was a metabiological nightmare that left a permanent *stain* on the annals of human conduct. Fed on a steady diet of murder and lust, and with an unconditional license to carte blanche depravity, he would have made the perfect Nazi. Blood was his favorite moisturizer alright and Sin never slept in his bed, each morning he'd put pesticide in his slave's cornflakes and his henchmen were no better. Patricians *exchanged* slaves for carcasses, then made love to them time and time *again*. Concentration camps sprang up in several provinces to house priests and single parents, that's when Dread led the dance with rodomontades the size of encyclopedias. He committed gratuitous atrocities that make current acts of Satanic ritual feel like Benjamin Netanyahu's Bar Mitzvah. Banquets *ranged* from sautéed Scythian babies to giraffe necks served on huge timber skewers; all the best cooks in the Empire were kept busy turning pets into pies and dying gladiators into sausages.[1] (When they ran out of food they cooked the cooks.) As an imperial pastime (and with matricidal provisions à la Orestes) he would spoon out the brains of chosen victims and feed them to his pet crows. His Giant Pig-strangling games attracted thousands of competitors from the Yorkshire Dales and you could even rent your own saber-toothed tigers on a week's free trial and let them loose in the local leper colony. There's no doubting that evil was his recreational drug of choice and boy did he sniff a lot of it. Every feast to the Gods resembled Nazi Remembrance Week in Warsaw, it eventually became the condition known as the Absolute Nevertheless with do-it-yourself violence disconnected from precise rituals behind the sub-block of a month at the Körperweltend show. But it would be a *lie* if I said that things have improved since then. Take me for instance, talent still unrecognized and superiority unrewarded it really pisses me off. In fact my latest temper tantrum's already on YouTube. But what if I *depart* from my Enlightenment agenda, from that marriage of matter and mind in the practical manifestation of the organization of space and the managed mastery of my emotions, what then would *qualify* my dying other than some cheap thanatic theory dear to the post-romantic *heart* and the pathetic rationale that it'll be a permanent solution to my hair loss? Things are going so badly in my version of corporate internationalism that my Other, the Shadow, recently coerced me into a disconnection from venture capitals. Does my asshole-in-the-*heart qualify* as an authentic contortion or must I *depart* from all reference to organs and endorse the *lie* that my favorite ecology is the one of hypothetical existence?[2] I say what I have to see and it's *ranged* identically in the essential supplement to being real. It's the casino of destiny *again* and soon my body will be a prime hunting ground for junior bacteriologists, my brain removed and *exchanged* at vast profit for puns and linguistic accidents that come directly out of some Abu Ghraib etiquette manual. They say life is the light of a man, in which case it's my duty to blow out all the candles and die as badly as possible in private revenge on all the world's illuminations. The *stain* of the human that *reigned* for centuries might be indelible, but my *blood-stained* coronet remains the *good* promise of a kingdom to come in King Minos' labyrinth—and yet I get the feeling that would only be a whiff of the *call* to *all*-star sentimental humanism if ever I've smelled one.

1. Not to mention all the public castrations of primitive artisans in the Coliseum, on which see Vossius and Bosorius fol. Cccxxvi in Shimmelpenick's revised edition.
2. Tom Conley's definition of 'Pataphysics.

Music playes. Enter Cleopatra.
That's a very good point, but it's no good beating your *breast* complaining about the forgotten lessons of the labyrinth, *best* resign yourself to the fact that death's

the price of growing up. When we were young the end of the world had already happened in the morta nova style. Now, *confined* to me as your sole remaining *friend* and in a relationship that's worse than most communities of two, you should *grind* your teeth and put an *end* to masquerading as Elsinore's number one Sex Pistol. I admit, blowing up heritage architecture for the fun of it seems rather aggressive for an Egyptian Queen, and hardly qualifies me for giving sound advice, but prior to that the only thing I'd ever blown up was a party balloon. I *love* to think on my own misspent *youth* outside both architecture and community. *Above truth* is the oneiric house we live in, the street enters the house via astrophysics and voila a *new* epiphany rejuvenating my dream of motorized gondolas on the Nile. However, when you touch the door it feels like the latch remains, but the foot of the stairway becomes the toe of a victim and, from the window, *dear* to your contacts, is a *view* to where Norwegian metaphysics disintegrates. It's *there*, on the agnostic side of God, a little below his left ankle, that the consequences of the greenhouse effect can be seen. New buds arrive *there* by train or taxi, it is Spring and international at the same time. Thanks to the entire siderealization of space, terminal encounters of the fourth dimension come into *view* via compound transparency phenomena; the illusion of playing blackjack with Saint Francis of Assisi quickly passes into terror at the thought of joining Frank Sinatra among the ranks of the symparanekromenoi.[1] Festoons of uncertainty merge into diatribes around a hidden point of dispute. *Dear* to your heart is a *new* found enthusiasm for aeronautics out of control, by which *truth* will emerge via parachute as a representation of Martin Heidegger thinking about a stone. *Above* him an orchestra made up of Hitler *youth* assembles to play the requiem of Adolph Loos, and listening to them will be what *love* would have been like in Saigon at the *end* of the Vietnam War. Teeth will *grind* in the mouth of a *friend confined* by his self-centeredness to the *best* of all possible parentheses and only then, calmly stepping out of an inferno of special effects, will the epigone emerge with an open trench coat over her street credentials, beating her *breast* at the thought of another Saturday alone with you.

1. Not to be identified with premature burial, the term refers to "Persons who have buried themselves while still alive" (Karsten Harris "The Voices of Space" in *The Ethical Function of Architecture*, MIT Press, 1998: 195, a book from which some of this monologue has been

sampled.)

Hamlet

That's a case of the pot calling the kettle African-American and I think a little more noblesse oblige might be in order, I also thought we were going to talk about *me* on the subject of those dead heroes whose autographs are embedded in the sidewalks of the theatre district of Valhalla, but all *you* come up with is an incomprehensible digression en route to a personal insult. Not that it matters, I've passed beyond *correction* and criteria into some advanced state of cellular decrepitude. Come to *think* of it my lingering hypochondria needs another *infection* to finally put it to sleep. However, with your lips to God's ear instead of your eye on my *drink* we'll have a democratically *renewed* relationship in no time. Unlike Courbet I've never been big on originality, I'll take the grand style carried in the general idea anytime over his kind of Bakhtinian slum naturalism. All that talk about a *hand* on a latch in an oneiric house *subdued* my appetite for *brand*-name praeternaturalism. It's also enough to make a sensitive prince puke to think that semiotic unawareness *breeds* that aesthetic irresponsibility some call psychic automatism and that art history doesn't *provide* the necessary credit lines to those uncreative *deeds* that elude legitimation. There's no need to *chide* my frequent rendezvous with microbes, better *chide* my peeled-off tattoos, especially the one depicting those *deeds* of Joseph Rykwert in defense of Renaissance concepts of perspective. That said, your own life really does *provide* the template for a perfect figure without ground. I'm tired with the poverty of thinking, thought *breeds* a *brand* of pathogen that only thought itself can tolerate. Personally I leave all my thinking to the Pentecostal avant-garde, but not to be *subdued* by actuality let's give a *hand* to the *renewed* Parmenidean tenet that it's basic to living to think. I don't need a *drink* to insist that there's a fundamental problem to cogitation, the fragility of its balloons suspended as clouds above characters in action, our own included, render its permanence unendurable. Odiol of Saint-Médard described a hysterical *infection* that struck several pilgrims in Marseilles, it took the form of an ability to *think* a lie and at the same time utter a *correction* to its consequence. It's a little like cocktails during Happy Hour with a Tamil Tyger, or a suede sandwich in Candlestick Park the moment the earthquake strikes and *you* hit *me* with a bat into a fundamental parity with crying aloud.

Enter a Courtesan.

Remember that dream about the *dead* armadillo and the dwarf not tall enough for high spirits? So much more enigmatic than mine about performing group sex in a spin dryer with Vasco da Gama and eighteen of his sardine-sucking nautical lunatics from Lisbon (that trick really did convince me that the world was round and radically changed my perspective on both the Bermuda Triangle and the Big Bang Theory). Placing ads in the Wall Street Journal "Attractive blonde looks for sex and possible friendship, personality irrelevant" gave me high hopes of having a distinguished career of sleeping for cash with international leaders, but these days my idea of a stimulant is sucking on a Fisherman's Friend and all I dream about is my own carbohydrate shortage and the plunging dollar. Unlike the Prince of Denmark I was *bred* to believe that dreams (as distinct from the other bedroom activities) constitute a form of cognitive excrement, a way for the mind to *dispense* with the day's phenomena. (God knows, I need to do that in my profession.) It's hard to believe that I was actually baptized by a Bishop in full pontificatibilitis and still managed to end up spending most of the time on my knees giving blow jobs in the people's Republic of the Pissoir.[1] With all that non-stop meat munching I'm beginning to regret quitting my day job as a ventriloquist's dummy in The Vagina Monologues; I recall one john from the monastery tried to recruit me (along with Rosa Luxemburg) as a nun for identical work in the convent, but it's much more certain who you *are* in convents and it's hard not to *sense* the constant danger of being caught up in liquidating quiddity at prayers. Granted, I'm hardly one of the white lilies of womanhood (being the meatpole magnet that I am) but I'm more than familiar with life's little ups and downs and ins and outs and that allows me to take pride in my glamorous functionality. I also take *care* not to *wrong* those door-to door sex toy salesmen who keep *alive* my hope of a return to the narcissistic stage of the sex industry. Working in Paris out of my massage parlor on the Rue de Pox proved quite lucrative until the authorities airbrushed out the pubic hair on my work permit. Wherever life throws me I always land on my back. If only I could retire my *tongue* as an anxiety disorder I could turn my thoughts to celibacy and finally heed that call to the cloisters. I'm going to *strive* to target my totals with one of those new swivel joints, and if my sordid lifestyle will *allow* me to get *ill* I'll turn my sickness into a professional career. Hermann de Valencienne once took a Danse Macabre troupe touring across the entire breadth of Europe; cripples and midgets with leprosy received sitting ovations with such untumultuous applause that everyone's *brow* would *fill* up with devotion then laughter as they shouted "we're not stunted we're miniaturized." Speaking of ovations, that CD of Gospel Blockbusters Through the Ages that my last trick left on the bedspread was really something, it almost convinced me to renounce my atheistic whoring, *fill* my face up to the *brow* with soul cream and believe that there's at least a good recording label out there pretending to be God. But my own sexual indetermination, the incessant busts by the vice squad and my *ill* treatment at the hands of my pimp *allow* the Negative a way to squash every hope I might have in an eternal orgy to cum. In fact, given the risks of my profession, it'll be one small step from a carnal to a charnel house however much I *strive* to reform the skill of my *tongue* and keep classic fallatio *alive*. In my script, potential is always complex, a glass misplaced on the Lost Credenza of Antioch slides the *wrong* way from 911 into 2001. I couldn't *care* less about the flower-shop flop-house moralists who decry my profession, best preserve my *sense* of the tragi-comic as a week-end hobbyist now that philately and numismatics *are* finally extinct. I'll *dispense* now with well-*bred* homilies; the sun's bright in a clear blue sky, the air unclothes the mountains as light drops with a silent thump, and with the noise of lawnmowers filling the air it seems a beautiful day to be *dead* and buried underneath the wolverine droppings on the neighbor's lawn.

1. I didn't want to admit it in the main body of this masque but my most recent trick was old enough to be my father and knowing my mother he probably is.

Exeunt omnes

Scene 3. *Enter Antipholus of Ephesus, with Jailor.*
Okay, it's a fair cop, but it would be *untrue* to deny the fact that your brain completes the way I happen and, given the circumstances of the double scission, I've started to readjust to our anomalies. I'm sick of all those rumors about infinity and first causes, being here is equivalent to being nowhere, just get it over with. My friend, it is only through magic that life remains awake.[1] But given our state-of-the-art interfacial consciousnesses it takes a miracle to

177

get up from bed. Meanwhile, there's other philosophical wonders to explore. Anaxagoras, for instance, the night he introduced Mind into cosmology in order to explain the presence of order in Nature—I bet he never experienced a Summer in Darfur. That said, there's a stubborn asymmetricality to this intimate occasion; we resemble a bad plot for a Restoration Comedy. I mean when *you* accused me of a cataclysm and I heard a catechism, Lord became laud, bawd became bored, red read, decency dyssentry and hymen highway men, even The Lord's Prayer became the Lord's Test-Match. It's quite an exasperating *feature* of communication not to know what the other person actually means, caught up in the homophone of the moment. Or take the *night* Edmund Spenser brought that viviparous *creature* from its locus amoenus in Hölderin's Hyperion and placed it on the pillow right next to my head. The *sight* of its teeth made me divide into several streets and turn left into the first available panic. I felt seriously similar to a stray chicken in a world of foxes. I didn't *catch* its name or the *part* it played in your own short career as an interfaith counselor (not to mention that unsuccessful venture into drive-thru dentistry) but I'm sure it proved disastrous, like your Operation Desert Kafka a few years ago.[2] Yesterday, when I woke up in bed to feel a defanged cobra, wrapped aound me, it was enough to put the *latch* down on the door of my *heart* for good. Then, jumping *out* of bed into a *blind* condition of dystopia and *about* to comment on the non-relation of our relationship, woosh damnatio memoria, my entire *mind* went phucking blank. A funny thing the *mind*, it's in the brain but not of it, and *about* as experientially accessible as a Cabbage White is to a *blind* lepidopterist. Gilbert Ryle wrote a book on it and both Christopher Smart and Antonin Artaud went *out* of theirs. Having one allows one to indulge in the phenomenon of inner speech so nobody needs to join the Lonely *Heart* Club. Mentative essence is relational and the only way for it to move from one to two is via three, it's vital to invention and to *latch* on to quick countermoves in mahjong tournaments. A *part* of it is reserved to house memories and *catch* (via recollection) the *sight* of transient events. One event that I remember, before becoming a vampire and *creature* of the *night*, was buying a ciborium and eighteen identical reliquaries of the True Cross in Istanbul, each inscribed "Merry Christmas from Pontius Pilate." It seems nothing's single anymore, let alone genuine, but there's lots of innovation. In fact, I recently heard that

Christianity's trying to revamp its image by renaming the Holy Trinity Snap, Crackle and Pop, which makes perfect sense if the Holy Ghost actually was the olive branch between its own beak and if Christ had been buried alive under a giant mound of buttered popcorn instead of crucified. My Holy Trinity's the same as Catherine the Great's: drugs, diet pills and plastic surgery. Staying with the Trinity, I hear the Holy Ghost has developed a fear of heights and refuses to perform any more of those high-altitudes annunciations (the ones that made him a living legend during the Quatrocento). One *feature* of my mind that I'm particularly fond of is the way it always thinks before I see. That's the reason I said what I said and why I seldom think as much as *you* do. It's the combined and consequential legacy of Merleau Ponty and Donald Trump. Now, having said that, all things become revenant and the fortune ferris at Horizon Park halts the allure of *untrue* allegory data.

1. Stefan George.
2. It's telling you choose not to mention your grand schemes for selling cocktail ice cubes to the Inuit and sand for the bottom of bird cages to the Bedouin.

Enter Mariana and Boy singing.

> "I met a girl called Enola Gay
> where the whistling gondolier crosses the Styx
> she was built as a flying crucifix
> and off she flew e'er our first date was through
> with a hey nonny hey nonny no,
> up and off to a distant shore,
> and the land turned to light
> where she left her card
> with a hey nonny hey nonny no,
> and the whistling gondolier coughed up a cloud
> that vaporized empires, pagodas and crowds
> and we tattooed a tombstone on body-print skins
> and a president told us a new life *begins*
> with a hey nonny hey nonny no."

Good words lousy jingle but I now *begin* to understand why we became pioneers in kidney transplants rather than psychiatrists. The glitch in analysis resides in the *sin* of its practitioners. Imagine Freud kayaking the white waters of your unconscious from noon to nones. I prefer reading leaves in a tea-*cup* for solutions to my psychoses and fear of being buried alive, but we end up *agreeing* (in those rare moments when I'm not singing) that Death is a pathway not a place. Yet it still doesn't explain that tendency to burst into song at the slightest provocation. I grew *up seeing* myself as the perfect idiot in the Village of the Damned, seeking a way to *assemble* the *best* reasons for sticking my head down a disposal system to unbleach my blonde hair. Right now, when something's happening nothing happens. Life seems to *resemble* some version of chronic *indigest*ion and if this is Shangri La I want a herb garden. Crisis becomes a discipline as *alchemy* enters the disarrayed ranks of complementarity and, *true* to *flattery*, the autumn remembers this and covers *you* in leaves. *You* really are a phenomenon for the new age of percipience and *flattery*, trapped in the dream of a *true alchemy* that would return us to the Promised Land. As for me, I'm happy that my *indigest*ion's stopped playing havoc with my thinking. The fact is we both properly belong in medieval dream literature as two emblematic cucumbers born with gout. We *resemble* the *best* encore to oblivion. Shall we *assemble* then, in the exterior decency of ignorance,[1] *seeing* the pure illusion of a Godot (as I've given *up agreeing* to wait for the splendid hour that never comes)? Meanwhile, I think I'll stick around and await that *cup* of prussic acid and look back on *sin* as a proven method of good gout control then eventually *begin* to reduce my excursions into contemporary voice.

1. "Les bienféances extérieures de l'ignorance." (Fontanelle).

Enter Iago.

This masque is quite the cocoon. We started with Polonius confessing to his love-affair with death and since then the old spider's spun its web out of that identical sentiment to a claustrophobic, repetitive tautness, so I won't be slackening it. Does anyone have a spare atomic bomb I can use, or a secret footnote with a trap door in it? Seemingly not, but at this point I'm pretending to be one of Shaykespiere's most complex villains getting ready to ask if you *grow* your own nightmares *so* they end in other peoples' tax returns and wait for them to flower into unprecedented rebates? Like the *rest* of us I'll take a cauchemar over this constant petit mal of fiscal anxiety anytime. In a life of *uncertainty* it's *best* to settle for the *tyranny* of the obvious; I know *things* may be improving in cognitive linguistics but Death still remains the prevalent pseudonym. From Los Alamos to Las Vegas it's a candid arc or abyss slung across the concept of the perfect day. For all *intents* and purposes *kings* may end up paupers after life, and with *accidents* my only certainties it's becoming *clearer why* life is not my forte in this purple sector where the shrapnel shrivels before the Grand Grimgribber of the flavor-splash. There's nothing *dearer* to my heart than to *lie* asleep dreaming of an intimate body search by Columbian customs officials each dressed up as the Cisco Kid. How a uniform turns me on! Saint Polycarp wears one all the time around his mind when he's claiming a *lie* can be a truth about to happen. Take my own truth for instance, after having been poetry for a hundred and eighty one pages, I'm finally emerging as a dialogic structure in prosaic space. I was hoping you wouldn't say that, I mean there's nothing *dearer* to the spirit than to remain a disruptive category of fictitious being, which explains *why* this is a Divine Tragedy and makes *clearer* how we all are characters played out in the final seconds before unveiling the ultimate stalag to be the unreadable. But I should take the invisible ink of the dark to some other metaphor, a final question seems pertinent to the *accidents* of what I'm saying: "What is Death but a man in language? The 'I' which sits upon a throne of *kings*?" For all *intents* and purposes *things* are just as they've always been; I've outlasted my Principality of Paranoia, parsing the names of those who are numbers to tease out the *tyranny* of life's little ironies. The *best* form of *uncertainty* usually manifests in anger management classes where your favourite TV pedophile bishop or one of the *rest* of those de-frocked evangelists tries so hard to spread his blessings on a bunch of soccer hooligans while struggling to *grow* accustomed to dodging slices of left-hand bread.

Exeunt

Scene 4. *Enter the King with diverse young Lords, taking leave for the Florentine war: Count, Ross, and Parolles. Flourish.*

I *loved* the way mathematics always came to the aid of philosophy in the twentieth century. Take set theory for instance and how it *proved* the blatant contradiction in Hegelian becoming. But look what we've become—several unrelated knots in an allophonic strand leading backward to a morose people laughing from the sacred center of a Portuguese sardine (and with the breath to prove it). They say Florence can be nice during wartime, but the *doom* and gloom of the *weeks* ahead is yet to *come*, so let's put a little botox in our *cheeks* and face up to it later. Against a backdrop of "deep time" we seem to have *taken* the residual as our line of flight; we represent the cosmos precisely by not knowing it. At Glastonbury, where wild dogs *bark* at the Tor, the Arthurian cycle is *shaken* by the critical difference between a Druid and a Dryad. Such fine insights are the *mark* of an even finer being and open up the possibility that a brain as smart as mine can *remove* an iceberg in its path. Yet thinking is the most difficult of deaths, the body *finds* itself in *love* with thoughts still scattered across a multiplicity of *minds* and because of that I always strive for the perfect congruence of sanctity and degeneration. "There's no stability here on the lower east side of the Renaissance. Andromeda holds the Baptist's head above the Mother of Innocents and retires into the *minds* of those permanent residents of the posthumous. Don't you *love* how a bird is a bundle of multiple responses and *finds* itself unable to *remove* the *mark* that holds it in a mutinous lucidity? *Shaken* by a sound it flies off returning to a favorite stream as a system through sallows, a confluence of accidence and catastrophe in Rilke's dream of a world of pure relation until taking permanent residence in two abbreviated atoms." I said all of that without knowing a word of what I meant. Language does that to you sometimes, putting the *bark* before the dog without a mouth. I should have *taken* that short cab ride to the beginning of the past, cleaning my four *cheeks* of what's to *come* in the *weeks* ahead, before the day of *doom proved* an end to the careen of meaning across entities having *loved* my life of regal reticence I can finally welcome the Cataclysmic Circus into bed.

1. Pascal.

> I show that I have understood a writer only when I can act
> in his spirit, when, without constricting his individuality,
> I can translate him and change him in diverse ways.

> Novalis

Scene 5. *Enter Suffolk and Queene.*

I'd *love* to help you fund-raise for those mass infant burials in Bangladesh, for a baby's face is never young, from the day of its birth it bears the scars of its future that we cannot *prove* will come in happy gestures to its mother's fingers— turning itself toward experience as if its vulnerability had wandered. I *hate* being knowledgeable and equally *frown* upon the novelties that *accumulate* at the turn of each century such as Van Gogh's mind drowned in the acrylic of a fading heliotropic potential—that's why I've made my date with the global genome. Mind you, it's a relief that we're biodegradable from our necks *down* despite the plutonium inserts. Now that the end is in *sight* and the last Summer *winds* through its final sunshine, perhaps it's *right* to call on *minds* better than our own to plan the final *day.*[1] But if death turns out to be time regained, I think I'll make a *call* on the body of Proust reposing in its ponderous syllables and *repay all* his debts to the neo-morticians of Paris. Perhaps it's time for us *all* to *repay* our debts to those fertility forecasts that stabilize my calendrical rhythms by living a leap year every month, then making a *call* to future prosperity anomalies and that way pull off an act of incomprehension not unlike Newman's illative sense as misemployed in this sentence. That would be the *day* that the global deficit solidifies into its own gift basket, captivating *minds* as well as bank accounts by the *right* kind of largesse. Then I'd definitely share the limelight with glitzy Egyptologists whose complex theory of the pyramids *winds* up as the agit-prop of Yemeni make-up artists, at which point my soul would assume the form of a pharaoh dessed in a three-piece suit. What a *sight*, *down* through the entrails of ultra-fine "*accumulate* cookie" body-tubes to finally arise the simulacrum of a family resemblance! Looking back without a *frown* or trace of *hate* on the Age of Certainties it seems incredible that we lived to *prove* that *love* takes its roots in the ones, like us, who need stability.

1. Such as?

Exeunt

Enter Orlando and Jacques.

Did *you*; know Jacques; the semicolon; isn;'t found; in a; printed English; book; before; 1589 and that we've already tripped over nine of them? I'm currently rereading an epic poem that consists entirely of punctuation marks. In Canto 287 a woman and *true*-to-the-end vegetarian called ":::" *cured* her lover from a comatose *state* ";:;;" with the following magical charm ",,,!!,;::::',!!!?,," It was as thrilling as a drive-by colonoscopy and it sure as hell *assured* me that there are things less gripping than the annual reports of the Commission on Applied Comparative Atrocities. Reading it clarifies how meaning resonates in its absence and not in its installation. I didn't *anticipate* I'd be *needing* assistance but to my surprise I did. It's hard to conceive in it a community of sentences, yet I'm finding a surprising *meetness* in the sparse deployment of question marks, *feeding* my desire for the minimal, and a far more rewarding experience then listening to that Polish ambassador speak entirely in consonants. Incidentally, how was your transit from nature to culture? Mine had the *sweetness* of a veritable nightmare, it sure seems as if the Locating Angel missed its mark. After being rendered unconscious by a tornado in Baton Rouge I got stuck between the naïf and the sentimental before the *purge* of Warsaw came up on me *unseen* and dropped me back into self-reflexivity. My nervous exhaustion's been building up over the past thirty-five years and I lost my *urge* for the ethical obligation when I inherited the late Pope's swastika collection at which point my entire historical perception dwindled into dates.—Wordsworth had a similar experience at Tintern Abbey which caused Leopardi to throw up on his selected prose. But I'm *keen* to know why your face looks so hauntingly accidental? Not exactly a mistake but a becoming still on its way to being there. I'm also *keen* to find out your favorite sexual position. I like the one where the man's stripped naked, gagged, tied down on the bed with nylons and the woman finishes the ironing; it always makes me feel emotionally suspended at the point where the *urge* to immortality greets a sizeable chunk of non-existence. Will an *unseen* parsec *purge* us of the *sweetness* not to come?

I think not, but how can we know for sure? Before we "know" "construction" we need to "construct" "knowledge" but that collapses our tactical vectors into strategic circumbilivagination with the cephalus of the episteme *feeding* off its own coccyx. There's a *meetness* to knowing that the man who first stuttered invented the wheel and all its attendant, delirium.[1] Stop getting so pristine in your sentiments, always *needing* to *anticipate* an answer to a question never asked. Rest *assured* we'll have all eternity and its constant *state* of zero haecceity for questions without answers. *Cured* of the need for *true* knowledge, abandoned to the dialectical manifold an ant gets entangled in a sovereign silence—that ant is *you*.[2]

1. The reference is to Orpheus (I think).
2. Attendant, confidant, infant, peasant, servant etc.

Enter Timon and Stewards.

When we were Greeks and *spent* time together in the Agora, where pure forms preoccupied our thinking, we were *content* with a knowledge no *greater* than the fact that we are born several and we die one.[1]—We rose *anew* each day to no *better* truth than that; however, in the "*true* event" heaven might prove to be a countryside of pure mathematics. But enough of reflection, my *fever's* back and I'm coughing up Asian flu again and that bad habit's returned of yelling at corpses. It seems I'm not *fitted* out for professional eternity and was *never committed* to the finer intricacies of the pleasure principle. What I urgently need is a different idiosyncrasy, something along the lines of a compulsion to work while whistling. All my life I've hoped to *win* an award from some travelling exhibition of world famous idiosyncrasies, but my *fears* of abnormality seem to have stifled that ambition. Caught *within* a space between terror and serendipity even my *tears* taste of paint, at which point I always remember the plight of Joanna Southcott, made pregnant by the Holy Ghost—a historical event more enthralling than the entire French Revolution. She died in *tears* of a dropsy *within* a year before giving birth thus ending all dreams of a new millennium. It might allay your *fears* to know one always dies towards the past. I know you've not had much luck in a cut-throat world but you did *win* the Shroud of Turin in last month's Papal Lottery[2] and now it's a table-cloth for our own last supper. I've always been more *committed* to the aleatory than to Coptic theories of embarrassment, although I've *never fitted* in with those who have the *fever* for the Imaginary. In fact that rumour about me turns out to be *true*—I HAVE applied for a once only membership in the SICS.[3] *Better* to be posthumously entertaining than livingly immiserative, or perhaps I should start *anew* on some *greater* campaign than the inevitability of death? Who knows, I might find myself *content* doing research on Lithuanian recipes for human procreation in the National Library of Scotland (the Earl of Bute had a couple of interesting suggestions for knotting and gendering in a cistern),[4] or indulge in the pleasures *spent* on ear-ring alterations by collage.

1. Socrates in Valéry's *Eupalinos, or the Architect.*
2. What jubilation when the last pink ball rolled into place, a 44!! And they say God prefers odd numbers: seven days to a week, 365 days to a year, three persons in one God?
3. Society for the Invention of Creative Suicides.
4. Cf Othello IV.1: "a cistern for foul toads to knot and gender in."

Exeunt

Scene 6. *Enter Suffolk and Warwick with their weapons drawn.*
I adore being named after an English county as much as I love the feel of everyday things like this ticket you gave *me* to the Darmstadt Symposium on Man and Space. That was prior to this sword and dagger routine and before the bad attack of apocalyptic transformation turned us into competing technologies (courtesy of you not paying our joint annual *fee* to the Syzygy Monster)—it certainly *fits* our pattern of becoming-elsewhere. At this point the greatest temptation that could be *tendered* would be to enter singleness when Being, in fact, always shows itself twice.[1] It's the entire history of Speech and Writing, Jacques Derrida wrote a musical about it and it became one of the all-time *hits* on Broadway. Paris Hilton played the leading role, a schoolgirl called Alice who *remembered* that the alphabet was a *crime* against humanity brought upon us by some evil Egyptian called Toth played by Denzel Washington. Even Gayatri Spivak's *taken time* to write a prologue to it. I'll see if I can summarize the libretto: Language plus two equals translation minus one—unfortunately, language doesn't have the larceny of poetry at its disposal. It's important for characters like us, *shaken* by the diremption of presence and lacking the metaphorical *steel* arrow to shoot from the equally metaphorical oak *bow* of différance to *feel* that the limits of LANGUAGE are those contours

of tiny articulated architectures called letters. Were we *now* in such a city a blot would be a vision, but *now* I *feel* where words arrive no thing may be.[2] However, we don't have to *bow* down before the *steel* edicts of the coco-centric, that play's *shaken* the bananas off all the branches of Western Philosophy. True sounds now reach the ears across an infinite deferral between a subject and a life. I think it's *time* we published a raunchy novella and got ourselves interviewed in the Etudes Rabelaisiennes. Methinks not, it's *taken* a long wait to admit that our planned disintegration into non-organic identity has surprising appeal. Soon we won't have to worry about writing or being picked out in an identification parade on *Crime* Stoppers, or being *remembered* as the two goofs who parachuted off the Eiffel Tower. All *hits* have been *tendered* and if the job *fits* the *fee* then you and *me* will remain a paragraph from the lost pornography by that Man of Space.

1. See Gilles Deleuze, *Essays Critical and Clinical* p.93.
2. Stefan George has "where word breaks off no thing may be."

Enter Petruchio and Hortenso with meate.
Should we talk about future tenses, now that we're actually not that which we thought we were, or do you feel the *reign* of the continuous present will *maintain* our equilibrium? Right now I feel more an I myself than a me. Urban demographics have *shown* that the auto-parasitic carnivore has its lapidary qualities; imagine this chunk of meat cooked over a single-*bevel* grill in a plaza, as you suck your very *own* host into semantic entropy, then *level* out and leave in various lexical directions. It's *good* to know you're still authentic and that the cyborg *spies* haven't drained you of all your originality. Despite being ectoplasm over metal skeleton with stains of synthetic *blood* around your *eyes* you're still capable of *seeing* how one's knee bone's connected to one's thigh bone. Compared to me you might well be *deemed* still "one of them," that is, the *being* you once were, but given that *esteemed* condition of transmogrification's already taken place let me ask you what tense you choose to live in? As a new-arrival in the inhuman, perhaps the flatulent tense in honor of everybody who phart because they don't know how to laugh? I myself want "to live in the imperative of the future passive participle—in the what ought to be;"[1] it'll be a good tense for my microchips and it's *esteemed* highly practical in the more

exclusive Crisis Ethics Clubs. We've so many tenses to reflect on—many barely usable: the perfective imperfective (as in *being*), the subjunctive, the pluperfect, even the present slips away *deemed* the regimen of a non-event. Speaking of which I was quite touched when I received a personalized gravestone as my retirement present, I only have to carve in my last four numbers. Ah, dolce padre, I think you're still *seeing* life the way I see death: as a sunset into syllogism; we'll need to keep our *eyes* alert as the descent beckons. It's a clown's way, playing life for laughter, with jokes in the shells of jokes about the life *blood* of a cab ride to applause. But what really matters is what's on the other side of this curtain, there may be *spies* analyzing all our *good* punch lines on the *level* of our *own* lowest common denominators. Yet the adage is sound: to have all in the moment, that's the *bevel* of the quest. Do you realize that we've never been *shown* the proper way to die, let alone how to *maintain* our life supports? [Ed. The answer to that question recedes right now as suicidal parents interrupt their lullabies to think on the *reign* of the concordia discors occasioning the loneliness of the long-distance mortician.]

1. Osip Mandelstam, "Journey to Armenia" in *Complete Prose* p. 236.
2. Dante's *Inferno* Canto X.

Enter Rodrigo and Iago.

It was winter in the singular and *me* and *you* were together, and as I was thinking my old black dog went out into the garden and was indistinguishable from the snow that had fallen, but it was actually the dog who fell and the snow barked back. It seems there's an abyss in my logic; true, I'm *more* than happy to have invented pessimism and granted, I've never met a mind I didn't plunder, but I'm beginning to sound like a concept without a percept. Rest assured, it's because the world is utterly unintelligible that it's so fantastic. For instance, why is it that our *bold* ribaldry finally rivets us to the image of a human corpse in Spain? Death sings all the time in Andalusia, a *score* of lyrics each reflecting the cadences of Lorca's land. It's prudent to *hold* onto that truth which makes death seem so obvious. Frankly, I *missed* out on the aesthetic *part* of nonentity and find it hard to *subsist* in a life that's as exotic as Type 2 Diabetes. In the figure and the fictive life of Don Quixote we encounter a being for whom the everyday is extraordinary. As for me? Well my revolution won't be televised, life's so boring in this place, nothing happens apart from the odd, accidental miracle. I haven't been cheerful since 1348 and only then because I caught Bubonic Plague. I've been phoning Death for eighty-nine years and it still hasn't returned my call. I'm bored to the point of innocence. Oxydized, I'm freezing into place without admitting who I am. My *heart* beats an *eternity* in seconds and I *remain* a *memory* of a happenstance in the *brain* of a Thompson's gazelle. Just imagine me as Quixote pallid at a wind-mill as my wilted *brain* engages the clouds above La Mancha, cutting a cumulus in half with a misplaced Aragonian delusion. There's a *memory* keeps returning of a wise man at a window staring in awe at a chorus line of recently deceased orthodontists; such recollections are the story of my life. But it's no worse than malaria, in fact boredom and unhappiness like ours is the condition of the gods, and in a way it's a relief to know there's an end at the end after all, rather than a royal command to *remain* alert for *eternity* obediently counting the beats of your *heart* for strictly regimental purposes. Given my own ability to *subsist* on elective affinities and your *part*-culpability in every chance encounter that I've *missed,* it may *hold* true that it's the life among the parts that's difficult. I'm sure it's possible to *score* a symphony for silence on that last reflection, but it'll take the mind of someone *bold* and *more* ambidextrous than either *you* or *me* to conceive death as the non-organic adventure of a soul.[1]

1. Petrarch.

Exeunt

Scene 7. *Enter two Drawers.*
Suppose I'm unlucky enough to die second, what epitaph should I inscribe on your tomb? "Miserimus" perhaps[1] or "Here lies one whose name was writ as Walter?" or summarize perchance those ugly disputes in pandeca-syllabic couplets about those immaculate contraceptions *you* had with Pope Clement IV? Incidentally, if you're planning to run for Pope yourself it would *be* prudent to read "Jesus for Beginners," preferably in Catalan not Latin, and preferably not on an undulating fiscal imbalance, for there "the only fertile way is repetition."[2] I remember the time we helped Sisyphus carve a comment on his stone; it was a light bulb moment in mythopoesis: "Nous avons les

embryons desserchés" writ in perfect Portuguese. There's no *haste* to obtain cosmetic enhancements when dead, but when I join your corpse and *lie* beside it in the Merry Morticians Funeral Home, it might prove fun to continue our conversation telepathically on our respective slabs. Why not, since "Death is absolute and without memorial"[3]—who knows, it could end up being the trip of a lifetime. Comments like that ruin my complexion. What of those events that have no *past*, and *defy* transcription? I'm *told* the date that has been will come again, but I've no *desire* to return to some *old* Department of Sumptuary Studies, reinflated and pulmonary with an air of self-esteem. In fact I *admire* Bataille's destination for subjectivities in a form of immanence he likens to a wave among waves. Dead ancient mariners aside, I have to admit I hate the *sight* of a healthy body; rather than focusing on exercise, diet and well-being I prefer to concentrate on novel styles of self-destruction. It's precisely what I find so appealing in Dr. *Strange*love—taking oneself and everybody to obliteration after counting the number of body bags needed before lift off—that's what I call democracy in situ my venerabilis inceptor of the via moderna. Eternally, it's the superficial corpse that matters, yet we *might* take hope in the fact that we can *change* the way life happens. Why not imagine being a contact lens and drop onto my left eye, viscid but firm and round, the resulting *change* of perspective to the way I see things *might* help solve the enigma of Dante's epic that haunts us both. *Strange* to grasp *sight* of a meal in Tokyo Deserta with your breath caught between Quillan and Axat and still not able to *admire* the florid prose of Justin Smith.[4] Last week I fell asleep into the phrase "of possible experience" and dreamed an *old desire:* that in dying we recall what in dying we are trying to forget. I'm *told* it's still possible to *defy* all odds and settle in a state somewhere between the comic and the tragic. The *past* may well *lie* ahead not because of an eternal return but owing to the reversed polymers in our chromosomes. But I'll add in *haste* that this isn't intended to *be* a compliment to *you*. It simply means we're back at square one. Or perhaps not, if we imagine death turns out to mean not imagining at all.

1. Wordsworth wrote a sonnet on this word he discovered written on a mysterious gravestone in Worcester Cathedral bearing that single word and no other.
2. Gandhi.
3. Wallace Stevens.

4. Why does McCaffery insist on throwing into this ridiculous farce esoteric terms? I thought Quillan and Axat were minor Mesopotamian deities until I Googled them up and found them to be nearby towns in southern France. If he insists on writing in English (some of the time) then at least let him use family place names like Borrego Springs and Seven-Mile Creek. On Justin Smith see his *Troubadours at Home*, 1899.

Enter King Richard (disguised as Georges Bataille).

It's a *crime*, when you look at what my life's become— a radical untelegenesis that no one understands. With my chakras all clogged I feel utterly redundant as a monarch. I used to be considered the greatest chameleon of statecraft, a veritable tortoise of genius, now I'm so internal all the *time* to everything that it's impossible to remember me as me. My memory emerges from *showers* of recollections in a style of migraine that feels uncannily analogous to fetish cults in West Africa. Despite that glass of dock, comfrey, cinque foil and betony after every meal, I'm still looking for a cure for the King's evil[1] so it's hardly *politic* to mention that at the extreme limit of suffering nothing remains but the conditions of space and time.[2] Oh, mutabilis, dear name! I harbored serious aspirations of becoming the next Pope until a nun assured me that I had to truly believe in God. During the Wars of the Roses, the then current Pontiff was a member of the Lancashire Hitler Youth and later the Merseyside Wehrmacht, no doubt fantasizing the crucifixion on a swastika of all those six-million tax payers who happened to have the wrong blood type and the wrong shaped nose. It was a shock to realize how genocidal justificaton boils down to profiles and cosmetics. It's calm, however, in these *hours* of solitude without God, especially now that I've stopped sniffing all my paralegals' portfolios. A *heretic* like me *calls* for a language released from *discontent* then *falls* in love with nouns. It's no *accident* that Love and Language remark the old stilnovist dilemma when experiencing the pure event of words.[3] I *gathered* long ago— before *hate* became my last great attribute—that it's a case of dichterbereuf— the poet's calling to *unfathered* progenies across a bereft *state* of abjection. I don't want to *state* the obvious but a truly tragic poem is one that recognizes the tragedy of language itself—such poems are born *unfathered* into contradiction. To love a poem is to *hate* a poem[4] but an echo is a recollection *gathered* to be ripped apart. Old Woman Language, withdrawn by *accident* into her dream of not dreaming as nostalgia *falls* into *discontent* and *calls* upon some *heretic* of

191

temporality to transport her for a few *hours* to a new admissible paradise. The poet stands metaphorically behind his debt, juxtaposed by her bright red endnotes. Is it therefore *politic* to speculate that God may be a radio that someone's forgotten to turn off? Without Jean Cocteau to answer this question I'll let my head deviate into generalities and stay the opposite of backward, looking out there, speechless where *showers* of destruction are cleansing *time* of its *crime* against the Proxy Tabulator.

1. For full details of this pathetically provincial remedy for scrofula see Daniel Roberts, *Remarks on the King's Evil, or Scrophula; with an Account of a specific Medicine for the Cure of it.* London, 1791, (if you can find a copy).
2. Hölderlin, in his Notes to Sophocles' *Oedipus.*
3. See Giorgio Agamben, *The End of the Poem.*
4. A sentiment of Georges Bataille.

Enter Exeter with a Coffin.
This so called coffin turns out to be quite the Pandora's box, carrying it around sure teaches me the meaning of mortality. Incidentally, these hemorrhoids have turned me into a veritable anus mirabilis—(or is that a case of judging the hole by the part)? Either way it's nice to pause and meditate upon the Latin verse inscriptions carved on ruined pedestals, and to always find the funerary urn placed beside the lovers' bench. I think I'll become a poet when language is finally dead and I'm free from the *control* of differential signs. It's part of my vision of recovered infancy but my *soul* has always had a passion for the fantastical. For instance, when I visited God to discuss our mutual budgetary crises, I found the floor of his study littered with plans for the architectural renovation of Heaven. Terrific I thought, God wants a new urban order. His problem turned out to be surprisingly human: how to realize floor-plans as three-dimensional designs. I suggested a vast biblical theme-park as a narrative solution to the visual problems inherent in his Führer Gallery, at which point he suddenly disappeared. Do *you* remember when asemia was our greatest technology, liberating the *art* of writing from language into the *free* poetics of the doodle? My *heart* skips a beat when I think of every dollar I've *spent* on crayons to *savour* that condition of a writing without Writing.[1] Now all the talk's about community and the infinite restlessness of identity.

(A kind of "It" between a "Me and Us"). But as we're in the Epoch of the Great Escape why don't we *rent* a town with fourteen exits, each leading to the same precipice? I'd love the *favour* of a chance at *ruining eternity* as a way of *honouring* the *canopy* placed over all my thwarted desires. I mean it's hard to bundle up my truculence, life today's as bad as southern hospitality with all its bourbon and Cotton Bowls. But imagine the sight of a tattooed Genghis Khan under a *canopy* of stars *honouring* the dead at the Alamo according to medieval theories of entropy. Which makes me wonder whether *eternity* is shorter than infinity, both seem to have a way of *ruining* the details of the past. Take Benny Methuselah from Nantucket serving great pastrami from the same location on Washington Street for over three hundred years before delivering his last dill pickle to the Lord of Shadows—and we don't even have his memoirs! I'd be doing myself a *favour* if I took a walk outside these words I am. I could *rent* one of those pastrami sandwiches, sit down on this serenity flask, and *savour* the unforgettable expertise of Etruscan gastronomy now that it's all been forgotten. All that trans-fat must taste fabulous and given the state of espresso after Euclid, with its indisputable affinities to the consequences of an undiscovered botanical paradox, it'll prove a veritable noctes ambrosianae. I'm sure a day *spent* indulging in the pleasures of the stomach sure beats a *heart free* of cholesterol. Then there's the *art* of dying *you* told me of, the preparation for a slow but tidy passing in a long-term care facility for the derelict, hoping death will usher in immortal life for the *soul*, or at least, life as it should have been: unassuming, subservient to *control*, non-demanding, in fact, just the regular corpse in an unmarked grave.

1. See Roland Barthes, "On Masson's Semiography" in *The Responsibility of Forms. Critical Essays on Music, Art and Representation*, trans. Richard Howard. New York: Hill and Wang, 1985: 153-56.

Exeunt

End of Act IV

Laughter is the depth of worlds … the human ambivalence is that we cry at death, but when we laugh we do not know we are laughing at death.

Georges Bataille[1]

Act V Scene 1. *Enter Rosalind and Celia.*

I know *you* suffered badly at the bicentennial celebration of the Treaty of Augsburg, but that suit of armor and chain mail vest made of the best see-through polyester still looks great, and with a little spit and polish to your armorial crest and forty minutes of consensual frottage (with yours truly) my darling will *be* as good as new. Happy obituary; people can keep their Sapphic modernity and stuff it in the next available fin de siècle. Still, I *treasure* the memory of when we last met slightly east of The Florist's Directory, it was a *pleasure* that no aerobics manual could *kill*. I quickly learned the *skill* of same-sex excess among the erotics of Lesbian Landscapes, which threw me *back* to your own desire for a fully accessorized feminist bishopric. Given the *wrack* and ruin of current Europhallicism I'd say our stance against the hegemony of the priapic is definitely paying dividends. It was a Moral Victory to see that snippet on YouTube where Arnold Schwarzenegger loses his testicles to a short-sighted and infernally hungry squirrel. As our fortune *grows* it *shows* to the world why it's always sunny when we share a dildo. The *hour* has come when finally we're together as two apprentices to a sexual *power* commissioned by the Anti-Christ of Patriarchy.[2] I've always admired that *power* to turn words into delicious entrées, yet every *hour* we're together *shows* why I'm attracted to malfeasance. I know issuing death threats at the local nursery's taking it a little too far but I'm moon-struck, under a planetary influence and, to a monstrous genetic throwback like me, the feeling *grows* that we've always been the Royal butchers of the King's two bodies. Your mind's complexity, my love, matches the intricacy of the Lindisfarne carpet page, I fear this *wrack* at the *back* of your cognitive *skill* will *kill* the *pleasure* in our passionate nights of cloning. I *treasure* a splash of romance, but a kiss on your lips requires macro-economic coordination, after the smooch there are inconsistent trajectories to the blood-splatter pattern leaving your plasma on my teeth. So it might *be* a stepmother's blessing to have *you* in bed pondering whether it's God or plain bad luck that controls the extension of orgasm into this cabinet of curiosities.

1. I'm getting truly pissed off with all these quotes from yours fekking truly. How about some gnomic adages from Leon Trotsky (who's still to be mentioned apart from that jazz band) or Must-have-a-Camel Atatürk aka the Turkish Delight.

2. I.e. Margaret Thatcher.

Enter the two Kings with their powers, at several doores.
So many Kings and too few monarchies to put them in! It was the same problem that plagued the Jena Romantics' Oscar nominations with their poetics of gloom and *woe*—in my *esteem* they touched the acme of the unbearable. I thought it was "storm and stress" not "gloom and woe?" All your comments and actions *lack* accuracy: celebrating Christ's birth on Bastille Day and Fidel Castro's on the Fourth of July. In the present instance you *seem* to be confusing the high Romantics with such mid-Victorian duds as Ella Wheeler Wilcox, capturing the dark—even *black*—side of the emotional spectrum with her gloomy thoughts on poverty and sexual repression. Those slum landlords were a *disgrace* to Industrial Capitalism, but Karl Marx predicted correctly that the *Bower* of Bliss would be available to the Proletariat when the workers decided to *face* off against the bosses and claim *power* for themselves. It's a *shame* you never married into the lumpen and had some uncultivated *heir* to pass the class-struggle on to. The fact is we reign in the common *name* of Calamity *Fair.* It's also *fair* to say I have so many favorite anxieties that collectively they form a pretty comprehensive millennial blues. But as Monarch and above-average idiot, minor poet, convicted warlock, and Cherokee translator of Robert Frost, I did make a *name* for myself outside regality—sufficient to land me the direct *heir* to a syndicate of young satirists complete with idylls fitting for gutter and gallows. It's a *shame* I didn't stay longer in the Harlem Renaissance and assume the *power* of poet laureate (boy, they needed one like you all need a shower). Let's *face* it, I'm proud to be a King equipped with all the accoutrements of

aristocracy: no cell phone, no ipad, no Droid. I've loved eating fruit ever since Chaos slipped on a banana skin, but each plum I pluck from the palace *bower* reminds me of the *disgrace* I felt at knowing that I never once attempted to sit on one of Albert Speer's experiments in Nazi Chippendale. *Black* clouds always *seem* to hover over all my self-ratifications, I seem to *lack* the capability of holding on to my self-*esteem* long enough to even fax myself a compliment but *woe* betide those micturating heterarchs who yell "I told you *so*."

Enter Lear.

Things just got a little worse and a lot more surprising—that corpse that winked at both of you just gave me a *kiss*. My jockey never told me *this* could happen but look at my *lips*. Matthew Arnold sure got it right this time. [1] They say the life of a man is the most precious oblation to deprecate a public calamity, [2] but last week ranks as a personal catastrophe for a three-legged nag like me. I'll have to alter my *gait* and get involved in some new participation mystique where I can bring my own coefficient of weirdness to the fore. When the *chips* are finally on the table it's spoor's vamoose. To *state* it bluntly I gotta *stand* up and *reap* the corn from the *hand* that slaps me, *leap* out of rutting into recreation whorehouse, or anywhere else that *confounds* mah appearance at Kentucky Derby time. Mah ass juss *sways sounds* from trundle mops to semitones as the band *plays* ow's about dat Chastity Waltz? [Ed: One of the problems being a King is that the responsibility *plays* havoc with one's sanity. It *sounds* strange to admit that King Lear thinks he's the talking horse in Ed Dorn's Slinger, but judge it for yourself, dear reader. The evidence so far presented in his monologue *sways* assessment towards delusional egomania and *confounds* the *leap* in faith required to imagine this masque to be a plausible fiction. But then again, Caligula made his horse a senator and this horse sounds like a pony gelding to be reckoned with.] Unnit sure does! Cozzarmuz sober as November and today is March, for an hour at least, so it's arbeit up among da exclamation marks! Gonna lend a *hand* to some bum rap and *reap* da hand dat whips me, and *stand* against a *state* dat's rotten to da *chips*! Change mah *gait* 'n gallop into cheese 'n pouting tell yawl that it's mah scene ain yower *lips* ginst *this* asser mahn's cawlled a "*kiss* onna hoss's mouth!"

1. "Truth sits upon the lips of dying men." Sohrab and Rustum.

2. Edward Gibbon, *The Decline and Fall of the Roman Empire*, Book 50.

Alarms to the fight, wherein both the Staffords are slain. Enter Cade and the rest.
Hell, what was all that about? It seems to be another case of writing under the influence of smart quotes. It's all *well* and good to resort to the vernacular to deliver a houynym soliloquy but it hardly helps us realize the *dream* of a perfect language. Speaking of perfection don't cry *woe* is me when I inform you this slaughter before you demonstrates how death is the perfect axial event, a contact equivalence leaving reputation at a zero point—and yet a corpse yearns for symmetry. I rather like the idea of having a bumper sticker on a hearse that reads "Death has no inner signification." It might be taken as a little *extreme* in this part of the political spectrum but it's *so* close to the *mad* reality of a different truth: that Death's both an ontological condition and a proper name. With your looks I might have taken the *bait (had* it been offered) and walked *straight* up to the Goddess of Atrocities to put my *trust* in the tactic of fishing for compliments. I used to feel it a duty to prove myself to the world, now I can't wait to leave it. Don't *blame* me if I don't get us from life's analogy to *lust's* homology. It's a *shame* the future is only this vicinity and it's a *shame* too that every morning I wake up happy I'm not one of you and, thanks to that, feel less in touch with your *lust* for the present, but it sure allows me to focus on the prospect to come. The River bin Laden insinuates among the flock of Talmud geese heading west into Flamingo Whississippi where, in the evening, after bible class, the dead run for their lives. You can *blame* it entirely on me and my avuncular disposition towards your pocket John Adams for getting us caught trafficking in such an aberration, and you can *trust* me to invent three more deadly sins before I die, sins *straight* out of the Brussels Yearbook for Boys. Remember the fun we *had* feasting our eyes on that treasure trove of homoerotic pornography? It was the perfect *bait* for a *mad* surrealist like you. Personally I found it *so* graphically *extreme* that I cashed mine in for a User's Guide to Becoming Emily Dickinson. (I mean who needs a window in a fortress of solitude?) *Woe* to those who *dream* of the rewards of a chaste life—you know as *well* as I do that Nefertiti ranked virginity on a par with malnutrition. It's nice you can be funny about such a serious thing but *hell,* you gotta add acid to that humor if you're gonna turn a smile into false teeth.

Exeunt

Scene 2. *Enter Rosencrantz* (believing he's a midget) *and Guildenstern.*

If I had to *compare* myself to yesterday I'd have to admit I'm somewhat shorter, but then again I've always felt height's wasted on tall people. My minimality is due to a *rare* defect I acquired from mixing occult Haitian voodoo protocols with southern Californian organic root-vegetable cocktails. Still, I like the *ground* up to my chin this way, it makes me feel like one of those grotesque caricatures immortalized by the Master of the Salzburg Psalter. Growing up I was the smallest child in my village outranking heavy industry by a single lullaby; in those days I would *go* to sleep to the *sound* of hunting horns in pursuit of the final unicorn and felt destined to become a transcendental empiricist. Both my mother and my father hated me, but luckily I soon realized that parents are as bad as private property and fools dream wiser than the wise. I'm quite talented at flaunting my own ignorance so let's get back to what I don't *know.* That dream, for instance where I'm in my mother's bedroom and the air *reeks* of stale onion. A Mennonite hunchback, known to everyone as Ethel the Paraphrast, approaches, replaces all our cutlery with plastic then confesses her *delight* in Renaissance theories of cloning, at which point my *cheeks* turn *white,* my *head* develops a *dun* hue finally turning to bright *red* and, in place of my right eye, a miniature *sun* appears wrenched from the heavens to dangle on a chain while a bruised octopus floats across the skyline. Nothing under the *sun* can explain that whirlpool of enigma. Perhaps it celebrates the evolution of subjectivity into the general proposition that "a potential 'experience' of dying is not the same as an 'actual' experience of death plus its 'departure value.'" Right now I'm *red* at the neck and on the verge of a *dun* disillusion, unable to answer why all the rest of us have guardian angels while you have your own patron saint. I mean your *head* and *white cheeks* seem the same as ours; you *delight* as we do in dancing pastors and other evangelical outreach programs, so why the privilege? It *reeks* a bit of micro-mismanagement in the Cherubimic Promissory Department. I *know* Theology was never a good neighbor, always fussing in its tight corset over what constitutes *sound* repentance after you *go* wild for a bit at the local discotheque for single parents in a passing tribute to the libertine. That's why I'm retiring to the *ground* that's giving way beneath me, preserving my fascination with the transcendental—and the *rare* chance of it happening. Incidentally, why is it always me who ends up playing the back end of our pantomime horse? From where I'm bending your asshole seems my wormhole into a cosmic short-cut. Some day it will be good to *compare* your dream of Corybantian antics to come with the fact that my face, in all its splendid confrontations, always remains behind me as the most memorable of post-industrial landscapes.

Exeunt

Scene 3. *Noise and Tumult within: Enter Porter and his men.*
I hope the *proceeds* from the National Catastrophes Telethon go to a better cause than us. At the end of our *deeds* we can look back and say life was a peaceful dream interrupted only by two North Korean helicopters, but what a *place* to end up in, and what a burden to *bear!* The pub's closed, the troubadours' gone home to take up telemarketing or first philosophy, the whole town's suffering from colony collapse disorder, and a child's walking-tour through the Paris catacombs turns into an enigma of tiny unlocked rooms. It's time to *face* up to the fact that death comes without tears as our active handmaid. So you mean we've come all this way in life to be confronted by the incontrovertible fact of our inevitable demise? I *swear* that sounds like essential desertion. At the end of a life we gaze at a gap and gulp? It's comparable to being *alone* at a Christmas eve party, delirious with jungle fever and discovering there isn't a Father Christmas. I prefer the *bold* premise that a tragedy is the comedy of the upsurge and each *groan* in life's rewarded with a corresponding laugh in heaven. But lo and *behold* from that beating *jewel* named your *heart* you tell me the *cruel* hand of aesthetic taste will guarantee there'll be nothing about us in the archives of *art*.[1] I once believed the soul to be a genetically modified form of skin complaint, but via those polyplicities collectively called creative evolution, I now realize why my soul has become your voice and sounds like Death in its new false teeth. Despite the *art* of conversation this entire *cruel* world's become my coffin but in saying this I hardly reach the *heart* of the existential crux. Whether it's a *jewel* or glass trash that we *behold* the same old things pertain. Heady riots, a child's *groan*, *bold* rapes in a schoolyard where a bull meets a duck in bed and the teacher calls it systems analysis on the same old mythological TV set beside the porcelain swans who *alone* remain

unaltered in their elegies. I *swear* I'll *face* up to the causality within and *bear* out my *place* in summation as all the *deeds* I never could be, while Nietzsche *proceeds* to apply his gay science in a boot camp for babies.

1. Freddy Footnote here again. Try to imagine the archivist as the colporter of the phenomenon of time. It sure bites back at the glitter of Quintilian.

Exeunt

> Our birth is nothing but our death began.
> Edward Young

Scene 4. *Enter three Murtherers.*

Robinson Crusoe thought cannibalism valid as a last resort, but the majority hold it an aporia in the ethical, an absolute negativity employed in the unenunciatable encounter of death with turpitude. Lévi-Strauss describes it as more a kitchen distinction between cooking and being cooked, of remaining in the land of the living rather than ending up on its plates. Carl Lumholtz opined human flesh the greatest delicacy known to the Australian aboriginals, and it was also big among the Aztec Tupinamba. More recently it became an astounding hit when it entered the nouveau cuisine of the Barons' Wars, a Lord would offer his non-vegetarian guests a choice between serf and turf and a charcoal burgher for the main course. My understandably late sister-in-law was a wet-nurse to cannibal triplets on the east side of Chicago until she was naturalized into the new job of being eternity. Should we turn ourselves in for finger printing or break off these electronic tracking tags and wander the world? People accuse us of being corruption's wardrobe, but we're only the necessity of all our contingencies. What we *lack* however is a good sense of *black* humor of the kind made famous by Caligula. I want to do my *part* when Petrarch comes to Denver, after his great escape from Bunyan's *Grace* Abounding, and rent him a house with a nice view of the local crematorium. I don't have the *heart* to have him *face west* into that propaganda theme-park ycleped Instrumental Reason and I *even* dislike that *east* view over the Rockies into *Heaven* as a well-earned destination via all the *pain* immortalized along the glitzy boulevards of hagiography. That said, a corpse is far more complex than a simple theological proposition. I mean, language buries us at birth inside a proper name and an insistent being-toward-mortality. What was the name of that famous advocate of death-for-death's sake, Pol Pot? Where would Death *be* without him and his killing fields? You need 3000 military historians per square inch to cover all his exploits. I was convinced by G. M. Trevelyan to become the official Cheerleader for the Khmer Rouge, and after I did Christopher Hill insisted I plunder his entire lexicon. In Pee Pee's em oh obligatory matricide followed the birth of each new male and if you were literate, lived in the city, watched television and could write your name correctly on cheques and envelopes or had a degree in higher education you were immediately decapitated on purely ideological grounds. Still, it must have been fun sitting under the guillotine with a flask of saki watching all those heads drop off. Personally, I find the idea of decapitation a little too Cartesian, but a death into scattering is quite appealing, and who knows, considering our sins and deceits, we may get elevated to saints, our bodies disinterred and broken up for auction among several congregations: your skull in Paris mine at the Warburg Institute—and eventually we may actually make it into the Gallia Christiana. It's not that I *disdain* living, but it seems to *me* that the urgent problems in the world are eliminating both the pleasure principle and the pursuit of happiness. What both you and *me* need is a sublime fiction to hold up with *disdain* before the Commissariat of Shadows but it would *be* a real *pain* in the butt if some drag-queen called Desiree, with a face like the late Yasser Arafat's, reminded us that the coordinates of subjectivity have switched from ideological to familial wars and the constant murder of grandparents. Good *Heaven*, do you think Joseph and Mary's proved a smooth relationship, and in an era of pram bombs why would anyone want to bring up a human baby *east* of Alcatraz or *even west* of Martha's Vineyard? Today, for instance, I met one, *face* red and contorted, screaming away in its fiberglass stroller and smelling like a part of Rio de Janero; they're without doubt the most un-utilizable examples of becoming-life. When Augustus Caesar legislated against the unmarried citizens of Rome, he declared them in some way slayers of the people, but I suppose I'm still too wrapped up in the pursuit of my own pre-adult self to appreciate the rights of others younger than myself and I've neither the *heart* nor the saving *grace* to *part* with an iota of my egocentricity. In fact, I think my existence is constantly just beginning, but when you shake my hand like that it feels as if your entire soul has entered my arm as a *black* suntessence desperate for departure across the entire *lack* of an armpit.

Enter Hamlet, reading on a booke.

Midnight is the cruelest month extending its blackness over correspondence, memorial perhaps of research without aim, or as Zeus said while annotaing history backwards, "this narrative is far too bright." Perhaps I should write my own memoirs, call it "My Life in Elsinore," however I had coffee and a croissant with Christine de Pisan recently and she insisted that in the beginning everything was poetry. The miniscule mark in the margin, the squashed mosquito between pages 8 and 9, the snotte caught on the decorative chapter-head, the shy gerund on its first date with "Propositional Language," the primrose dried and pressed with its residual butterfly attachment. Then the sonnet appeared with its fish-net typography and celebrity endorsements, taking over the East Bank and settling in every worm-holed title-page it could find: "Astrophel & Stella," "Amoretti," "Delia," "Idea's Mirrour," "Fidelia," "Parthenophil & Parthenope." There were daily pogroms on the limerick and haiku; sestinas were forced to wear a yellow star sewn on their covers; blitzkriegs killed countless families of innocent nursery rhymes; clerihues and odes were abolished by decree. Then came the mass deportations to anthologies and school text books; a few lucky ones escaped by quotation and erratas into the transatlantic liberty called free verse to join the ferns and tree stumps in ecopoetics around Thoreau's railway embankment. Others indulged in the prose vistas opened up in one of Emerson's transcendental balloon trips with complementary champagne on landing. A few brave ones remained to join rengas, epyllions and villanelles in brave resistance groups. Frankly, I've always loved those Elizabethan sonnets that we once were, but for *me* poems aimed at eternity blatantly avoid the sheer ephemerality of a life-toward-catastrophe. It's usually disasters (rather than catastrophes) that bring foreign words into parlance: holocaust, tsunami, hurricane—they litter language as do the cadavers they induce. Speaking of cadavers, do *you* remember that *gaol* we visited during the last outbreak of patina scent—and the *guard* there called "Nancy Boy," who posted *bail* for his mother's murderer? His crowning approbation was to end up in the *ward* for the morally incurable, believing Walter Benjamin had double *crossed* him, turned him into Theodor W. Adorno, and left him *forsaken* in the basement of the Frankfurt School *engrossed* in the wilderness of his own arcades. Still, it's better than being *taken* hostage by those first-nation casino theologians who structure chance at the margins of the possible.[1] I still find it preferable to *be alone* than by myself in the charmingly *me* of self-identity, immured from the constant *groan* of others. That caterpillar I squashed last week and gave to Lady Gaga offers the perfect image of philosophy's aporia—an epitaph for who is being what and why. So much death and so few lives to put it in. This next question to myself may provoke a *groan* and I know it sounds a little over-pensive, but I wonder if after death I might enjoy the phenomenon of fossilization, or simply dissipate into a sky the color of wintermute? Either way it seems to *me* infinitely preferable to a life spent in pursuit of softer skin and early morning yoga classes, or standing *alone* in some semi-obsequious panic attack, ready to *be taken* to see for the umpteenth time that film adaptation of Mel Gibson's Life of Satan. I'm *engrossed* by these *forsaken* times, *crossed* by the forces of the cemetery and the maternity *ward*, perhaps it's better to *bail* out of existence for good, change my crown of thorns to a chaplet of laurel and join the gang in Hekatempyllos. At least the dead look content, unlike myself trapped in a life of theme dinner parties, whose hosts make the prison *guard* at the *gaol*-of-your-choice dress up as Saint Francis of Assisi and feed *you* bird-seed. How did Cocteau put it? The cult of a ruin hides the sound of the shock of intelligence against beauty? But what if this is Königsberg and the year is 1783 and Kant is dressed as Santa Claus and a wallet surrounds us, then, emptying our money, it returns two lips from *me*, sealed as a lipogram conceals its own embarrassment?

1. Robert Musil.

Enter Polonius (disguised as Ezra Pound).
What was the name of the printer's pie I ate in that Tyrolean dialect? Honorificabilitadinitatibus I believe. It's about as palindromic as a Dallas salad and far less nutritious; I remember it took longer to pronounce than to swallow. I wonder how many U.S. Presidents have created neologisms that

have lasted like that one as they tiptoed around the complex euphemisms of the Oval Office? I also wonder if "protosyphilisticationalitize" is a valid hapax legomenon, if it is it would render my good self the greatest wordsmith since that mother-of-all-nonsense Sir Thomas Urquhart force-fed the Society of the Writers to the Signet with page upon page of "Logopandecteision" and his sheer "hirquitalliency at the elevation of the pole of a microcosm." You can submit those two to the Unregistered Words Committee if you like, I've lost my appetite for anything other than radiant clusters, Chinese ideograms, vortices and *free* contrastive phrasal doublets—owing to that, it pleases *me* to think of my life as my favorite pair of shoes. Marcel Duchamp avoided the *abuse* of art for art's *sake,* endowing art with its own identity by simply granting it its own problematicity. Thanks to him I can *use* my life as a ready-made, not that I'd equate it with anything so dignified as a urinal or a bottle rack. There's an odor to such words as *"take"* and *"bind me"* with their aroma of rhetorical exhaustion and impotence, the *kind* Tiresius experienced as a drag queen, campaigning in the Waste Land for *free* verse and claiming now is the time for modernism. To my mind time is *still* utopian in its least pessimistic form, for instance, by the "time" I met Yeats I'd already intellectually murdered most of the poets of my generation; it's a canonic trait of *mine* to do so based on an old premise that poetry *will* always replace "what it is" by what it "has to be." Unlike *yours* truly [points to Hamlet], my aim was always to avoid poetics. In fact I thought Constructivism my instant passage to fame until Amy Lowell arrived with her two-volume Life of Keats wrapped up in some post-epistemological tarpaulin manufactured by *yours* truly, with a living octopus under her blouse named Utopian Expressionist Architecture,[1] it instantly made home feel like a foreign country. Now nothing works of its own accord, if you get a headache it *will* last for thirty years and *mine* after fifty *still* keeps throbbing. The more oblique the truth the more banal its impact, for instance, that any social interchange extends the limits on *free* expression (it certainly didn't for the Hunchback of Notre Dame). It's the same *kind* of impression when you listen to a cadre of longshoremen admonish tenement therapy for the homeless. Or then again, imagine *me* as a dead modernist poet reading Finnegans Wake for the first time and feeling it's all been stolen from my notebooks. It's such a *bind* being a poet in a cage, and why does everything *take* so long to happen? Ten years to write a sutra, two decades before it's your turn to *use* the shower, fifteen years of appellate court before a self-confessed mass-murderer from Tallahassee finally gets his wish to die in the electric chair. It was for the *sake* of profit and profit alone that a concerted tactical *abuse* of boutique symbolism brought down the Berlin wall. I didn't buy a piece but now I wish I had, however it did please *me* to win a lifebelt from the Titanic in the *free* lottery for the cause of the impotent pentameter.

1. The blouse not the octopus.

Enter Ophelia.

Did you know that a heart palpitation in a coroner's building *will* usually put you in mind of Coleridge's 1795 Lectures on Poetry and Religion: that heroic attempt to ground Christianity in domestic sympathy? It certainly grounded me—in the poor girl's Septuagint—but it seems a tad ridiculous for me to be an atheist and still avoid the delights of the flesh. I try to convince myself that a little carnal intercourse wouldn't *kill* off my virtue any *more* than gazing at Simone Martini's Annunciation *will* convert me to ornithology. Frankly, I find jouissance a nuisance (beyond the kissy bits) because you always end up sweaty and exhausted and in need of a shower which I hate having, but I'm told the bit in the middle can be really good. Like trench warfare in the dark you never know what's in *store* for you in the hot symplegma of flesh, as you finally fall asleep *still* hoping for the sun to rise and *shine* on a *gracious* state of post-coital depression. When I think of *your* own penchant for hard-ons I remember all that sexual phobia I picked up from looking at too many Rubens; they left me believing sex to be a dark, *spacious* terra incognita illuminated by the occasional distress flare and *thus* I didn't read The Joy of Sex again until I took up Scrabble.™ You need to know a lot of organic chemistry to be good at that game. It *still* amazes me how the letter values change. If you're playing in English then the Z tile counts for ten *plus* a bonus dip in the sack, but if you're playing on a Polish board the Z tile *will* only count as one. I know life's never a straightforward thing but the rag-time fractals around here make you feel as if you're trapped in the string section of the ozone layer performing Rakmaninoff's Rhapsody on a theme of Paganini's for the rest of your life.

In fact *will* somebody please call a referendum on mortality *plus* provide an explanation why the only safe place for a human being is a mortuary slab? [Silence.] Back to the game then, I have an innate gift for bullshitte, but as the board pattern develops it always at some point reminds me of an aerial view of a death camp with letters lying as *still* as corpses in the prison-house of language. *Thus* rules the law of the great comparison, but it's *spacious* up here above the board, from the peak we're looking down on tiny guerrilla phonemes criss-crossing a village to the north of somewhere else. And over there, in that graveyard for dead letters, all the contemporary ways to stay unread line up for inspection. But what's *your* concept of time when alone and doing nothing? Is it a sentiment Shagspere enjoyed in the *gracious* pauses between his writing? I know it's hard these days to *shine* in the ranks of the minimal but I still believe it's better doing a little bit of nothing than absolutely nothing at all. Unlike "at ease" "at all" *still* seems to set you alongside the most impossible relations. Take, for instance, you and me at the *store* this morning arguing over free *will* and the mythological merit of Hesiod's Theogony then realizing how many *more* great philosophical names start with H. Homer, Herodotus, Hermione Hickey (and her horse Hippy Hoppy), Heraclitus, Hobbes, Hegel, Husserl and Heidegger. But then again there's Himmler, which seems to *kill* the theory and certainly *will* if we add the name of Hitler to the list. But that name was spurious, his real name began with an S, like Stalin, but Stalin wasn't his real name, and Sshaekspir was the Earl of Oxford dressed as Francis Bacon, which goes to prove that in this era of infant prodigies we should be wary of giving names to babies.[1]

1. Well yes and no, Freddy Footnote's done his research. Adolf Hitler was the son of Alois Schicklgruber who subsequently changed his surname to Hitler (deriving it seems from Hiedler). As for Stalin, he was born Iosif Vissarionovich Dzhugashvili.

Enter Ghost.

Why does Steve McCaffery always insist on dressing me up like a corny character out of a gothic novel? Here I am fermenting in my armor, brushing the cobwebs away and gleefully embracing the fact that we're one more sonnet closer to death. It took seven transmigrations into the Mabinogion before I finally encountered the Spoils of Annwyn as Gaston Leroux's Phantom of the

Opera (and got to sign a lot of autographs along the way).[1] I wonder if after Cardinal Newman joins me among the slot machines of Hades he *will still* need his copy of The Dream of Gerontius? *You* remember that memorable passage? It's the one I *hold* to *be* his greatest thought: "The grass springs up in the morning, at evening-tide it shrivels up and dies." Of course, not all deaths involve shriveling, there are many other eschatologies, decapitation, for instance, and the *untold* death of Arthur Cravan, pugilist-cum-Dadaist and *none* better at the art of disappearance. I'm told self-guillotining's been around for centuries which goes to *prove* that nothing's as dead as the idea of death itself. *One* can still *love* being a sleuth of the morbid and find the opportunity to *fulfil* a not-for-profit weekend job as a gnome of the further if not the future. Perhaps arriving *there will* require some extra time for all the living to prefigure their dying from the temporal condition of *near*-death. If it commences *near* the bedside light it *will* start *there* at the precise moment a life decides it best to *fulfil* the missions of others. That's why I *love* precision, no *one* can *prove* that the *none* of entity embraces the *untold* in every testimony. To *be* static is to *hold* distant from the image bending *you* to mortis. At which point the *still* harmonious old poet *will* forget to announce that death is actually a gift from life and life the meadow in the middle.

1. Thus dating this speech to no earlier than 1911.

Ghost beckons Hamlet

Enter Hamlet.

I've never understood what people get out of Sumo wrestling: two fat guys each trying to push the other out of a circle, but folks love it. Etymologically speaking the lover is the amateur, therefore I'm glad I *transferred* my passions from that born-again Christian pottery club frequented by Ophelia to these fresh pursuits of horror, such as a chance meeting with a giant dressed in cobwebs. The best thing about my current plan to retreat into myth is the strategy of surprise, so much grander than reality (where if you *erred* you would always *face* the consequences). Myths come fully equipped with a goddess to help you *not* get lost in a *place* as unspeakable as Indiana. Perhaps Aphrodite, that patron saint of the sexual instinct, might assist me with a *plot* I'll call "My

Quest." In the first episode, after reformatting my birth-control coordinates, a handsome prince with a German sounding name is *tied* by metal *hooks* to the trunk of a withered oak and I *ride* on passed him into further perils and ordeals. It *looks* like I'm mired in the poetics of the platitude again, but structural ethnologists say most myths have their basis in a cultural truth, even though the majority will *be* related to unconscious fears such as nail-biting, reflexology and bed-wetting. Some of them blend facts with *lies* to form thinly veiled allegories. Snow White, for instance, is all about the American Civil War, others are secret recipes, some cryptographic maps to hidden gold mines and secret Cuban cigar stores in Palm Beach and Miami. I *see* I've been letting my *eyes* wander over too many tales of imaginary voyages again. Perhaps if I cast my princely *eyes* over the front page of the Elsinore Gazette I'll *see* that in these dire times of *lies* and xenophobic disemboweling, poverty proves itself to *be* an international luxury. It *looks* like the rest of the *ride* down the midden-heap will prove about as gripping as that Revelation of the Monk of Evesham I seduced myself into reading. Yes, I know about the era of the Elzevirs and the spread of learning via smaller formats and why *hooks tied* to the end of string form the basis to the *plot* of your favorite book,[1] but this is hardly the *place* to debate fly-fishing versus fate. Why *not face* up to the fact that you *erred* in your choice of being *transferred* from the mass graves of Treblinka back to early modern Denmark, but always remember that the Post-Modern never gives you a second chance to pass through death and not know of it. It always gets you there. Oops, it's time for my aerobics class, bye bye.

1. Isaak Walton's *The Compleat Angler*, 1653, which proved to be the Moby Dick of the moment.

Exeunt omnes

Scene 5. *Enter Caliban.*
Holy psheeet! What's brought I'ze here ain't good enough to get I'ze out from under never known what *be* more unproper than to think Hell coldern Heaven un if you ask *me* coals round alcawl means a real guilty Chrissun even if your brother turns out same us that there devil sure as hell ain't never bin *told* to *trust* an *old* dose of polar mytheme like that afore cussing *unjust* an awl to git

that toxic Texan intimacy *suppressed* round these parts nuff to cut your *tongue* on a Mississippi windblast *best* git back to awl that book learnun ass done as a *young* Immaterialist but thankin these days giz guys lark uz uh headache awl dem *subtleties* in that pooped out ole policies uh mine[1] makes awl *youth* glad they passed em by real quick fer a newer model dang *lies* year rand here means *truth* gone drinking sassaparilla bourbon by the barrel still bet it's *truth* to say that with some *lies* a lingering from *youth* hostel dormitory protocols an awl of um predicated on a distruss eh others not like in these parts awl lickety split n fine n dandy no *subtleties* here no destiny fabricated uz a *young* thunderbolt collapsing on uh rubber giraffe juss damm *best* booze this side Golgonooza splits yer *tongue* inner shreds eh blue grass pardner don't know what yawl got *surpressed* dahn that gullet uh yers but yerl grow surprised ahm sure to learn yer granmah fell dahnstairs to her death er else ah pushed her plain *unjust* to un *old* gal like that un have to put yer *trust* in lasticated stockings *told* life's cheaper when yer dead uhn no need clean yer teeth but then agin ah never did pleased *me* juss to keep awn chewin un spittin tuhbacky un *be* President uh sumthun or other still misprouncin awl mah words in another State uh de Union Address.[2]

1. Sure seems sad day when ten o'clock's gone stubborn 'n ah sure as Hell missed out on them misery coupons (craw crows flight alright) but how about a candle lighted up to celebrate the work 'n thoughts eh Joseph Wright eh Derby?
2. So much for eighteen years of elocution lessons.

Enter Cassio (disguised as Donald Trump).
You said an "Immaterialist" Mr. President but to what point? The *pain* that registers in such a question articulates the influence of pesticides on *slain* pets, concurrent *injuries* to the throat, and the massacre of millions of tiny entomological *foes* through friendly fire. In these days of Al Qaeda and open immigration policies you can't tell your *enemies* from your enemas and, (given the way that you pronounce em), your "terrorists" from your "tourists." After having enjoyed a photographic memory of everything you've killed you end up with a legacy smelling like a decomposing hippocamp. Heaven *knows* you deserve it, having failed your last five ontological inspections you should be permanently excluded from the universe, but you're a little too compact to

decompose and your dreams of empire aren't complete. I know if I owned the City of God I'd *bide* my time until the price was right then subdivide. Temples *might* be converted into condominiums with a couple of angel roosts set *aside* for sale to a Starbucks franchise—what a *sight* that would be. You see, there really is an *art* to making money. I know we're heading toward solar death and before that global warming, overpopulation and mass starvation, but what's in it for me? Sure, I've got a mean *tongue* and a callous *heart* in the *wrong* body but raising children the way you raise chickens on your Texas ranch opens up new possibilities along the chain of being. Just think of it, the *wrong* amount of polystyrene in their diet sent by mistake along a concatenation of omega-three aftershocks might provoke the unfortunate commingling of their neurons with your coup d'états! But I've set my *heart* on something more grandiose than innovative cookery: to beat God at chess and the severed *tongue* of Hieronymo tells me I can do it! Saint Anselm tied him once in a Cincinnati darts tournament but later admitted to Saint Peter that God deliberately played to lose. I suppose that's what the *art* of omnipotence is all about, having a motive for being generous, keeping all your adherents in *sight* of an effigy of yourself, and giving them something to construe as hope (a little like your own foreign policy I suppose). As for me, I put hope *aside* along with all my argyle sox the day my Treaty of Versailles expired. It was then I realized that the eyelid presupposes the coffin's hinge—till death do us close. I *might* simply *bide* my time until laughter proves a fitting epitaph. Who *knows,* perhaps the answer lies in the workings of the four-footed landscapes of invariance and the human voice that takes up their mute horizons, singing them to *enemies* and *foes* alike among the *injuries* precipitated by the Cubo-futurist *slain,* when mistaken for Cossacks dying in *pain* and coughing up semantic sound trans-rationally, unable to pronounce the phrase writ "not to speak."

Exeunt

Enter a Sargeant of a Band, with two Sentinels.
Forgive me if I'm totally *wide* of the mark, and if what I'm about to claim seems already *belied* by the current metaphysical status quo, but I take it to *be* plain *bad* luck we landed here in this part of the cosmos where God is

canonically absent.[1] I mean *you* never hear or see him. I constantly yell out "Here I am in a play going nowhere" and "me voici" (in case he's French) but there's never a reply. It makes me *mad* to *know* I'll never draw a response from a transcendental signified, but it does provide a good excuse for prayers and witnessing the occasional *near* miracle that turns a tiny unknown village into a multi-trillion tourist resort for optimistic cripples. I take it that's Lourdes, but check out Los Angeles, *so* named after the angels who never even visited, with its billions of gallons of holy water piped in via the Colorado river every day—*so* much for the vox clamans in deserto I'm told about. I mean, if I *were* lamenting hypoesthesia or back *pain* I could do something about it, but in this condition I'm a rudderless *express* with no idea of where or what to explore. Take Arminum for instance, should I approach it as a town or a metal? As for Saint Veronica, I *disdain* the fact that she never even existed.[2] But life's too short to haggle over hagiography just *press* on fantasizing Death dressed in skin-tight leather, the butch, tattooed bouncer at one of life's discotheques. Speaking of death and desire, I don't want to live longer just thinner—about the height of my own *press* clippings. But more importantly, will I still have a life-in-death-beneath-futility, as the Germans might concatenate it? Probably not, but I *disdain* those neo-Thomist doubters of optimism, I've still got lots of good thoughts to *express* in the style of Lancelot Andrews as my humble contribution to a better world. However, anchored in the actual I'm limited to being a Principality for Pointillism, but perhaps this universe is actually that other world, a little north of the American Southwest afterlife. I personally prefer my interplanetary shopping sprees to those occasions when I have to explore the nether regions as a classic Latin hero avoiding *pain* the way the Pope avoids the contemporary. We *were so near* to perfect communication the day I convinced Jack Spicer that oranges were words not citrus fruits we *know* by their smell outside the definition of their rind.[3] And then the *mad* flight back to *you* and your alibi for *bad* memory, hiding your syntax in what used to *be* my vocabulary, *belied* into believing this discussion was being broadcast over world-*wide* video.

1. I dig what you're saying sarge. Victor Hugo spent his life trying to depict God verbally and ended up with *Les Miserables* and *The Hunchback of Notre Dame*.
2. The name derives from Vera Iconica (i.e. the true image) referring to the image of Christ's

face imprinted on the towel with which she wiped his face. Replicas of this precious Christian icon are widely available in the Vatican as well as the more commercially minded churches and cathedrals. Courtesy the miracle of globalization all of them are now manufactured by non Christians in China.

3. I couldn't resist yet another arcane reference to an arcane poem. Masochistic aficionados can track the reference in Spicer's "Six Poems for Poetry Chicago." I'm still working on the riposte (under the pseudonym of Frederico Garcia Lorca) "Six Rejections by Poetry Chicago."

Here an alarum againe and Talbot pursueth the Dolphin, and driveth him. Then enter Joan de Puzel, driving Englishmen before her.

Why isn't that dolphin in water? Perhaps it's one of Jacques Cousteau's legendary inflatamates. Any fool may get into an ocean but it takes a Goddess to get out.[1] Is this a rave or a happening? Don't just travel there, do something to it, that's what I always say to those costumed cry babies called the enemy. See that lance corporal over there? Just hold the dogs and let him through the wire then kick him in the tostesticles and finally kill him before finding out if he's a communist or not. The dream of warfare is to recover its infancy in which case shall we rape first and pillage after, or is it best the other way around? I've always prefered the spoudogelois approach, find a victim then laugh at it.[2] I think a little vituperatio puellae is in order coz a well-behaved woman never makes history, and despite being downgraded from a Weapon of Mass Destruction I'm still deadly coz I take presumptuous temerity over diffident timidity every time. I'm a missioned Maid and that's why I do Armageddon weekly and it's also why I made the 1812 Overture my Lord's Prayer. Remember it's always the victim's fault. Geeze, I'm glad I turned my hostility from my aversion therapist and returned to altering English men into English bodies.[3] With my expertise in aerial predation I seem to have fully recovered my reputation as Elle's Angel. Well, that was the best battle since my victory over puberty with all its primeval behests echoing down my chromosome tunnels. Incidentally, that was a nasty attack of the hermeneutic sublime a minute ago and right under my cockpit; it's eighteen thousand feet as the crow drops and I feel like a destroying angel with vertigo. The god of the bee is the future as Maeterlink recalls (which reminds me to confess that last apiary I attacked gave me quite a buzz). Those Heinkels and Stukas are proving quite a *pain* in the ass but it appears their Red Baron's turned a nasty shade of posthumous indigo. Give us a few extra thousand parachutes plus more megaphone diplomacy and we'll definitely *gain* the momentum, must almost *be* time for a lunch break shall we land? I know truth's always the first casualty of war, but why are we playing out this scene from World War II? It's time to switch to decaff. I think you're spending way too long looking down the Aristotelian telescope from the wrong end, and too many replays of Muhammad Ali's and Rocky Marciano's Greatest Hits, why don't we take a pause from the cause. Come on, as late as 1310 Marco Polo still didn't believe World War II was over. Being a *man* and a sexually experienced virgin at the same time, I'd say *you* were fishing for historiographical compliments; that said I *can* safely skip *alone* into any scenario to which I'm not *invited* because I know that the weapons of my own war are not carnal[3] lodged as they are in the panegyric enumeration of ineffability. Isn't meaning marvelous? Mallarmé was *prone* to it the way I'm *delighted* by the possibility of semantic cannabis in villanelles. Not to *dote* on my own insightfulness, but "without meaning" also "supports meaning" in Mallarmé's poetics. Unfortunately, I *despise* blank space, it's like that extra unwanted grace *note* at the end of a requiem hymn. I wish my *eyes* could hear sounds, discern the high trill of a warbler in spring, the crocitations of a raven through summer, but could I then call them *eyes*? There's something casuistic to *note* in the construction of continuities, it's a tendency that I *despise* as it goes flat against the wish I *dote* upon: the sudden break that renders apothegm a testament to syncope. That's why I'm *delighted* by Francis Bacon's choice of the acroamatic method as a "quiet entry" into the reader's mind. Oh by the way, because I'm not *prone* to obfuscation I've been *invited* into Parnassus' select group: the Poetry Foundation (a little like Freemasonry or going it *alone* at a MENSA Tournament). *Can you* point to a better thinker than Bacon who proved that by adopting expansed hieroglyphics[4] as models of the universe the supercession of the Chain of Being is more important than the Book of Nature?[5] I may have been born with the brains of a Barbie Doll, but *man*, it drives a little French girl like me insane to think that conflict can *be* the second scripture and I can *gain* a truth in a simple wave of my sword. I think of the grave as Death's reversible vagina but this Virgin Queen's next accessory is a chastity-belt; thoughts are less important than words these days where *pain*, like the imagination itself, remains a purveyor of second-hand suicides. It's a different order as the world turns as chinkers in your pocket, not in your mind. Where the hell did I put my rubber strap-on and hey who invited these Chippendales with twelve stripograms?

1. Jack Spicer (slightly modified).
2. Those French have never got over Agincourt. (*King Henry IV* Part 2).
3. Paul, Corinthians II 10 4.5
4. I take the term from the title of a book on Sir John Denham's "Cooper's Hill" by Brendan O'Heir.
5. Francis Bacon, *De augmentis* VI, I.

Here a Dance of twelve Satyrs.

Exeunt

> In history as in nature, decay is the laboratory of life.
>
> Karl Marx

Scene 6. *Enter Autolicus, and a Gentleman.*

People think fate *denied* me the Kunstwollen and that's why I like to *hide* my critical opinions in the decorative-versus-abstract debate tossed into that Paleolithic junkyard called art criticism where it deserves to *be*. Nietzsche said a love of aesthetics *grows* in inverse proportion to the Apollonian propensity in real estate to expand towards Dionysian consumer compromises, in which case cut me out. *You* know, I don't mind being relegated to *those* megalopolitan cubicles ycleped condos, where not even the *rents* cover the price of a doorknob, just don't leave my life like language does in a remnant of the Scottish Enlightenment. *Mine* has been a life of perpetual *ornaments* among the more select agro-alimentary secretions of City Halls and that's why I thoroughly dislike those comments of yours reproving my *state* of being-towards-curvature-and-contradiction. That raises an old serpent once again, the Old Jewish Cemetery in Krakow, a testimonial to how a *loving* of pure *hate* was the 20th century's most enduring contradiction. I *hate* to change the subject but yesterday I Googled God and came up with a link to a clinic for the treatment of cattle now housed in some abandoned Serbian cotton-mills. I'm *loving* this *state* of living as the siege of Sebastopol, in the past the "other way" had been a missing mile, but now it's sort of like William Cobbett as the transition between Ben Franklin and Robert Pinsky via Adrienne Rich. My time's come and *yours* too to start *reproving* that favorite historian and note the fact that Fascism and its consequent *ornaments* of atrocity (*mine* included) elucidates the different fact that Hitler is the name of the event called Auschwitz. (It *rents* the heart to recollect *those* were the days of the best wine in France.) In your mind's eye *you* see sunlight that *grows* to *be* a host of golden daffodils, thus nature enters literature. Let's leave Romanticism alone to fill out its de-nazification questionnaire, I think it's time for a jaundiced gaze at the event horizon.[1] Should we stay for Jerry Springer's final thought, or should we *hide* in absolute erasure? So far neither of us has *denied* that to draw up nothing meets hypostasis in which concentric circles form an ideogram a pain slips out of—and into a language to think it.

1. The De-Nazification Questionnaire, or *Frageboden*, was implemented by the allies in 1946, whose many questions contained the following for women: "If you had to go to bed with either Churchill, Stalin or Hitler who would you go to bed with? Not surprisingly, most German virgins answered Churchill, no doubt remembering his rousing words on radio towards the end of 1942: "It will be long, it will be hard, there will be many ups and downs, blood will flow, but above all there will be no withdrawal."

Exit

Enter Ariel a Water-Nymph.
How did I ever survive the Picturesque and *still* live to experience the difference between doctrine and ritual? It *will* be good when I've successfully cloned a bit of anarchy again, it's the only *kind* of alternative to the serenity this evening casts around the muttering poet, ruminating on the way in which puzzles become pretzels. *Me?* I'm done with poetry and its pastiche line-breaks, as with most other things I've left the muse far *behind*. I grant *you* I was a skilled mechanic in Georgian poetics, addicted to pastoral montage just before the birth of cinema, but I've long felt *discontent* at the prospect of a Parnassian vocation. Let's *face* it, the poem has always been an ideological state apparatus ensuring the writing class's

domination over the reading class. Look at Mallarmé (yes, him again) pharting into his galligaskins and grinning behind his moustache and goatee, *bent* over his coffee-table edition of the Larousse Dictionary of Semantic Obfuscations trying to *chase* common sense into the gutter and make it *stay* there for good (not to mention all that surplus value he extorted in the form of mounds and mounds of critical exegesis). He should be reported like e. e. cummings was to Stanton A. Coblentz, head of the League for Sanity in Poetry. Bring on the Ballad of Sir Patrick Spens anytime, I find a cup a day infinitely preferably to un coup de dès. The dearth of words scattered across an insufferable plenitude of empty space gives one the feeling of being back in Montana again. Same thing goes for art; I think the raison d'etre of a painting is so the viewer can exercise her right to punch a hole in it. And feel free to *dispatch* any of my opinions *away* to the Board of Ethics, I don't care what Levinas says, there's nothing arche-original about my face, it was designed to be Narcissus friendly and *catch* the eye of every horny sailor. There's always a *catch* to a poem when it's far *away* from its *dispatch*; the mind wanders to a distant obelisk or dolmen, then a clinamen occurs in the monotony test, performed upon a yard of letter A's.[1] It's impossible to *stay* relaxed when one appeals to posturepedics to *chase* a symbolic lamb clenched beneath a *bent* right arm straight into a hecatomb—and all of this via the history of the automobile: unconstitutional tire rotation, insurrectional volcanic magma for sectarian oil changes. I can't *face* another verbal equinox or landing as a Christian remedy for oblivion in the relation of morphology to *discontent* and toxic growth in a hypothetical fish tank courtesy of Herman Melville. See, poetry let's *you* get away with saying anything. I mean I could have said "a baboon's *behind* reminds *me* of the *kind* of free-*will* that's *still* happening" or even worse "if this is Guantanamo Bay I must be God."

1. A test devised for the analysis of tones in tonal languages; words believed to have the same tone are repeated one after the other, producing a monotonous effect; if a word with a different tone is inserted into the sequence, the monotony is broken, and there is acoustic assurance of the tonal difference (Gleason).

Exit

Scene 7. *Enter King of Fairies solus.*
I'm sorry to ruin the evening by talking, but I have to say I'm well aware that

problems are solutions disguised as question marks, yet how do I get *out* of this mess? It's like living out a scene in Frankenstein's laboratory. No *doubt* a fetus often wonders what the afterbirth will be like, but I'm somewhat different. In fact, I remember turning up at the Congress of Vienna[1] as a feminist pronoun from a decent squire's second marriage, neat and demur in my apparel, waiting for the grammar-in-law that never showed up. Poetry's born out of such a *hell* of disapprobation, disappointment and dejection, it even alliterates and, for poet and *friend* of poetry alike, "the chronicler of morselation waits upon it." What a phrase to start your car with while spilling your morning coffee as you fumble for some change at the toll-booth to happiness! Do you prefer the Death Wish to the Death Drive? For me the latter requires too much gasoline. They *tell* me all the allegorical highways are being repaired, some *fiend* of a contractor taking *pride* in putting in a brand new anagogic fast-lane to get us safely out of the literal control of the *devil* and efficiently back into the thoughts of God. The entire Renaissance will turn green with envy when it's finally finished and has its off-ramp this *side* of the catabolic. Encouraged by the temporal coordinates across the arcs of new symmetrical Chinatowns and the complex personalities of the fighter pilots flying above us, Being will cease as a precondition of ontology and emerge out of the ambient *evil* smells as a purely gaseous event. (I don't mean the *ill* smell of afflatus but the *fair* radiance of immolation traces.) Nightingales will drink gasoline prior to self-conflagration according to one of several Phoenix-impact projects *still* in effect since the reign of Nordic mythology. It's time perhaps to send mythology to the laundromat. Looking on the downside, however, I *despair* at the prospect of my thoughts giving God a migraine; I even *despair* at the thought that a deity may ever happen. There's *still* no roads running to God's heavenly car park and it's a *fair* guess there never will be. I may sound *ill*-advised and inspired by the "*evil*" of negativity, but on my map every place is a non-place asterisked for emphasis, every galaxy carries a superscript that takes you to a footnote or a *side* gloss, and each footnote is a hole in determinacy. As you're reading this, I might be playing golf with the late Sadam Hussein in Baghdad or Kabul because the *devil* went chasing butterflies. The course might be a vast battleground, the bunkers shallow graves, and the eighteen holes car-bomb craters. The grass is pristine and the golf cart carries me, like the Pope mobile, with *pride* toward the clubhouse, where crowds of dead marines and Iraqui fetuses applaud me as the golfing *fiend* I'm not. But what if suddenly at an annual convention of lawn-mower manufacturers the concept "ground" became "depth" and the concept of community became restless? There's a pot of gold somewhere in the center of a rainbow but the desert is the place where viewpoint never happens. You could *tell* a *friend* that *Hell* is a temporary *doubt* your mind is in and that way pull *out* both the troops and the golfers.

1. 1815.

Exit

Scene 8.

> So the man finally realizes himself, he should die, but it would
> be necessary to do that while living—while watching himself
> cease to exist.
>> Georges Bataille

> In [the Imagination] I am stronger and stronger as this
> Foolish Body decays.
>> William Blake, Letter to
>> George Cumberland, 12
>> April, 1827

> Where other men must suffer grief in silence,
> a god gave me the power to speak my pain.
>> Goethe

> She came back, my unknown god! my pain!
> my last happiness.
>> Nietzsche

I have not long to trouble thee.—Good Griffith,
Cause the musicians play me that sad note
I named my knell, whilst I sit meditating
On that celestial harmony I go to.

Shakespeare

In the battle between the world and you, back the world.

Kafka

Enter Richard and York.

Isn't it great to have a body that breaks down? In my case the word disarticulation springs to mind, no doubt a fitting preparation for some of the archaic Greek mysteries on the bleak perimeters of an Easter Uprising; I'd far rather be reliving my halcyon days at university than pacing the halls in this House of Pain. I heard a cleric on Al Jezeera claim that pain is experience and experience is happiness, but it's ridiculous in my case. So this is what "welcome to second childhood's" all about? feels like I'm turning into the Elephant Man. I seem to be anatomy's "je ne sais quoi" from the inside out, morever it's hard to tell which end of me's my face. Hugh Heffner told me x-rays are among the quickest ways to become a skeleton but I seem to be doing quite well on my own. Now that I'm coughing up blood and reusing it as toothpaste I must be the perfect self-sustaining ecosystem. Time methinks to join the masque of death's old comedy,[1] perhaps I should offer myself as the subject of a snuff sonnet. Ah sempiternal pulchritude, they say there's nothing quite like it—Oops!—There goes my other eyeball rolling down to join a growing pile of fingers and teeth—and with all that spinal fluid squirting out like fountains of crème de menthe even my own children don't recognize me. I should try to gather up all my shedded parts and form an acrobatic troup. Last week I suffered from water on the brain until Scroope gave me a tap on the head. Most of me's transformed into an adventure playground for larvae and yesterday the Court Physician mistook me for a rare strain of athlete's foot imported from the Black Lagoon. It's hard to make a high five with only three fingers—and one hand.[2] I feel like something a camel stepped in after dropping me and, given this condition of incurable delapidation, I'm sure not destined to become an exquisite corpse, but it definitely beats supper with Liza Minnelli, or being boiled alive with two-dozen lobsters, or waking up a turkey only to realize it's Thanksgiving Weekend. Yet medicine is but the physiology of the sick man and to look on the bright side, I'm sure glad *you threw away* that gangrenous left buttock it was a *fiend* to sit on—and those pustules are so terrible I think I'll have to bleed myself again in a *day* or two.—My nostrils flared up years ago with the chronic sinusitis I picked up in Martha Stewart's bedroom (but I've always had a yen for emphysema) and I suppose that dose of gonorrhea I contracted as a fetus rendered me prone to blindness from birth. (No wonder the Pope loves meat.) I might still get nominated for a few Emmys for my leading role in some geriatric sit-com full of jokes about biodegradation but now the dragon pain is wrapped around my corpse the *end* must be near. This fever's making me so hot I need a transfusion of ice—it'll soon be time to flute off into my autumn twilight and *greet doom* with a *sweet* sans souci as I skip into the afterlife to *come* inside the black belly that eats birthdays.[3] Please make sure to donate all those bits of me to the New England Journal of Medicine—and don't forget to get a tax receipt. Now that I'm turning living into leaving I'm ready to be anything in the ecstasy of being ever.[4] As the world's second Zimmer frame monarch (after Lear) I may not have reached the ranks of the grandly tragic but at least my life's been pitiful and I still have my reservoir of optimism. In fact I'm not doing too bad for a near-neomort, stripping Nature down to her bra and panties for a final tickle fight. I've got full power in one ventricle and being a blind cripple is still new and exciting, also—as that strumpet the Queen herself pointed out—living with genital herpes can be a surprising pleasure. Wisdom is not the opposite of sickness it is its younger twin and now I know that I can go straight up to Our Lady of Perpetual Autopsies and shout "marry me today!" Unfortunately I'm in a constant *state* of anadiplosis, it's a similar condition to that pertaining to the modernist novel, triumphant in its debris of reflexivity and collective consciousness. At least for the *sake* of possible corporate strategies I should reconsider all my options, I'd *hate* to *make* the same mistake as those handicapped veterans in Les Invalides, painting their prayer books with flowers from dawn to dusk and chanting homilies to the Reign of Terror, or those Jewish souvenir sellers during the Hep-Hep riots in Frankfurt.[5] My tributary memories remain fresh and Morpheus still handles all my lullabies. What can we *make* of the iconography of our times? Anamorphically a flat map turns out to be an elephant at the moment *hate* and fear emerge (for the *sake* of *state* security) and paranoia becomes the cardinal rule of biopolitics. *Come* to think of it (and recollection's *sweet* if uncertain these days) I was with H.D. in Egypt the day she changed her name to Humpty Dumpty in a desperate attempt to effect the *doom* of Imagism by the power of a weighty nom de plume. I've always preferred asterisks to proper names—they link persons to the sky. Well, I think it's time for me to *greet* my fate after I *end* this rant by not signing it. Every *day* I wake up feeling like a used Q-tip dropped on Bosworth Field, bent in the middle with the white cotton yellowed at both ends—just look at my hair, the sight of it's enough to make a raccoon sick. With my remaining organs now open to every bacteriophage that lives on the earth I look and smell like the *fiend* from Walmart swamp. Granted, I may stink but it sure beats getting clean in the shower-block at Auschwitz-Berkenhau (wasn't it Villon who proved that to be a vagrant is to be immortalized)? In my prime I used to have scabs on my chin but they never caught on with the general public. Yea, yea, I know I'm well on the way to becoming kitty kibble, that Death's not far *away*, maybe as close as that black vomit I just *threw* up, but life is not a book to be read twice[6] and hopefully I'll be heading to that discrete and seasonable silence in a manner befitting a garrulous king, awaiting a celebrity postmortem carried out by Jack Kevorkian or Dr. Conrad Murray. I heard Ann Rohmer on Breakfast Television claim that as a person is dying the entirety of their life passes fleeting by, but I'm more excited by the prospects of what's to come. I bet it's full of gossip in the nation that is not[7] and no doubt deliberately designed to undercut the mandatory attendance at Orphic choirs and lutenalias with their ballads about the slanders of the Saints. When I'm dead I'll be able to talk to anyone I want and it won't be God who makes it possible, but Lucian of Samosata. Imagine, talking to Walt Disney in his ice-palace and the ashes of the Wife of Bath while listening to Brahms whistling the end of his unfinished symphonies. Who knows, memories of being alive might all come back in leopard skin. The demise of a king like me is never an aureate hagiography, but when death does come I hope it comes like Schlegel's words on viewing the Dresden Madonna.[8] Such a calm savagery's contained in the posthumous voice that whispers "I died for Beauty" don't *you* think?

1. A. C. Swinburne.

2. Although, if the truth be told, I have to admit I lost my right one due to masturbation—guess I should have listened to the Queen Mother.

3. Jack Spicer's description of thanatos.

4. Sir Thomas Browne.

5. These early nineteenth-century pogroms of German Jews are prophetic of the rise of Nazism.

6. Avicenna quoted in Santayana's "Dialogues in Limbo."

7. A. E. Housman.

8. "The effect is so immediate that no words spring to mind. Besides, what use are words in the face of what offers itself with such luminous obviousness."

Dies

Enter one with a Recorder.

God speed ye time-worm pilgrim of this world, rest in that haven where all tempests cease. In other words, oops, sorry I'm late, I assumed you were asleep recovering from prostate surgery; will the corpse of a king accept a kiss from a wounded man? [Kissing then turning to soliloquize.] Interstitially between two nothings I was falling asleep in pain, among my dribble and trembling, but *then* I remembered *men more* dead than alive than me: Terezina, 1945, Desnos found still breathing amid the *dross* of stinking corpses—and what was in *store* for those unsuccessful mass-suicides of Social Realist painters during the pogroms and purges by Stalin—the *loss* of limbs, eyes, ears. Spayed or neutered we are as Pascal at his gulf, yet in the *end* I'll settle for death without resurrection. I mean what's so special about a resurrection? I wake up with one every morning—and who wants a posthumous eternal return especially at Christmas? It will be so good to be free of the mandatory potlatch and Yuletide *excess* and *spend* less energy buying useless gifts that no one even wants in the first place, like a box of handkerchiefs or an eighteenth pair of identical socks. It'll also free me up from that unpaid *lease* on my Ferrari and the *gay* mainstream of boutique consumerism. It's a pity though that the Republic of Echolalia never worked out and we all grew up to lament the *dearth* of Masonic management consultants, I was quite looking forward to an infant President. (Through the vast *array* of my knowledge I've never forgotten that the greatest pickpocket on *earth* is the child.) I want to be through with this *earth*, its dazzling *array* of state-of-the-art dinettes and the corresponding *dearth* of charity concerts for unemployed anaerobic flute players. Ironically, the thought of death actually gives me a *gay*, new *lease* on life, a renewed urge to *spend* a little time preparing for a simple passing without the *excess* baggage of an ars moriendi. It's also reassuring to know that death's not necessarily the *end* of functionality, you can make a free gift of your organs on the back of your driver's license and a clean, fresh cadaver is great for educational dissection. Statistics show that during the eighteenth century more empty coffins were buried than full ones[1]—there'll be no *loss* of ability to keep on generating capital. Take Jeremy Bentham for instance, that tedious founder of Utilitarianism, he donated his entire skeleton to the University of London, fully dressed and complete with a top-hat on its skull—it turned that institute into a veritable Mecca for heritage tourism with more visitors than students walking its hallowed corridors towards the Regents Room; the cafeteria was always full and you could buy miniature versions of him on the end of key-rings at a local souvenir *store* run by a Viet Cong veteran. There's too much *dross* in living, that's why I now welcome a little *more* complementary wear and tear from Johnny Decay. I also believe that if you're angry with the world you should kick it, *men* in these parts don't do it enough, spending all their time philosophizing on origins and telos instead of the practical power of the foot. Take Dr. Johnson, for instance, when he kicked that stone and broke his toe he demolished Bishop Berkeley's entire philosophy of subjective idealism. What a Prelate he turned out to be with his new theory of vision, it was a national relief when he sailed to America and started the San Francisco Renaissance. I can't wait to die and listen to my last words,[2] but now my voice is fainter and it might be time to write against the silhouette of Petrarch in his own death throes, sandals to the light, a rattle of "Laura aura morta" *then* silence, death and a catafalque beneath a flag.

1. The popular term for a nefarious body-snatcher was a "Resurrectionist."
2. Viz. "Annihilation ho down, here I come!"

Sleeps

Let us not talk about disease but about death. If nobody
had to die how would there be room enough for any of
us who now lived to have lived. We never could have
been if all others had not lived. There would be no
room.

Gertrude Stein

For hym death greep the right hand by the croppe
That is moche knowen of other, and of him self alas,
Doth dye unknowen, dazed with dreadfull feare.

Sir Thomas Wyat

Come in and shut the grave after you.

Kenneth Patchen

Dead! all's done with.

Robert Browning

Enter Hamlet (dead).

Dead at last! I should have done this more often, it sure is an efficient way to
get out of the city. The sudden jolt did me good and it definitely put an end
to my career-virginity in Early Modern Princedom. So Ed Dorn was right all
along, you don't disappear you reappear dead; at least my vocabulary didn't
do this to me. Every *night* I think back on that *bright* idea I had to stay alive
with you, my body, as a final friendly disinhibitor. I thought I *expressed* my
case for a quick demise with great conviction in my famous rampart soliloquy:
laceration, conflagration, anguish, you name it, there to greet me at the end of
this old mortality in decline. I learned quickly that Death always meets you
before you die and dying wasn't all that unpleasant—a final thought upon the
category "I am here" then voilà the writer disappears in traversing a brink.[1] It
was great, a moment before death I felt myself floating around the light fixtures
gazing down at myself asleep. Having come into life on a fielder's choice it
finally feels like I've done something with it—a sort of mortification in the

fine art of left-hand measurement. My passing drew quite a crowd[2] wearing their trousers at half-mast, but it was just my luck to be the only casualty at my own funeral. We'd got as far as the "ashes to ashes" part when—imagine my surprise—a sudden flaccidity took over my rigor mortised backside, it was so embarrassingly loud that the congregation gave the undertaker a standing ovation. Some even flipped to the relevant page in Gone with the Wind (to Margaret Mitchell's chagrin). Thank God someone had the good sense to have me cremated. (All my life I'd dreamt of having my ashes scattered in the main showroom of a Business Depot). It ended up being the dry and compact death I always wanted and, with a sunset to match the dormition of the Virgin, it spoke the paradox of urban turf wars when tweaked by a rare instance of metropolitan friendliness. Having squandered my fortune on alimony payments and phone-sex charges it's quite a relief to be deceased. After playing a CD of greaest hits sung by the Mormon Tabernacle Choir I had a requiem mass in Braille sung in the capital D of Dyslexia. Unfortunately, I'm without my beard and moustache trimmer and so I might eventually get mistaken for a saint, which could be fun, but I did remember to turn off the stove and unplug the plasma television and I'm sure glad I refinanced my Forever Flask, it makes a perfect Center for Tomorrow. So this is death? Apparently it happens all the time, but this is hardly the Palace of the Posthumous I had hoped for— being dead I feel like a man unborn. I'd long been fascinated by the ontology of the after-life, and have long known that the ultimate Hell is other people, but what's happened to the viragos of Valhalla dressed in boiler suits I'd heard about, and the torrid arguments with Satan and his arcades ambo—and what if the majority of guardian angels turn out to be mere concepts in contingency and no better than the average security guard? I had high hopes too that Death might prove to be a second womb but I feel like I've slipped between the cracks of an arse that never pharts. Charles Wright believes "the dead *are* constant in the white lips of the sea." If that's the case then I can't wait for the first tsunami, it's as dry as a nun's nasty (as they say in Brisbane). With so many "down here" I expected it to be noisier but you don't hear a thing. Sweet God, it is lonely to be dead.[3] That said, you all should join me down here, despite the anxiety of my questioning, there's absolutely nothing to disturb you. In fact I've never been so happy since the time Polonius came down with tonsillitis at an illegal yodeling competition in Tangier.[4] Hegel thought sound to be a mechanical light with more soul than steel but here, with neither soul nor body, one is free to rediscover the joys of being beyond your being in absolute non-entity. With no *unrest* and no *care*, it's the perfect arrival where God exists but not the world.[5] *Except* I don't *approve* of being *kept* in the dark about who or what he is. I was assured by John Calvin that God was omnipotent, eternal and got pissed off very quickly, yet I haven't run into him. I thought he might have the decency to put in an appearance but nada, zilch. Buddhists speak of the consolation of ignorance, and a corpse reduced to ashes in an urn is seldom curious, but I'd *love* to know why truth disappeared with the differential calculus. It also doesn't *please* me that there's no one to talk to but that's the case for everyone I suppose and it remains a moot point whether or not souls have personalities (as mine's still undeveloped and I've yet to meet another) or simply float around as virtuous clouds of iridescent gossamer. But nobody's *ill, disease* has disappeared and you can *still* stay awake and think after the light's turned off. That's what I call dormitory democracy—Nothing! It's only that it's everywhere. The one thing of life that I do miss is the constantly heavy prospect of actually dying, but my hypochondria's not gone, I *still* worry about contracting a *disease* and getting physically *ill* without a body precisely because I haven't got one. *Please* send my regards to that French guy who invented the mind-body split, it sure helps me cope with death down here. I *love* the fact that two parts of me, *kept* separate, have different fates—one conflagrates while the other thinks on. That said, the disintegration of becoming in Saint Cyprian's death was quite scary.[6] I heartily *approve* of imaginative martyrdoms *except* to drag it on for sadistic reasons is something I don't *care* to think about. I'm grateful that I arrived at the gates of the City of Death courtesy of a minor taxi accident and who knows, maybe death goes by so fast I'll be back in time to die again before those Grammy Awards. You always walk alone in Paradise but here the neighbors apparently go on for miles. The first thing I did was try to join the neighborhood watch but I've yet to meet a neighbor. There's no vandalism (so far) and no *unrest* for which I'm grateful as *are* all the others (I expect). Sociologically speaking it's a perfect community, however it feels a bit like being in a Trappist Monastery after news arrives that the Pope's just died, but, just as there, it's a good place to think (I hope). (In fact, I'm now beginning to question that adage of Emerson's "Good as is discourse, silence is better and shames it."[7] Maybe my thoughts will now be *expressed* telepathically through the *bright* expanse of the *night* not knowing if there's anyone listening. Then, finally, through all the silence I'll realize why sound is a little more than dead princes should hear.

1. "The sovereign individual who exists in the instant who is not separated from himself by promising himself reconciliatory ends, does not imagine death; or at least not the anguished interruption of death, and the anguished destruction of its expectation." (Quoted in Michel Surya, *Georges Bataille. An Intellectual Biography*: 493.)

2. Mainly people who wanted to make sure he was dead.

3. Jack Spicer (when alive).

4. I have nothing to hear and I am hearing it and that is music.

5. A thought borrowed from Antonio Delfini.

6. Beheaded with the bluntest axe in Carthage.

7. In his essay "Circles."

Oh Death! That art so dark and difficult.

Guido Cavalcanti

Enter a Soldier (dead).

That's great, dead for a ducat, so I turn out to be another case of Morte pour la Patrie like all the rest. Karl Marx assured me that it was precisely because Napoleon III was nothing that he was able to signify everything. That's hardly the case with an honest ostrich-man like me.[1] Just another green bottle falling off a wall—and if being a peasant conscript on top of the wheel of life was inhabiting the best of all possible worlds then stuff it, I'm glad I'm gone. I was thrilled, however, that the cannon ball that killed me was signed "Babe Ruth" at least it helped me start death on a sporty note. But what a fate to end up lying next to the charred remains of Josef Goebbels and not able to pronounce his name! In the Wars of the Roses Ricardian poetics hid in moor-bog and cloister dust awaiting the eye-sockets of wild guitars. Back then Laurence Minot was Lorca with Death his Lord Chancellor. Perhaps to die young was my reason to be. Still, it was a surprisingly long career I had as a suicide bomber; for someone in my line of work the main challenge in life is to disappear as soon as possible.

After a life like mine I think I've earned the right to be canonized the patron saint of both air fresheners and gingivitis. Unlike Finn Mac Cool I'm glad I had my wake before I died, it made much more sense and now, paradoxically, I *find* being *blind* because dead *clears* a *view* to vistas beyond *tears* I never dreamed of. It's *true* the saints thought death to be an embarrassing giggle across eternity but it's much more original; with *no* ethics to *denote* interpersonal directives it approximates a pure marriage of discourse to ellipsis. *So* what, if my soul turned out to be the coffin I was put in, at least I've got a place to stay until it rots. I don't want to *dote* on it but here I lie, and not begrudgingly, at the complete arrival. There's no place like elsewhere, that's why the mental traveler never returns, but where now are the voices of silence? Right here, I guess, where the world can't see my corpse nor ever hear my voice again. I'm relieved that I died nameless given that I've done nothing. But I still don't see the point of an everlasting after-life—I mean immortality's a future like the past. I know Lorca told Jack Spicer that "the dead are notoriously hard to satisfy" but what am I suppose to do now in my non-coincidence as a now-become-a-then? I can think on and on, but that's simplicity itself, what I can't do is set *aright* those wrongs I failed to correct while living. Praxis has *fled* alright, out of *sight* of the *head* mortician. Incidentally, what's the difference between a mind and a brain? my posthumous *head* spins trying to answer that one. Is it like the difference between a soul and a spirit? Ah, the enigma of those finer distinctions in the great Mysterium. Meister Eckhart knew it well through those millennia of mysteries, his *sight* gagged by the truth of the Aristotelian sign. But something *fled* from philosophy when Cyril Connolly dubbed Pa Ubu "the Santa Claus of the Atomic Age" that was when Sister Wendy came along with a mission to set the general public *aright* and convince us how important art is, and why if we *dote* over the delicate brushwork in a minor landscape courtesy the Hudson River School we'll exude the fragrance of Madison Avenue style good taste. I wish she'd spend more time in her convent praying for the bereft souls of the damned rather than wasting time pontificating from art gallery floors. It happens all the time in life, some used car-dealer turns out to be a member of a Rosicrucian cartel intent on monopolizing the pharmaceutical industry. Enters then the Philosopher King to heroically interpose, but he conveniently dies in an air crash only to be replaced by a puppet dictator handpicked by the CIA.

So what does it all *denote*? At this early stage in my demise it's a predictable catena of interrogations: will heaven come with complementary napkins and wine glasses, or should I move to Hell for a superior model for posthumous unwinding? Anyone would think I'd actually paid to come here and that Death owes me something. *No* doubt it's *true* that the thought of lip gloss on the mouth of Mephistopheles, or even the remote possibility of kissing the ghost of Liberace in between strawberry daiquiris, *tears* me apart with anticipation. But the *view* from this pauper's casket actually *clears* my senses; I may be *blind* to the living, yet somewhere I'm sure a voice is telling me, don't worry, you'll *find* yourself alive again in a very short time.

1. A seventeenth-century term (perhaps earlier) referring to a soldier.

Exeunt

> On him lies heavy, who, too known
> of all, dies unknown to himself.
>
> Seneca

> Into his Heart ne'er pry's,
> Death to him's a Strange surprise.
>
> Marvell

Scene 10. *Enter Lear, Foole* (disguised as Shakaspear), *and Gentleman.*
A proud monarch dies to enter sedimented history. Sure, I've known the loneliness of command and after queering the entirety of Christianity I couldn't wait to see what I'd do next, but I never thought old, crazy Lear would end up dead like this. Praise be he who has removed my responsibility for not being there. I had hoped death would be like someone closing a book—and it was. And, maugre the embarrassment of dying with a full bladder, I said to myself they'll be plenty of time for a pee in Heaven. It was smart of me however to lower the public impact of my regal demise by having the forethought to post my picture on the back windows of all the hearses with the words "Coming

Soon" written in electric-blue Gothic letters beneath it. During life I turned a *blind* retina to my daughters' shenanigans, tried to *mind* my own business among the tribes triumphant, warding off my autophobia with bog trotting and bungee jumping, so imagine my thrill at disappearing into nothingness only to find out, to my utter despair, I'd landed in a veritable geographica abscondita. Theoretically speaking, it leaves a lot of room to move around in but then again in practical terms you're fixed in one place, caught in the anavocity of complete and utter stasis. My battle cry was always "Death before Dormancy" but death's as bad as metaphysics with its reductio ad unum. I'd like to say I died with both *eyes* closed by God but in truth I passed away without understanding a word of Wittgenstein. From birth my dream was to become the perfect stiffy, always believing death would be translation into infinite form, not this hourly larval transformation into some neighbor's fertilizer. (I also never thought I'd wet my coffin like I did a second ago.) Pontifications of that sort, your Majesty, betray a severe *defect* in the misprision of post-mortem disabilities. Come on, cheer up, we're dead as well and it could be worse, at least we're rid of the body and all its peccant attributes. I must say it feels great to be here as one of death's alumni—a few I *despise* but I never hear a word from them nor from those I *respect*, my son Hamnet, for instance, such a brief life granted to him on the shuttle between word and idea. Now he's just another one of those flirtatious transcendentals destined never to be thirsty again. I *moan* his loss more than I lament the hours I used to *spend upon* a final draft of my Timon of Athens, that play incidentally was a waste of time, ink and paper for both Greece and me. Now that I can't write or get drunk with a *friend* for the *sake* of the good old times I can think continuously and remember all the things I previously *forgot*. Take the Cartesian reduction for instance, (admitted it came after my life, but a Bard of Avon's allowed a little poetic license), isn't it merely a variant of Parmenides' assertion that thinking and being are the same thing? If that's the case do I still *partake* in being, *not* exactly alive but still a cogitans? I'm sure it's *not* as simple as that but I know I'll need axiomatic verification for any potential transfinities in order to *partake* of the full geo-tourist values of an after-life in the virtual. You see there's even technology after death. I *forgot* to mention that when I was alive and hard at work on the Scottish play, for the *sake* of on-stage verisimilitude, people believed I posited my theory of the I as an Other via that old gimmick of a Banquo-Macbeth correlation which proved to be just another inconsistent mathematical formula framed retroactively in language. Not even my closest *friend* knew that I actually based it *upon* my variant anatomico-historical presentation of the Henrician monarch-in-parts; it was my splendid English version of Osiris![1] I used to *spend* a lot of time wondering why there was never a crime scene investigation at the Globe when those plays were presented, but I shouldn't *moan*, that was way back at the very end of the sixteenth century. With all due *respect* to pessimism, there's not much I *despise* these days, though I do wish that during my life I had just once conceived a concept. Despite a congenital *defect* my *eyes* always saw the particular in a manner so unlike the *mind* of Hegel, with his Spirit and the Negative vaguely mumbling on about the end of history, and all the time *blind* to the singularities of each golden boy and girl surrounding him.

1. That's not what I heard. Anne Hathaway tells me that the main reason was that the original manuscript of the history plays disappeared when he went to photocopy them for Sir Walter Raleigh and inadvertently passed them through the shredder. Signed: Sir Francis Bacon (Mrs.)

Exeunt

> A complete life maybe one ending
> in so full an identification with the
> not-self that there is no self left to die.
>   Bernard Berenson

Enter Ghost of Banquo.
My caput mortuum has quite a posthumous headache, those ghost hunters are truly tenacious, here I am a supernatural protagonist with a stiff upper lip and terrified for my afterlife when all I ever wanted to be was a genius locus in the Scottish corner of Hell.[1] I'm told I should take it as a complement to have been booed in the Bronx but that's little compensation for my current condition. *You* tell *me* to *state* categorically everything that I *abhor* and *hate more* than immortality but the task *exceeds* my *skill*, besides, it's a little too late for post-mortem therapy. There I go, I'm already a dialogue again. After all life's *deeds*

through good and *ill*, *day* into week into year, it makes my ego tremble to think that a self, though double, can be an emptiness exposed to the absolute plenitude of nothing. Such a *sight* is enough to make one *sway* away from discourse analysis for good, but it *might* have its beneficial consequences; I mean it sure leaves a space in which to wish away every given non-identification. Alone in this condition it *might* still pertain that truth is what is sensed.[2] Meanwhile, back in life, amidst the *sway* of fortunes and in the full *sight* of Judgment *day*, the cockroach without *ill* will fulfils those *deeds* assigned to it by evolutionary commands before retiring into its next available sublation. No *skill exceeds* that creature's appetite, it swallows everything from tractor-trailers to Liberation theologies.[3] From dust to dust? That's a pretty cruel life-script for anyone with asthma. Coughing through life and continuing after death? A *more* apt scenario would be from soup to soup at which point each person enters biosis with a menu between her teeth and one asks about the soup du jour before inquiring into the specials of a lifetime and one's in luck because the venison comes with antlers and there's cream of mushroom instead of French onion which most people *hate* and *abhor* as much as sago pudding and cold spaghetti sandwiches, so one then asks what kind of mushrooms and the waiter might *state* "shitake ma'am" if one's a woman and she takes it as an insult and slaps him in the face and he brings her some wooly linguini with squid in a squirrel sauce instead, then she asks what those funny colored things are and the waitor answers vegetables and one reinquires if they're a new invention and life continues through exciting decades of routine questioning just like Plato's dialogues, and the interrogatory space is dust free, and I play *me* and *you* play yourself, and there's never time for living or dying just deferring, and before the complimentary smoked salmon manifests the woman asks if it's Pacific or Atlantic and the waiter disappears inside the kitchen never to return.

1. I take it that would be fire without the brimstone and porridge for every meal.
2. Epicurus.
3. I take my inspiration from this Welsh Triad of Wisdom: "Three things that will always swallow and never be satisfied: the sea; a burial ground; and a king."

At any given time the living see themselves in the

midday of history. They are obliged to prepare a banquet for the past. The historian is the herald who invites the dead to the table.

Walter Benjamin

The dawn light is before us, let us rise up and act.

Mao Tse Tung

The Dead never lie; it isn't worth their while.

Edward Sackville-West

Enter Macbeth (before Banquo).

I thought death was unauthorizable, that time in me I shall never enter, in other words the perfect exteriority. So how come the illustrious Banquo has returned to life again? By my last calculations your body should have reached the larval stage of decomposition but voilà the great return! It goes to show that the lottery predictions of Mystic Meg are not completely infallible. I'm hoping for a brief encore as I was beginning to appreciate your life as a fading memory flushed down the toilet. There I was perched on the edge of life's next great adventure after coveting a neighbor's wife, brushing up on my conversational Swahili and preparing to proof-read a text by Pierre Ménard, when, fan my fly, your reappearance simply happens; I bet it was part of a plea bargain for the general resurrection of the dead. Incidentally, that "Coping with Death" brochure would have benefited from color illustrations. In your case death surely was a "dialectical central station" with a turnstile.[1] The burden of the posthumous on the survivor, of course, involves no longer speaking to the dead ones but about them, in any case you're reemergence has proven quite a disappointing peripeteia. So, welcome home to the same old pshit—how was it being dead? "It" turned out a surprisingly short eternity and distinctly worse than the original *fall*. I was hoping for something I could applaud and *call* back for an encore, but nothing exists on that *side* of ontology except a pure community of the silent and asocial, and that sure ain't a place for me to *be*. Like that Sasanach Keats I'd long been half in love with easeful Death and after many hesitations (due no doubt to that psychological crisis induced when the "gilt of the kilt" meets the "warren in the sporran") I finally learned how to escape life. But I soon came to realize that Death was not my style of cheekbone. In fact it felt like a root canal in Projective Verse when utterly anaesthetized so I find it hard to admit "je suis porter le deuil." I must say though the truly periscopic way to see Heaven was from a path by the river Styx and from the lawn walls around Thanatopia where the ghosts of witches paced in the cool of evening.[2] Now I've got my friend back from the dead he'll instantly become the *pride* of the neighborhood, *you* can join us all on a sub-committee for local epitaphs, explain if a resurrection differs from a revolution, and help pay for a block party planned in your honor. So, have a great day as they say in the supermarket, I left the strychnine in the cupboard next to the transcendental signifieds and exterminated angels. At this point a little champagne might alleviate the excruciation of your return, but tell me the *reason* for coming back, *may* I ask if the food wasn't up to scratch, or perhaps God ran out of ice cubes and good jokes? I was told Ophelia and Cordelia both came back because they found the rents too high; it seems God was a cruel landlord. I imagine all the archangels were shivering in slum tenements when they weren't out panhandling pennies from Heaven for the Pope. It must have been like National Socialism on an Easter Sunday in the Second Galaxy, or part of some ancient seasonal myth like the end of baseball and the beginning of the football season. I must say, the news of my resurrection seems to have fallen on deaf ears but I was there, I saw, I returned, a life, a war, the same old Dante! I consider it *treason* to *betray* my trust in a friend and I hope my answer doesn't *prove amiss*— and please keep in mind that our *love* for each other *is* still as messy as any massacre, but I came back via a Deus ex machina, it was little Thel, short for Thelma I expect, that character in an early work of William Blake's that stages the clash of innocence and infancy. It *is* a carefully constructed chiasmic text that completes itself in a silent illustration approximating the death of language. Thel, lamenting the purposelessness of life, receives a welcome from three infancies: a water lily, a cloud and a worm—water—air—earth. The final response anticipates fire because it arrives in the form of a catechism, in the face of which Thel turns in horror and flees back to the Vales of Har.[3] Sound familiar? Thel found no *love* only answers. Would it fall *amiss* for me to go on and try to *prove* a reason or *betray* a penchant for her regression? Thel returns to a discourse of the Father in the encounter with interrogation. A physical virgin, she has lost the more important pucelage of infancy and, through that *treason* called language, she no longer enjoys the safeguard of a body without speech. (I thought I had such a safeguard in death but language kept me thinking.) *May* I go on? That infant body without speech or *reason* subsists within the silent discourse of the final illustration, which, in its taciturnity, depicts infancy astride a controlling power. (If *you* look at the design it shows babies on the back of a serpent and one even looks like me.) Without that *pride* of language, Thel figures a threshold between innocence and experience, between infancy and the socio-linguistic nightmare of the construction of the self. It may *be* that this shifts us back to square one but not necessarily, for in Thel human speech gives way to Natürsprache, the kind we read about in Jacob Boëhme—(Blake was familiar with the ideas of that great German mystic), or equally James Howell's Dendrologia where trees confess in words a covert history concealed from readers. Laying to one *side* the seminalities of influences it seems my own death was too Cartesian, but one can infer from Thel—the text—less an Ovidian metamorphosis than a human return to that condition the French term en-fans, to speak without speech as in a scream—but also a *call* to the gestural, to a hieroglyphic choreography both instant and determinate. Unlike me no *fall* can occur to Thel because no language pertains to innocence. How did Kierkegaard put it? "With innocence a knowledge begins that has ignorance for its first qualification." We too can join the cry of infancy, but stories like hers also teach us how to die. Through the bleak decades of my Age of Encryptment I too survived without words—a second infancy. The dead sat around me knitting the Quilt of Oblivion until a miser pointed a finger to his own name written in a puddle of algae and smiled after casting his heart into nonentity. Blake stages this onto-linguistic hesitation as the resurgence of pure figure against discourse and hence my returning to meditate on the meaning of those words of Tolstoy's on his own magnum opus War and Peace.[4] After your demise it became my practice to *lie* in bed at night with one *eye* open parsing a telephone directory of all the known malign deities (ours of course remains an unlisted number) and came to *see* why history—in one extended parapraxis—marks the pronoun as the great explorer of all those unknown continents beyond the self. In fact nothing wraps up, the soul and the body die into their respective scenarios of rot but the pronoun lives on. He will return in a little fat postman from Willendorf when announcing the death of his mother (Venus) to a neighbor. *Blindness* too leads to *constancy* but I advise keeping a diary of the weather inside your own version of the Doomsday Book. A *kindness* will be *lost* though in the negative irrationality of my purely intransitive thinking; it was the madness of Strindberg. *You* recall how memory comprises desire across a leap? *Most* meanings disappear inside some hermeneutic triangle but from the viewpoint of pre-originary sexuation *you* bring a greater challenge to the proof of the finite father. What precisely constitutes him? Will he come *bearing* an answer in print and full color, *torn* from the pages of a catalogue of wisdoms, and *swearing* the burden of his message, roseate as in French, a dictionary slung between his southwest memory terminals? Or will he come *foresworn* to secrecy and stretched out enigmatically into a rainbow of ideograms? The only thing *foresworn* in my life was to sing a song in a pianoless room. Hopefully we're now through *swearing* at urbanism and its *torn* denizens of the paltry *bearing you* a fake olive branch before supper. Beyond the monadic frame of the architectural body persists the soul of any city. The latter phrase was stolen from Lorca but remains redolent in *most* of Aldo Rossi's thinking. *You* know in Granada Lorca found what we have *lost*: an aesthetic of the diminutive—(it remains inconsequential that William Cowper too found this in the *kindness* and *constancy* of his own long poem The Task)— rendering a poetics of the precise formed and focused (beyond *blindness*) by a burning sun into a passionate ignition. At the moment one tries to *see* how keeping an *eye* on an echo helps deliver its indeterminacy in Galley Lane one comes to realize the *lie* of it all and why in these times of death-bed evangelism, one gets a sore throat from even reading Lorca.

1. Walter Benjamin, *Arcades Project* C° 2.

2. At this point the zealous and/or curious reader may wish to make the pointless comparison with Pound's 1962 description of Uzerche in *A Walking Tour in Southern France. Ezra Pound among the Troubadours,* ed. Richard Sieburth. N.Y.: New Directions, 1992: 33.

3. The name of a person not a place (as Dr. Freud would have quickly pointed out).

4. "If reading this book doesn't change your life it sure as Hell will take up a considerable part of it."

Exeunt

> The poor Penultimate is dead, she is dead, really dead,
> The poor desperate Penultimate.
>
> Mallarmé

Scene 10. *Enter Coriolanus in a gowne of Humility. With Meaenius.*

There's been a fault-line of facts throughout this masque: the old China tea-pot smiling at language, and a long campaign, this war between death and laughter played out before our *eyes* and all the time extraneous to authentic action. How could dying have lasted so long with "politics" and "history" in the way? For satirists—"les goguenards mes chers confrères"—the question posed is what *lies* beyond the linguistics of all this pantomimic nihilism? We've known for centuries that democracy was an uninvited *guest*, the invasion of the bourgeois into power at power's own invitation—yet power, like infancy, doesn't speak. I love the plain style of this written masque, in the Danish Grain our red wheelbarrow poet may claimeth, but I too love the pollution language must become when it speaks as singular voices shattering the *desired* d'étant and perfect reciprocity of self-clarity. I once dreamed I was a bat that felt itself imperfect. Deep in its *breast* an anxiety *fired* its little heart. High in the sky at night it rose a predator for the duration of its discrete targets: flies, ants, a peach or pomegranate. Being blind and without a *cure* in sight I can't *prove* a moral to this story of how lives *endure* the most horrendous tests. *Love, ground* into a powder paper power to *steep* in the wisdom of a fool *found asleep* inside the ratio of his body to his beard. I too fell *asleep* and dreamed I *found* us back together in the golden epoch of ekphrasis. Known as the de-scriptor I was celebrated in all the national academies of Mimesis then, suddenly from behind a *steep* incline Jackson Pollock simply happened, erasing my life of figuration into pure American *ground*. In art you get away with it, but can *love endure* such a con? It's hard to *prove* that living in the present is a *cure* for theology when God remains a puissance known as elsewhere, your friendly absence next door, in a room, and fills it. Guns are *fired* on his festivals, the *breast* of each believer fills with bratwurst, but the *desired* "ever after" never arrives. So let's walk back into that empty room and paint it.

Exeunt Marching after which a Peale of Ordenance are shot off.

(There's a pause in the détourne by which the final *guest* retires. The end is not the end but merely another sub-text of finality. In the heart of space a corridor remains, sub-linguistic in its beauty, shattered and torn between a whisper and a scream, unheard among the *lies* of a civilization and the *eyes* that refuse to read them.)

I show that I have understood a writer only when I can act in his spirit, when, without constricting his individuality, I can translate him and change him in diverse ways.

Novalis

Nonsense is an act of friendship.

Jack Spicer, The Unvert Manifesto

EVERYTHING OF ANY VALUE IS THEATRICAL.

F.T. Marinetti

AND EVERYTHING IS OPPOSITE TO WHAT IS SAID

Epilogue

Enter olde Gower.

I guess Hölderlin got it right, but with the gods long gone how is it possible to have a truly tragic experience? Well, it's time to drop the curtain and put the dolls to bed. I hope this consecration of artifice has justified our little tragicomedy and now that we're through in this rotting wooden O I'm sure it's left all of us with serious doubts about the theory of evolution, and shown the wisdom of my favourite proverb.[1] But let me read you a brief poem as my peroration. [Coughs.] Come syphilitic Muse inspire this verse (although I must admit it couldn't be worse). It contains fourteen end-rhymes from Shakisbeard—not my favorite poet. "'Dark ladies' he calls us, tiny words asleep in thin italics, all that's left of the Bard. Is that any way to treat a famous poet? Yes, if *love* of words might *prove* deletion is still poetry in the *thrall* of the prison-house that's everything other than a *remedy* for language. Recall the *perpetual* unrest inside those earthquakes called sonnets. Trust laughter as a logic *by* which the mind is *disarmed* of all entelechy. Once upon a hill they took a jar on a streetcar named *Desire warm'd* in the cortex of another poet whose fictions became facts becoming *fire*. A memory once in a garden grew but who cares about that? Why don't you lend a *hand* to Khlebnikov or Blake? *Keep* revolution your *brand*-name *asleep* in your very own parentheses and wait for the break-up to break out."

> (*asleep brand*
> *keep hand fire warm'd*
> *desire disarm'd by perpetual remedy*
> *thrall*
>
>   *prove*
>
>   *love*)

.

239

And is not love that nakedness of the other laid bare and taking place in love? Dark Ladies amidst dark laughter, winking a longitude?

[Long Silence]

I guess that wraps it up. We truly were the Tragic Comedians striving to bring tears of laughter to the eyes of Republicans and Calvinists and occasionally succeeding. Thanks for giving me and the others a local habitation and a name but now I'm off back to airy nothing. I'm sure we'll meet again in some different alphabetic combinations—perhaps as extractions from Barthes' Death of the Author, or Barnabe Googe's well-known Eclogues, Epitaphs and Sonnets, or even Thomas Warton's Letters to Thomas Astle now they're finally in print.[2] It was good being with you, but now it's time to finally make that move to Greenland with your wife, six children and the goat—and while you're at it, knowing Shakespeare is Cervantes, "keep on going. Towards Spain!" It's still there where we left it, three miles in front of us about eight billion years to the left.

1. If at first you don't succeed, give up.
2. Courtesy of David Fairer's eminently unreadable *The Correspondence of Thomas Warton*, Athens: University of Georgia Press, 1995 (775 pp. God bless those Southerners!).

CODA

Death does not finish anything: it prolongs completion.

Is my statement at an end?

I think so.

If it is not at an end, it would express fairly well what I wanted to say — ... [1]

1. Georges Bataille, Interview with Madeleine Chapsal. Quoted in Surya: 490, 493.

FINIS

NOTE ON COMPOSITION

The work preserves in reverse order and in mirror relationship all the end rhymes of Shakespeare's 154 sonnets. These italicized words are not to be repeated in that section. All italicized words in the main body of the text are taken directly from the sonnets and from a selection of stage directions chosen at random from the Norton facsimile of the first folio. I have introduced italics in moderation in the footnotes and allowed myself the liberty to update the more irritating antiquated spellings with their modern equivalents hence "You" for "thou" and "thee" and "gaze" for "gazeth." *Dark Ladies* is the first of several works planned to revisit and repurpose the classics, including Chaucer's *Canterbury Tales*, Dante's *Vita Nuova* and Lewis Carroll's Alice books. Owing to the unavoidable delays in bringing the manuscript to print there are several "contemporary" references that are now stale. Suffice to say that the majority of the text was composed over several years during the Bush administration and its attendant foreign policy.

Frontispiece: Vanitas-Allegorie by Jan Saenredam (1565-1607).

Note to page 7

The short quotation *détournes* a marginalium found in the Anglo-Saxon ms. poem Andreas: "Writ this odde bet; ride aweg; Aelfmaer Patta fox, thou wilt swingan Aelfric cild" which Peter Ackroyd loosely translates as ""Write like this or better; ride away; Aelfmaer Patta the fox, you will flog the boy Aelfric."

(Source: Peter Ackroyd, Albion. *The Origins of English Consciousness*. London: Chatto & Windus, 2002: 30.)

About the Author

STEVE McCAFFERY has been twice nominated for the Governor General's Award and is twice recipient of the Gertrude Stein Prize for Innovative Writing. He is the author of over 40 books and chapbooks of poetry and criticism. An ample selection of his poetic explorations in numerous forms can be savoured in the two volumes of *Seven Pages Missing* (Coach House Press), as well as *Panotpicon, Tatterdemalion* (Veer Books UK), *Alice in Plunderland* (Book Thug), *Revanches* (Xexoxial), *Parsival* (Rook), and *Slightly Left of Thinking,* which was published by Chax Press in 2008. His book-object-concept *A Little Manual of Treason* was commissioned for the 2011 Shajah Biennale in the United Arab Emirates. A founding member of the sound poetry ensemble Four Horsmen, TRG (Toronto Research Group) and the College of Canadian "Pataphysics and long-time resident of Toronto he is now David Gray Professor of Poetry and Letters at the University at Buffalo.

About CHAX

Founded in 1984 in Tucson, Arizona, Chax has published nearly 200 books in a variety of formats, including hand printed letterpress books and chapbooks, hybrid chapbooks, book arts editions, and trade paperback editions such as the book you are holding. In August 2014 Chax moved to Victoria,Texas, and is presently located in the University of Houston Victoria Center for the Arts, which has generously supported the publication of *Dark Ladies,* which has also received support from many friends of the press. Chax is an independent 501(c)(3) organization which depends on support from various government and private funders, and, primarily, from individual donors and readers.

Recent and current books-in-progress include T*he Complete Light Poems,* by Jackson Mac Low, *Life–list,* by Jessica Smith, *Andalusia,* by Susan Thackrey, *Diesel Hand,* by Nico Vassilakis, *Lizard,* by Sarah Rosenthal, *The Collected Poems of Gil Ott, An Intermittent Music,* by Ted Pearson, *Limerence,* by Saba Razvi, and several other books to come.

You may find CHAX online at http://chax.org